Feeding the Family

Women in Culture and Society A Series Edited by Catharine R. Stimpson

Marjorie L. DeVault

Feeding the Family

The Social Organization of Caring as Gendered Work

The University of Chicago Press Chicago and London

The University of Chicago Press, Chicago 60637
The University of Chicago Press, Ltd., London
© 1991 by Marjorie L. DeVault
Foreword © 1991 by The University of Chicago
All rights reserved. Published 1991
Paperback edition 1994
Printed in the United States of America

00 99 98 97 96   5 4 3

ISBN (cloth): 0-226-14359-7
ISBN (paper): 0-226-14360-0

Library of Congress Cataloging-in-Publication Data
DeVault, Marjorie L., 1950–
    Feeding the family : the social organization of
caring as gendered work / Marjorie L. DeVault.
        p.   cm. — (Women in culture and society)
    Includes bibliographical references and index.
    1. Sexual division of labor—Illinois—
Chicago—Case studies.   2. Housewives—
Illinois—Chicago—Psychology—Case studies.
3. Households—Illinois—Chicago—Case
studies.   4. Family—Illinois—Chicago—Case
studies.
    I. Title.   II. Series.
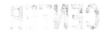
TX652.D473   1991
306.4—dc20   91-14447
                                                         CIP

⊗ The paper used in this publication meets the
minimum requirements of the American National
Standard for Information Sciences—Permanence of
Paper for Printed Library Materials, ANSI Z39.48-1984.

Contents

Foreword

The major story in my newspaper on the day I began to write this foreword concerned a natural disaster in Asia that was to kill over 100,000 people and their livelihoods. A "typhoon of unimaginable fury" had "swung across the flat coastal plains of southeastern Bangladesh, swallowing up villages and sweeping away food crops."[1] A photograph, spread across four columns, showed nearly a score of half-naked boys and men, reaching towards, grasping at, bags of supplies on a helicopter's metal floor. Once again, people had lost food, shelter, life itself. Once again, the survivors were naked before necessity, struggling desperately for food, shelter, life itself.

Feeding the Family is about the human necessity of food. To be sure, its setting, Chicago and its environs in the early 1980s, is far less devastated and calamitous than Bangladesh in 1991. Nevertheless, the men, women, and children of this more secure metropolis must have sustenance. At its most elemental, sustenance is material—a grain, a root, some milk or water. Sustenance has as well two other, linked meanings. First, as culture does its work, the material becomes symbolic, ritualistic, and linguistic. Grain becomes flour, flour bread, bread "the staff of life." Second, sustenance is intellectual and psychological. The mind and heart have their appetites. Indeed, languages and rituals help to gratify these appetites. Many believe that our need for such immaterial sustenance is one mark of the human species. So King Lear argues with his daughter Regan as she and her sister Goneril are stripping him of his retinue, his "household," and his dignity:

1. Barbara Crossette, "Official Toll Reaches 92,000 in Bangladesh Cyclone," *New York Times*, May 4, 1991, p. 1.

> O, reason not the need! Our basest beggars
> Are in the poorest thing superfluous.
> Allow not nature more than nature needs,
> Man's life is cheap as beast's.
>
> (*King Lear*, II, iv. 267–70)

Regan and Goneril are, of course, women, two of the most vicious female characters in drama and literature. Part of their evil lies in their refusal to feed their father properly. The great theme of *Feeding the Family*, a serious, valuable, and humane book, is that feeding others is women's work. Women collect, prepare and serve our daily bread. So doing, they care for us. The acts of feeding and caring, as connected to each other as earth to water, maintain and sustain the family. If women refuse to do this work, they seem to themselves and others like somewhat less malign Regans and Gonerils, "unloving" and "unnatural."

Marjorie DeVault has interviewed all of the women and some of the men in thirty families and rendered their "lived experience." Her ethnography illuminates four crucial questions about modern life. First, what actually happens in our homes and daily lives? Too often, researchers and scholars have been content to let novelists and gossips answer this question. Next, who cares for us? Who takes on the task, generally unpaid, of succoring the weak, ill, and dependent? Next, how do class and gender work together to structure our society and its tasks? More particularly, how do patterns of cooking and caring show this structure? For example, how does a woman who has married into the professional classes learn new, class-based practices? Finally, why do women accept a role, a place in our social organization, that is inequitable? Deftly, sensitively, DeVault shows women taking pride and satisfaction in the craft of feeding others. As deftly, as sensitively, she explores how difficult it is for women who wish to resist practicing this craft, even during our period of transition in gender roles. Men who genuinely want to do their share of the daily round of shopping, cooking, and serving also find it hard. They have neither a vocabulary for nor an image of family life to guide them.

Feeding the Family is a remarkable narrative about modern culture and society. It also poses a moral challenge. DeVault knows that we have needs that we must meet if we are to live—if blood is to circulate, limbs move, neurons fire. These needs are as irresistible and as powerful as a storm. DeVault also knows that we socially construct the ways in which we meet these needs. People must eat, but people also decide how they will eat. Culture and my family, not nature, put a spoon in my hand. Can we, DeVault asks, have both gender equity and a sense of sociability broad enough to encourage both sexes to take responsibility for the essential but mundane tasks of everyday nurturance? One reason why we shrink from gender equity is our fear that it will breed a world without such a sense of responsibility; in which no one cares for us if women do not; in which no one cooks for us—except a fast-food chain restaurant. *Feeding the Family* is equally aware of our fears and of the fact that, unlike a great typhoon, they are within our ultimate control. We can feed or starve our fears. If we choose to starve them, we can then feed renewed families and social organizations with the nutrients of our energies.

Catharine R. Stimpson

Acknowledgments

Being a girl child of the 1950s meant that I was recruited into the "womanly" project, extending over several generations, of caring for others in my middle-class family and connecting our lives with those of friends and relatives. Coming of age in the 1960s, and being involved in feminism, meant that I also became sharply aware of limitations built into demands for traditional womanly activity. Throughout my adult life, I have struggled with conflicts between my ambitions and my commitments to care and connection. A sometimes painful ambivalence about my own life has no doubt influenced my choice of topic for this study. I am sure, as well, that my work on this topic has been shaped by lessons I have learned from the love and support of family and friends. I am indebted to all those who have nourished me, and especially to my parents, Barbara and Vere DeVault, for their strong support of my work. I know that my concerns are informed by the example set by my grandmother, Mary Dean Williams, who worked at both caring and writing, and I have enjoyed sharing recent work with my sister, Ileen DeVault, a fine historian. I am also deeply grateful to my partner, Robert Chibka, for constant encouragement and expert editing, and for his efforts at maintaining our connection while we work in different cities.

This book is based on research I began as a graduate student, and my sociological thinking was shaped by many fine teachers at Northwestern University, whose Sociology Department provided a stimulating and supportive environment for creative work. I have benefited enormously over the years from the advice and generous colleagueship of my dissertation adviser, Arlene Kaplan Daniels, whose own research on women's "invisible work" is one of the important precursors to my study. Other Northwestern faculty who contributed most centrally to my thinking about the project include Howard S. Becker, Naomi Aronson, and Albert Hunter. Dorothy E. Smith, of the Ontario Institute for Studies in Education, served as a reader for the dissertation and has provided continuing inspiration and advice from the early stages of the project. Fellow students at Northwestern were equally important for the development of my project; foremost among them was Sandra J. Schroeder, "chair" of my "informal committee," whose careful listening and insightful criticism made possible the many discussions in which my ideas first took shape.

Colleagues in a number of institutions have discussed these issues with me as my thoughts developed and have commented on various drafts of the work. Though I could not incorporate all of their comments, I wish to give thanks to the following for helpful readings of all or part of the manuscript in its various stages: Cheryl Carpenter, Robert Chibka, Ileen DeVault, Timothy Diamond, Alison Griffith, Chrys Ingraham, Judy Long, Julia Loughlin, Michal McCall, Harvey Molotch, Adele Mueller, Barrie Thorne, Candace West, Judith Wittner, and the late Marianne Paget. I also benefited from comments on the research when I presented it in early versions at the University of California—Los Angeles and at the University of Massachusetts—Amherst, and I received crucial institutional support from the Sociology Department and the Center for Urban Affairs at Northwestern University, the Stone Center for Developmental Studies and Services at Wellesley College, and Syracuse University.

Of course, none of the work would have been possible without the generosity and patience of the women and men who agreed to talk with me about their household work. I want to thank them all and also to express my deep admiration for their skill in the conduct of everyday life and their eloquence in talking about it.

There is no spectacle on earth more appealing than that of a beautiful woman in the act of cooking dinner for someone she loves.

—Thomas Wolfe, *The Web and the Rock*

Introduction

Image and Experience

The image of woman caring—doing for others—is a powerful one. It signals a central element in our culture's sense of what a woman should be; it represents the appealing, wholesome best in womanliness. The image feeds misogyny as well: it can stimulate fear of the controlling, potentially manipulative power of the caring woman. Like any cultural image, this one both represents (though only in part) and helps to construct social reality.

This book is about one kind of everyday caring—the unpaid work of "feeding a family"—analyzed as activity rather than image or emotion (though I will also discuss how images of caring influence activity and emotion). My concern with this activity emerges at the intersection of two recent lines of feminist scholarship, one focusing on household labor and its significance for women's lives, and the other examining the paid or unpaid work of caring for others. Both of these lines of thought have developed as a result of feminist scholars' attention to previously neglected aspects of women's lived experience. Both aim to illuminate shadowy, almost invisible terrain that has been taken for granted in the past: analysts of housework have insisted on the significance of the trivialized activities of everyday maintenance (e.g. Lopata 1971; Oakley 1974; Luxton 1980), and analysts of caregiving work have called attention to the extent of women's largely unrecognized contributions to support for elderly, sick, and disabled persons (e.g. Finch and Groves 1983; Waerness 1984; Abel and Nelson 1990).

Caring work is activity that most women engage in every day, in their occupations, through voluntary activity, as friends and neighbors, and especially at home. Caring is not limited to women, of course—men too care for others in various ways (Cancian 1987)—but the culture's division of labor has assigned far more responsibility for care to women than to men. For generations, women's caring work has sustained life and community. For many, caring has been a source of deep satisfaction and pride. But women have also been constrained and oppressed by the burdens of caring for others. Often, caring has required the suppression of other capacities and desires. It has meant involvement in low-status, often unpaid work that has limited women's entrance into more lucrative work. In addition, traditional caring work has become part of larger social structures: women's work has supported traditional family patterns—with their characteristic benefits and costs—and has helped to maintain the divisions of gender and class relations. Through caring work, women have participated in the activities that structure their subordinate position in society. They have participated not only because of social coercion, but also because of deeply-held beliefs about connection and people's responsibilities to one another, and commitments to fostering growth and relationship. The activities of care, in short, spring from more than a single source and have potential effects that both enrich and limit the course of group life.

Currently, the notion of woman as caretaker (like other aspects of traditional gender relations) is at issue in many societies. Feminists have called attention to the enormous amount of unpaid work that women have been expected to do, without the social or economic rewards that accrue to paid labor (Waring 1988). In Western industrialized countries, this new attention to caring work has evolved as middle-class women have taken on more and more of the activities traditionally reserved for men. Increasing labor force participation has brought new conflicts as most women now attempt to combine paid jobs with the caring work they have done in the past: not just housework, but also caring for children, husbands, elderly relations, and caring for friends and neighbors through informal work exchanges and volunteer work in schools and churches. Poor and working-class women have often worked for pay, and have searched for ways to squeeze caring for families into lives of perpetual work and worry. Women of color, especially, have often been paid for doing the household work of caretaking that has allowed women in wealthier families to pick and choose responsibilities for care, emphasizing emotional or community work rather than the work of daily maintenance (Daniels 1988). Perhaps the most painful aspect of doing paid domestic work has been the irony of performing caring work for others, which limits caring for one's own family (Rollins 1985). Now, as middle-class women face similar problems and are no longer available to serve middle-class families as they did in the past, policy makers begin to identify the conflicting demands of economy and family as a "problem" for society. They begin to wonder who will take care of families.

These social changes are experienced as problems for women living their lives as well. Now, many women expect to be mothers who are also competent in a wider world, autonomous, committed to challenging careers. Changes in the workplace have made it easier than in the past for women to achieve and act in the public world. But these women encounter, at home, difficulties that result from a "stalled revolution" (Hochschild 1989). They confront the realities of the "double day" (Glazer 1980) or "second shift" (Hochschild 1989). There are too many demands, too much work in too many places, too little time to rest or play. Individuals find solutions to these problems of everyday life—some relatively easily and some at great cost. But individual adjustments do not solve enduring social problems. Often, indeed, individual strategies solve the problems of one group at the expense of another, as when affluent parents purchase caring work from poor and immigrant women who are economically vulnerable (Hertz 1986). Individual adjustments, moreover, leave the sources of problems unexplored. Prospects for change may hang in the balance: will the pressures of adjustment fuel a return to traditional patterns, or will this women's movement generate lasting changes?

This perplexing situation is a puzzle missing a piece, and that piece is the acknowledgment of caring work in all its complexity, as activity deeply compelling for those who do it and critically important for group life. Though necessary for maintaining the social world as we have known it, caring has been mostly unpaid work, traditionally undertaken by women, activity whose value is not fully acknowledged even by those who do it. Similar work done for pay—by domestic workers and home health aides, for example—has also been trivialized by an emphasis on strictly physical tasks. Caring, as activity, has also been obscured by the organization of gender relations and their construction in terms of "natural difference": by beliefs about women's "disposition" toward care, by the trap of economic dependence set for women by barriers to labor-force participation and wage discrimination, even by language that discounts the importance of caring. Social expectation has made this undefined, unacknowledged activity central to women's identity. In the same way, it has been defined out of activities traditionally assigned to men. Both men and women have learned to think of these patterns as "natural," and often seem puzzled by the new problems of caring created by women's increased activity outside of family settings.

As women have taken on more responsibilities outside the home, caring often seems a liability that limits the autonomy of anyone who does it. In order to enter the "male world," it seems, women must jettison caring. However, the feminist hope—that we will enter the public world and also change it—suggests that there must be another way to go. Though this other path may not yet be obvious, it will certainly require respectful attention to the life experiences that have been distinctively associated with women until now. The goals of such respectful attention, in the case of caring activity, might include at least the following: an understanding of the nature and significance of care; a vocabulary with which to discuss it; and a clear and honest assessment of both the value of caring and its darker side—the ways it can diminish the one who does it, and its negative consequences for those who get defined as "dependent." Eventually, such analyses can perhaps lead to new understandings about how groups in society can best organize the necessary work of care. But a deeper understanding of care must come first.

Problems of Knowing

I have used the terms "care" and "caring work" without explicit definition. In fact, I use these terms with some dissatisfaction, as the best available, but aware that they do not signal my intentions as accurately as I would like. My topic is activity without a name, activity traditionally assigned to women, often carried out in family groups: activity that I know from experience but cannot easily label. When I began to think about this research, I wondered how I might study the ways that women care for those they live with. Unable to see how such a goal could be framed as a "proper" sociological topic, I resolved to approach the topic through a study of "housework." For reasons that were only partly conscious, I began to concentrate on the work of providing food. The term is awkward and sounds rather odd, but I could find no term that said precisely what I meant. I meant more than just cooking, more than "meal preparation" (the efficiency expert's term). And "providing," of course, has been used for what the traditional husband does—it is linked to the wage that a woman transforms into family meals. While planning the research, I struggled with a variety of definitions, but found no simple and adequate label for the activity I had in mind.

This particular insufficiency of language is an example of a more general problem, a more pervasive lack of fit between women's experiences and the forms of thought available for understanding experience. Feminist thinkers have repeatedly demonstrated that the ideas and even vocabulary of the culture are rooted in men's experiences. Knowledge that comes from activity traditionally undertaken by women is frequently distorted or absent altogether from the discourse of the public world. Dorothy Smith (1987) refers to such a gap in social knowledge as a "line of fault" in women's experience. The categories "work" and "leisure," for example, emerge from the kind of paid labor that has become typical for men in Western industrial societies. The terms accord reasonably well with men's experiences, which usually include temporal separations between the job and family, and travel from workplace to home, but difficulties arise in the attempt to apply these concepts to women's daily activities. Whether or not they work for pay, women typically take responsibility for a wide variety of household work tasks at home. It is difficult to divide their activities into "work" and "leisure" because these women are virtually always on call, and their household work is often fragmented, picked up and put down intermittently as they respond to new demands. Many of women's family activities seem to combine "work" and "leisure": preparing an outing, for example, or taking the time to read to a child. Women themselves are reluctant to categorize many of their activities as either "work" or "leisure," even in a structured research situation, and instead label them "both" (Berk and Berk 1979). They define as their "leisure" those moments they can squeeze in among other activities (often while monitoring children's activities) rather than periods of time or projects marked off clearly from paid work periods (Ross 1985). Perhaps most important, individuals learn that the family *should* be a place for emotional expression rather than work, that it *should* be a respite from work; these shared expectations of family life provide an interpretive frame that allows the work done to meet those expectations to remain hidden. Clearly, the experience of family work would never produce the concepts "work" and "leisure" (Smith 1987:68). To use these kinds of words to describe women's activity at home is to use a language that is often inadequate. But these are the words available; as a result of this and similar conceptual incongruences, it is quite difficult to make the experience of family work a part of shared discourse.

Smith points out that such lines of fault provide opportunities as well as problems for the expression of women's experience. By exploring the contours of experience together (as in consciousness-raising, for example) and also critiquing the ideological forms of the culture, communities of women can both expose the gaps in social knowledge and also begin to develop alternative forms of expression. It is possible to speak of experiences without names, and that is my aim.

As a first step in this speaking, it is helpful to collect examples. One that informed my thinking as I began this study was a fictional portrayal of a particular woman's activity: Virginia Woolf's portrait of Mrs. Ramsay in the novel *To the Lighthouse*, which tells the story of a British professional-class family and their guests summering in the Hebrides. Mrs. Ramsay—mother, wife, and hostess—is a woman devoted to and absorbed in the work of caring for family and friends, and recognized by those around her as very skillful at what she does. Through a lazy summer afternoon, Mrs. Ramsay sits and knits, but she also attends to her children, her husband, and her guests, soothing those who need care and mediating their sometimes troublesome interactions. She has learned to pay attention and to be available to several people at once. She monitors their activities and strategizes about how to respond to them. She keeps track of sounds—the men talking, the children playing—which serve as information about ongoing events, and which could at any moment become signals of emergent needs.

Later, at dinner, Mrs. Ramsay accomplishes two tasks: in addition to supervising the preparation and service of the food, she brings the diners together so that they experience the meal as a particular kind of event. Neither of these tasks is sufficient without the other; both are essential to the creation of a "dinner." Mrs. Ramsay is quite conscious of these responsibilities. As the soup is served, she notices:

> Nothing seemed to have merged. They all sat separate. And the whole of the effort of merging and flowing and creating rested on her . . . if she did not do it nobody would do it, and so, giving herself the little shake that one gives a watch that has stopped, the old familiar pulse began beating.

She begins to talk to William Bankes and gently prods the others into talking with one another. By the time the soup is finished, the group has been united, "composed into a party round a table." The dinner seems like "order and dry land" as against a watery reflection outside, a "common cause against that fluidity out there." As the talk goes on, Mrs. Ramsay presides, and then ends the meal by rising at the proper time and leaving the room. She stands a moment in the doorway and, as she leaves, realizes that through her action the dinner is becoming the past.

While the theme of sociability dominates the description of the dinner, Mrs. Ramsay also has quite mundane concerns with the food itself, because of the way she deploys the food in order to construct a social encounter. The juxtaposition of these different tasks is beautifully illustrated in several passages that move back and forth from one to the other, as she observes and evaluates the event: "It partook, she felt, carefully helping Mr. Bankes to a specially tender piece, of eternity." Or, "Here, she felt, putting the spoon down, was the still space that lies about the heart of things, where one could move or rest; could wait now (they were all helped) listening." The examples show the simultaneity of diverse concerns in Mrs. Ramsay's mind: her personal meditations floating in and around her strategizing, the interruptions of her thought, and the interweaving of ordinary and sublime that this kind of thinking produces.

This scene also illustrates the delicacy of sustaining the interaction that makes up a dinner. Mrs. Ramsay must secure the cooperation of the others, and she directs and cajoles them into appropriate roles. Managing to achieve both subtlety and firmness, she signals Lily Briscoe to be friendly toward Mr. Tansley ("the glance in her eyes said it"), and—with a bit more anxiety about whether she will succeed—she silently warns her husband to control his impatience when Mr. Carmichael wants more soup. Carmichael, in fact, is unusual at this table, because he is so unaware of the demands of his role. "If he wanted soup, he asked for soup." Mrs. Ramsay notices his independence; from her position, it is quite unaccountable behavior. He presents a problem, which makes her work more difficult, but her reaction to him is also colored by a respect— perhaps envy—for his freedom from social demands.

Lily Briscoe's response to Mrs. Ramsay provides an especially instructive counterpoint. As the other adult woman in the book, she contrasts with Mrs. Ramsay in her rejection of Mrs. Ramsay's kind of work. However, she knows about the work, and is sometimes drawn into sharing responsibility for it. At the dinner table, she senses Tansley's need for approval, and she imagines Mrs. Ramsay saying to her:

> I am drowning, my dear, in seas of fire. Unless you apply some balm to the anguish of this hour and say something nice to that young man there, life will run upon the rocks . . . My nerves are taut as fiddle strings. Another touch and they will snap.

Reluctantly, "for the hundred and fiftieth time," Lily has to "renounce the experiment—what happens if one is not nice to that young man there—and be nice."

Though she doesn't want to do this kind of work, Lily is ambivalent, and feels somehow less of a woman because she refuses. At dinner she contrasts Mrs. Ramsay's "abundance with her own poverty of spirit." And years later, when the group has reassembled after Mrs. Ramsay's death, she cannot give Mr. Ramsay the sympathy he wants, and feels that she is "not a woman, but a peevish, ill-tempered, dried-up old maid." Lily feels the force of the social definition of "women's work," even though she rejects it. She has learned about the work, and since others expect her to do it, she confronts decisions about how to respond to those expectations.

Whatever judgments she makes, Lily seems to understand Mrs. Ramsay, while the men in the book are often mystified. Lily, growing up a woman and subject to social demands, knows about caring work. She has learned to put herself in another's place and to understand people's needs. Men are not typically expected to do this sort of work; they need not learn about it as they grow up, and therefore do not often have these skills of understanding others. They look at Mrs. Ramsay with wonder, marveling at her "magic."

This example provides important clues to the experience of caring work, but it does more as well. Lines of fault point to aspects of women's experience that are typically unacknowledged; they also point to ideological forms of thought that structure the interpretation of experience. Woolf's portrait of Mrs. Ramsay shows Mrs. Ramsay's experience, but it also shows the misperception of that experience. For those around her, Mrs. Ramsay is a particular kind of person, quintessentially "womanly": self-effacing, but powerful because she seems magically able to give (or withhold) the responses that uphold the lives of the others and the group itself. She is known for "who she is," rather than "what she does." This response to such a woman is a misunderstanding that is socially structured. Mrs. Ramsay creates experiences for others by acting in ways that respond to their needs. From the outside, her relations with others appear "natural"; from her own point of view, these relations can be displayed as a practice. Although her activity is labeled as an expression of inherent femininity, she is engaged in a skillful performance.

The qualities that others see as naturally feminine in Mrs. Ramsay are consciously crafted: a kind of work that she does. Rather than mystery and magic, thought and effort provide the foundation for her "womanly" activity. As the other adults in the book are occupied with thoughts about their various kinds of "important work," so Mrs. Ramsay thinks about the work that she does. She has something in common with Lily the painter: she is "making of the moment something permanent (as in another sphere Lily herself tried to make of the moment something permanent)." And William Bankes, the botanist, feels as he gazes at her "as he felt when he had proved something absolute about the digestive system of plants, that barbarity was tamed, the reign of chaos subdued." But Mrs. Ramsay's craft is invisible to the others, and does not count as work. Bankes, for example, makes the conventional separation between "work" and Mrs. Ramsay's "trifling" concerns: he sits at the table and thinks, "How trifling it all is, how boring it all is . . . compared with the other thing—work."

This account serves to correct much of the mystification of women's activity exemplified by the Thomas Wolfe quotation at the beginning of this chapter. Instead of seeing the caring woman from outside, as an "appealing spectacle," Virginia Woolf opens to view the complex work of caring and sociability, from the perspective of one who does it. However, there are significant absences in the portrayal of Mrs. Ramsay's work as well. Mrs. Ramsay herself does not cook; that work is done by another woman, a servant, whose existence we learn of only in passing, who does not appear as an individual in Woolf's novel. The separation of the tasks of cooking and hostessing in this account makes it possible to see more clearly here the work of service and sociability that are often obscured by combination with the more visible work of preparation. Thus, while the view Woolf provides reveals some aspects of caring work that are often ignored, it obscures and mystifies the material supports for a performance like Mrs. Ramsay's.

This example, then, shows a very specific version of sociability work: a formal dinner in a household with servants and a cook.

However, routine food work in the households I studied was similar in at least some respects. The women I talked with referred to their activity as something other than "work" in any conventional sense, as activity embedded in family relations. Many spoke of the activity as emerging from interpersonal ties, part of being a parent ("I feel like, you know, when I decided to have children it was a commitment, and raising them includes feeding them.") or of being a wife ("I like to cook for him. That's what a wife is for, right?"). Though they recognize that they work at feeding, and that the work includes many repetitive, mechanical tasks, their language reveals an unlabeled dimension of caring as well: some speak of their effort as "love," while others talk about caring for children as not quite a job, but as "something different." Such comments point to the difficulty of describing family work. If the activity is thought of only in terms of relationships and emotions, the necessary and arduous work of physical maintenance disappears. If it is thought of only in terms of the tasks like those of wage-workers—as discrete "products" or "services"—the most significant interpersonal parts of the work disappear. Women's own language suggests that material and interpersonal dimensions of these tasks are joined in their lives, and that these aspects of the work should not be separated in an analysis of what they do.

Why Women? Theories of Caring

Much recent analysis of housework and caring has been concerned with the question, why women? Do women choose to do most of the society's caring work, because of deeply rooted moral or psychological predispositions? Or do women "care" because they are less powerful than men, and must exchange caring for material support? These last two questions suggest the two most common answers, and can be understood as versions of the "difference" and "dominance" arguments put forward as explanations for the larger phenomenon of women's oppression (MacKinnon 1987). Many analysts of housework have adopted "dominance" explanations: they argue that women's responsibility for housework results from the active construction of a division of labor benefiting capitalists and male workers (Hartmann 1981b), and is maintained by women's economic disadvantage and patriarchal ideology (Feldberg 1984). Analysts of caregiving work have recognized the importance of power relations in structuring women's activity, but many have also suggested that women choose to give care to others, at least in part, because of predispositions toward such activity. In their emphasis on this emotional source for caregiving work, these analysts have drawn on theorists of "difference" who suggest that care and connection with others are concerns especially characteristic of women (Chodorow 1978; Gilligan 1982). Although these theorists agree that caring is not "essentially" female, but is structured by social arrangements, their analyses have typically examined caring as morality, virtue, or as an aspect of some distinctly womanly identity rather than as activity women engage in (e.g. Noddings 1984; see also Tronto 1987).[1] Thus, they reinforce the definition of "woman" as one who cares.

My analysis here will put forward a somewhat different argument about women's caring work, based on the concept of *social organization*. I do not assume, as do the difference theorists, that wishing or choosing to care for others is necessarily part of a womanly character or identity; rather, I emphasize the ways in which caring is constructed as women's work, and the power of this social construction. Unlike some dominance theorists, however, I do not emphasize coercion or the raw exercise of male power (though these certainly do sometimes come into play); rather, I am most concerned with the complex ways that women are themselves drawn into participation in prevailing relations of inequality. The argument is grounded in Smith's approach to building a "sociology for women" (1987), a specifically feminist version of an emerging constructivist sociology that combines materialist and ethnomethodological approaches. Smith, addressing the "problems of knowing" discussed above, argues that a feminist sociology should begin not with the categories and questions of a sociological (or other disciplinary) framework, but with analysis of women's actual lived experience. By lived experience, she means activity conducted in material settings—what happens in people's everyday lives—as well as the processes of interpretation that give meaning to everyday lives. Analysis is not confined to the everyday, however. Rather, the recovery of experience allows the researcher to locate the "problematic of the everyday world." This problematic—"a set of puzzles that do not yet exist in the form of puzzles but are 'latent' in the actualities of the everyday world" (1987:91)—serves to guide and focus inquiry. It calls for analysis that can explain how everyday lives are shaped by larger social relations.

1. Ruddick (1980) is an exception; her analysis, though conceptual rather than empirical, points toward an understanding of care as activity.

In Smith's approach, analysis based on the fundamentally organized character of social life can show how women's everyday activities are ordered by social relations extending beyond the immediate, local setting. Through their work, women are connected with organizations and institutions—families, workplaces, schools, stores and services, and the state. Typically, activities in these settings are organized by discourses that coordinate the workings of organizations and institutions in different local settings (Smith's example, for instance, is the discourse of "mothering" that teaches women how to supervise and support their children's performance at school [1987: chaps. 4, 5]). The concept of social organization explains how women (and others) enter social relations, actively producing their own activities in relation to the activities of others. It points to the importance of shared understandings about particular settings, recognizing that these are subject to change through negotiation, disputation and improvisation, but that they are always relevant to human conduct. By using the concept of social organization to allow attention both to women's agency in everyday life and also to the ways their activities become part of institutional processes, Smith aims to explain for women (as Marx did for the working class) how they can be overpowered by "the forces of their own life" (Marx and Engels, as quoted by Smith 1987:104).

This study focuses on the work activity of particular people in specific family settings. It is unlike many studies of housework, which take the work itself for granted and move immediately to questions of how it is divided and why, or to the examination of strategies for resisting or lessening the work burden. In my analysis, the social organization of the family setting provides a way of understanding both how women are recruited into the work of feeding, and also how feeding work contributes to women's oppression. Women learn to "care" because the production of a "family" as a socially organized material setting requires particular kinds of coordinative and maintenance activities. Women are not the only ones who can perform these activities, but the concept of "family" (maintained over time in its shifting forms by a variety of interlocking social discourses) incorporates a strong and relatively enduring association of caring activity with the woman's position in the household ("wife" or "mother"). In particular households, individuals engage in specific versions of the work of care, constructing located, idiosyncratic versions of family life. As they go about this work, in material settings, they refer to and draw upon cultural ideologies of family life (though hardly any households actually look like the cultural ideal). By doing the work of "wife" and "mother," women quite literally *produce* family life from day to day, through their joint activities with others. By "doing family" in traditional ways, household members sustain and reproduce the "naturalness" of prevailing arrangements. And those who wish to conduct their lives differently are constrained by the specific character of the work that produces "family," by the fact that discourses of family life prescribe particular ways of doing the work and make families (or more often, women) accountable for that work in institutions such as schools, workplaces, welfare offices, family courts, and so on.[2]

This kind of analysis locates the persistence of women's responsibility for care in a household work process that produces not just goods and services, but also "women" and "families," simultaneously (see Berk 1985 on the household production of gender). Such an argument does not directly contest the "difference" arguments which emphasize psychological development. But it operates at a different level, the level of social organization. It is an argument that is fundamentally about women's "place" in family life rather than about identity, an argument that aims to show how women are continually recruited—whatever their psychological predispositions—into participation in social relations that produce their subordination.

Bracketing "The Family"

In all societies, people have lived in small groups of cooperating individuals—labeled "families" by most scholars. In all societies, men and women have contributed differently to these groups (although the divisions between men's and women's tasks are not equally rigid in all societies and not always strictly enforced, and although Leibowitz [1983] suggests that this division of labor came relatively late in human evolution). But in spite of these broad similarities, small living groups have been organized very differently in different places through time: the particular tasks assigned to men or to women have varied considerably. Most scholars agree that in virtually all societies women are responsible for most child care and cooking (though in many societies with considerable flex-

2. This analysis parallels and also draws on the concept of "doing gender" (West and Zimmerman 1987), which will be discussed in more detail in chapter 4.

ibility in the division of labor the distinction is somewhat forced; in practice, child care is integrated with daily activities of both men and women, and individuals obtain much of their own everyday food and eat on their own or with work partners). We do not yet understand why food processing work is so consistently assigned to women. However, in spite of some apparent consistency, there is great variation in the specific organization of the work of feeding the members of different societies (O'Kelly 1980). Among horticultural people, women grow much of the household's food as well as processing and serving it. Often, women are powerful because they trade food items with other peoples (Robertson 1987). In some societies, women have been the ones to make decisions about distributing food to household groups (Brown 1975). Furthermore, although eating is a central ritual in all societies, it is not always done in family groups. Sometimes, women and men eat separately, and in these societies the cultural rituals associated with food may have as much to do with relations among men or women as between genders. Feminists argue from this kind of cultural variation that the gender-based division of labor—and the patterns of group living it produces—are social inventions that might be changed rather than natural or necessary forms of life.

This anthropological evidence is important to my concern with the dynamics of modern family life because it displays the constructed character of daily activity. It shows that the groups we call families are built on patterns of shared activity, and that the shape of such a pattern—who does what work in each society—produces a characteristic pattern of opportunities and relative power for typical men and women. The families described by most anthropologists are groups who live far away from most readers of this book, whose lives may seem unusual and exotic. It is perhaps easier to consider variation in group living among these people than among ourselves, where our kinds of families are powerful taken-for-granted realities for most of us. As in any society, the experiences that seem to arise "naturally" from powerful feelings about others are in fact produced, at least in part, by beliefs about how we *should* feel (Hochschild 1983). The feelings are quite real, but they are learned rather than inevitable.

When we speak about contemporary families, then, we refer to two kinds of realities, to both experience and institution (Rich 1976; Rapp 1982). As experience, "family" refers to the activities of daily lives: to small groups of women, men, and children who usually share material resources, who may work or play together, who sometimes love each other and sometimes fight. Experientially, households are sites of material interdependence, of care (both material and emotional), and often, of affection and respect. They are also arenas for social conflict (Hartmann 1981a), where power relations are reproduced. They are often dangerous for some members, and anger and frustration are taught along with love (Barrett and McIntosh 1982). But the word "family" refers to an idea (or social institution) as well. It is a term whose meaning has emerged historically, a construct rooted in discourse as much as in immediate experience. People hear and talk about families; they learn what families are supposed to be, and they work at forming families and experiencing them as they believe they should (Gubrium and Holstein 1990).

The dominant idea of family in Western industrial societies has developed as part of the construction over time of an ideological distinction between "public" and "private" realms (Zaretsky 1973; Garmarnikow, Morgan, Purvis, and Taylorson 1983). With industrialization, an ideology of separate spheres assigned wage work, outside the home, to men. Women, at home, were to do the work of transforming wages into the goods and services needed to maintain the household. Women's household activities acquired new meanings, partly through the writings of reformers who saw domesticity as a contribution to social good, and partly through the advertising that supported mass production and suggested that women needed a variety of new products if they were to care adequately for their families (Rothman 1978; Ehrenreich and English 1978).

This private, "nurturing" kind of family was promoted as a personal realm that would provide protection from the competitive world outside. A breadwinning father would be a public actor, while a subservient wife would devote herself to caring for husband and children. In fact, such a pattern was mainly characteristic of middle-class households, since working-class and poor households often required wives' as well as husbands' wages. But this falsely "monolithic" concept of family (Thorne 1982) has been influential throughout society. Social discourse has privileged the emotional character of family life implied by this model, and has devalued the economic interdependence that has been so important in working-class and poor households. In spite of some recent change, the ideology of family is still gendered and class-biased. Women are still expected to take primary responsibility for the caring part of family life, and the social discourse continues to emphasize a model of family life that assumes and builds upon a gender-based division of labor. It is a model that best fits the experience of middle-class, heterosexual couples, a model built on the images of agentic man and nurturant woman.

This discursive concept of family is mostly taken for granted, even by those whose family experience is often different. Some couples—the less affluent, single mothers or fathers, and lesbian or gay couples—find that they cannot divide household work in the traditional way. As these people struggle with the realities of their lives, they confront a discourse of family life that fits uneasily with their experience. The discourse, for example, names the roles "mother" and "father" in terms of a complex of gender, personality, and activity in which the elements combine, presumably "naturally." Thus, single mothers, no matter what kind of parenting they actually do, often worry about "substituting" for an "absent father." (And their worries have an institutional source: school officials, welfare workers, and policy makers, drawing on social scientific research, are quick to point to "family structure" when children have problems [Griffith 1984].) Mothers who work for pay feel guilty if they appear less available to children than full-time housewives. Fathers without jobs (or lacking power and control at their jobs) feel "unmanly," believing they have let their families down. And gay and lesbian parents often feel they are sailing uncharted seas: while they often want to insist that they are "regular families" like "everyone else," they also know that they look quite different from the family of social discourse, and that the complementarity of traditionally male and female activities cannot be taken for granted in their relationships. While an enormous body of science, literature, and even humor tells us how a middle-class man and woman might "do" family life, there is little public discourse to guide those whose relationships and material situations differ from the privileged social ideal.[3]

The social discourse about family is not static; ideals change over time, in response to material changes and the challenges of organized social protest. But the discourse of family is powerful and resistant to radical change. Over time, revised images of family life accommodate some new patterns, but usually in ways that preserve fundamental elements of social tradition. Alternative forms of family living often do not fit easily with established institu-

3. See Connell (1987) for a constructivist approach to conceptualizing gender that is consistent with this discussion of family.

tions, so that those attempting them feel pulled toward more traditional patterns. Serious talk about nontraditional options for family life goes on mostly "underground," in the alternative media and through the oral traditions of informal support networks and gay and lesbian communities.

Feminists have criticized traditional social scientists for allowing the gender and class biases of dominant discourses to shape studies of family life (e.g. Thorne and Yalom 1982). In fact, what social scientists have done is standard interpretive practice for members of the society: they have begun with a dominant concept of "family" and have investigated family life by studying groups that fit this social model (for further discussion of this problem, see Bernardes 1985; Gubrium and Holstein 1990). In studies of "normal" family dynamics, for example, researchers have often included only married couples in their investigations. Researchers who focus on the experiences of single parents have described their studies as investigations of "divorce" rather than "family" (and their research is usually taken up by others as part of a literature about divorce as a separate topic rather than as part of the discipline's fundamental understanding of "family"). This routine procedure in research—selecting only those cases that fit an established definition of topic—has in the case of family research been a powerful reinforcement of cultural discourse, with deeply conservative effects (Barrett and McIntosh 1982; Bernardes 1987). Knowledge about "families" (and therefore about caring in families) has come almost entirely from groups in which women and men have come together in traditional ways, have stayed together, and have conducted lives of at least relative conformity to social expectation. It is not surprising, therefore, that many of these researchers have failed to make analytic distinctions between gender and the work of care, and have reinforced the notion that women's nurturing activity need not be explained.

The work of feeding is always done in particular, material places, by and for specific people. In the discussion that follows, I introduce the reader to some of these places and people. I did not select these households, as many researchers do, because they contained traditional, "intact" families. I looked for households that included children, so I could consider the work of feeding children as well as adults. But I have included in my analysis of a household whoever lives and eats there: mothers and children, in all of these cases, and fathers in most, but also grandparents, aunts and uncles, and sometimes friends of various sorts. For those who live in these households, most of these people count as family. I will not be concerned with defining "family," or judging whether a particular group is "a family." But I will look carefully at these people's understandings of "family," at how their understandings influence the activities of household life, and at how they produce family life through their daily work.

My aim is to "bracket" the family. I use this term to refer to an approach that does two things. It focuses attention directly on understandings of "family," and thereby displays the operation of an ideology of family life in contemporary urban households (I use the term "ideology" here to refer to a loosely coordinated web of prescriptive understandings that underwrite prevailing relations of power [Smith 1987:54–56]). At the same time, this strategy provides a way to think about "family" as a form of social organization that is not inevitable. Once "bracketed," we can set aside and think beyond our usual beliefs about the practical or emotional necessity of family as typically constituted.

I begin with the assumption that caring is valuable work, and one of my aims here is to acknowledge the skill and social contributions of those who care. However, I will also question aspects of the current organization of caring work within the family. Since the ideal "family" that most people try to construct is built on women's service for men and implicated in class relations, caring is typically done in ways that reinforce men's entitlement and women's subservience. These patterns are not "natural"; they are produced by characteristic ways of understanding the family. Bracketing "family"—bringing family ideology into a frame that allows us to set it aside—will be a step toward disentangling the worth of caring work from its pitfalls.

Method and Organization of the Study

Following Smith's (1987) urging that we begin our analyses with everyday activity, my examination of the work of feeding begins with the everyday experience of doing the work itself. Drawing on detailed accounts of everyday routines in particular households, I analyze in some detail the "invisible" work that does not appear in most studies. Those who study housework have usually taken the meaning of this term to be obvious, and have relied on common-sense labels like "laundry" and "meal preparation" to summarize the content of the work (e.g. Oakley 1974; Walker and Woods

1976).[4] The definition implied by such an approach reduces house-work to a collection of relatively menial tasks; much of the work that must be done in households—and especially the work with greatest emotional significance—disappears from these analyses. Conscious of the "problems of knowing" discussed above, I do not assume that we can take the content of household caring work as obvious. Instead, I devote the first section of this book to examina-tion of previously neglected aspects of feeding work.

This approach to household caring activity relies on a "gener-ous" concept of work (Smith 1987:165–66), which extends beyond paid labor to incorporate more easily than standard definitions the variety of women's often "invisible" work activities (Daniels 1987). Such an expansion of the concept of work is implicit in femi-nist attention to previously neglected activity; in addition to stud-ies insisting on analysis of housework as work, it underlies recent interactionist studies examining a variety of activities not usually recognized as work, including, for example, "emotion work" in service jobs and in personal life (Hochschild 1983), "kin work" (Di Leonardo 1987), volunteer work (Daniels 1988), and the "interac-tion work" that women do in conversation (Fishman 1982). And it connects these studies to the recent focus on caregiving, and to new connections being made between paid and unpaid caregiving, only recently acknowledged as work (see e.g., Finch and Groves 1983; Abel and Nelson 1990). These investigations share an em-phasis on the processual, constructed character of work; because they refer to social interaction quite broadly rather than primarily to economic transactions, they point toward a new, more "so-ciological" definition of work (Wadel 1979).

Informants. My investigation of feeding work is based pri-marily on interviews with those who do most of this work in thirty households (thirty women and three men). The interviews were conducted during 1982–83 in the city and suburbs of Chicago, Illi-nois. All of the households I studied contained children, but they differed in several important ways (summarized below and in table 1). As I recruited volunteers for the study, I searched for informants whose situations would include a broad range of the different

4. Studies by Berheide, Berk, and Berk (1976) and Berk and Berk (1979) represent attempts to document the types of work that lie behind such labels by asking re-search participants to list the specific tasks included in each area of work. However, their procedures still result in a list of tasks, though significantly longer and more detailed lists than in most studies.

household types and circumstances found in contemporary cities.[5] Like any research strategy, this one has characteristic benefits and limitations. Its chief advantage for my purpose—close examination of a household work process—is that it allows a rich description incorporating multiple "versions" of feeding work, and avoids presenting any particular family form as "typical." Studying such a varied group, however, also makes it more difficult to identify the sources of household variation, or to investigate the specific cultural and food traditions associated with particular ethnic groups, than would be the case with more focused community studies (e.g. Douglas 1984).

The households I studied were ethnically and racially diverse. Members of eighteen households were white; they came from a variety of ethnic backgrounds, with second-generation Eastern Europeans representing the largest single group. Black families constituted six households, and were represented in all class groups, though most heavily among poor households. The four Hispanic households, including two with single mothers, were all working-class/white-collar families. Two households were racially mixed. Two households were Jewish, and two Jewish individuals were married to partners of different backgrounds; none of these individuals followed religious dietary prescriptions. While ethnicity is not a focus of my analysis, these ethnic and cultural identities are often evident in the interviewees' talk about their food, and I sometimes comment on patterns that seem to be associated with a particular cultural group.

My analysis focuses on the organization of feeding work through gender and class, but there are also significant racial and ethnic dimensions in the structuring of caring work, both within and outside the household (Glenn 1985, 1990; Collins 1990). It is

5. Since *de facto* segregation in American cities means that race and economic circumstance are strongly associated with neighborhood, I solicited interviewees from different parts of the city, knowing that the occupations and income levels of neighbors would usually be similar. Study participants from two affluent suburban neighborhoods and two Hispanic communities were recruited through personal contacts; participants from other neighborhoods were recruited through several organizations: a women's health center in a gentrifying urban neighborhood; a preschool play group in a predominantly white, working-class neighborhood; a women's labor-union group; a parents' organization in a poor inner-city neighborhood; and a subsidized day-care center in a low-income suburban neighborhood. My reliance on these organizational contacts may mean that the study volunteers represent a relatively active and well-informed group who are somewhat more likely than other urban dwellers to be involved in community affairs.

Table 1. Characteristics of Informants' Households

	All households	Poor households	Working-class/ white-collar households	Professional/ managerial households
	N = 30	N = 5	N = 15	N = 10
Household income				
Median	$25,000	$6,850	$24,000	$35,000
Range	$6,000– >$100,000	$6,000– $9,000	$12,000– $60,000	$23,000– >$100,000
Number in household				
Average	4.3	5.6	4.5	3.5
Range	3–9	4–9	3–9	3–5
Race				
White	18	2	9	9
Black	6	3	2	1
Hispanic	4	0	4	0
Mixed	2	1[a]	0	1[b]
Women in paid labor force	15	2	7	6
Single mothers	9	5	2	2

[a]White/Hispanic
[b]White/Asian-American

increasingly clear that the family caring work under consideration in this study is often somewhat differently structured, and that discourses of "family" no doubt have different meanings and consequences, in different racial and cultural groups. In spite of the race and ethnic diversity in the households studied here, I did not begin to understand the significance of these differences until relatively late in my analytic work. To fully explore these relations would have required, I think, a more pointed attention to race and ethnicity during the interviewing for the study, and, perhaps, changes in the scope of the study (so as to include more detailed information about paid work, for example, or extended family, and relations with wider communities). In the present study, I can only provide a few clues to the racial and ethnic organization of family work, and attempt to indicate the likely limits of the analysis presented here.

There were women living in all of the households studied, and in all but one case, women were my initial contacts even though I eventually interviewed three men as well. Since my aim was to examine the *work* of feeding rather than individual workers, my intent was to interview anyone, man or woman, who performed a substantial portion of the feeding work of the household. I was only partially successful. I did not interview the several children or parents of informants who occasionally cooked or helped with cooking. Nor did I interview the paid domestic worker in one household, whose main job was cleaning but who also did some cooking.[6] Several male partners who cooked occasionally or did some food shopping were unwilling to be interviewed, but I did talk with men in the three households where they did almost half or more of the day-to-day cooking. My assumption was that men who cook would share many of the perspectives of women who do the same work, and to some extent that seemed true. In chapter 6, however, I suggest that the family setting constructs feeding work somewhat differently for men than for women, and I discuss the hints of those differences provided by the few men I talked with. Though I talked with those who did most of the feeding work in these households, the omissions in my interviewing should be noted; although I meant to be open to the complexity of household reality, and included a range of household types, my research decisions constructed an interview record that simplifies experience, as any technique for describing social life inevitably does.

Male partners were present in twenty-one households; nine households (including all five of the poorest households) were headed by single mothers, three of whom reported that male friends spent time in the household but did not contribute significantly to household maintenance. The families included in the study were in a variety of life stages, ranging from women in their early twenties with preschool children to couples married for over

6. Indeed, this informant's account reflected the characteristic invisibility of domestic workers. Although she told me that the housekeeper sometimes cooks part of the evening meal, the housekeeper barely appeared in her account of everyday activity, which was entirely a reporting of "what I [rather than we] do." As I read the transcript now, I see that, as the interviewer, I colluded in the construction of such an account; with hindsight, I would include more discussion of the housekeeper's work. On relations between domestic workers and employers, in the nineteenth century and more recently, see Dudden (1983) and Rollins (1985).

twenty years with teenaged children.[7] Two of the youngest (and poorest) single women lived with their own parents, in what they regarded as temporary arrangements; in two Hispanic households, informants supported parents who lived with them; and several other families in working-class neighborhoods lived close enough to share some domestic life with extended family.

These households can be thought of as belonging to three different class groups. In those I will refer to as professional/managerial households, husbands were mainly "true" professionals or managers and employed wives worked in professional or semi-professional jobs; both men and women usually had college or advanced degrees. In working-class/white-collar households, parents had blue-collar or lower level white-collar jobs; they typically had high school or some college-level education.[8] Finally, the group of families studied includes a small number of poor households, in which families were sustained through intermittent low-level wage work and government income supplementation; most adults heading these households had no more than a high school education. As this description suggests, my assignment of the households to these class groups is based on an assessment of occupations and educational levels of both husband and wife in two-adult households; in a few cases, where a husband's and wife's occupations suggested different class positions, income level or neighborhood seemed to involve households in relations characteristic of one or another group (see note 5). My approach is informed by Marxist conceptions of class as process, or organized activity, structured by historically specific relations of production and distribution (Acker 1988). For the purpose of this study—understanding how family work and experience are conditioned by

7. Most children were between two and twelve years of age, though there were also six infants and ten teenagers. There were three sets of twins. Two households included only older children, and three teenaged children in two different households worked for pay and made small but regular contributions to household expenses.

8. In identifying these groups I follow those analysts who argue that distinctions between traditional "blue-collar" and "white-collar" occupations are misleading (I. DeVault 1990), and that the proletarianization of work (Braverman 1974) has produced a broad class of working people which includes both of these groups. Professional and managerial workers, though not technically part of a ruling class, are in locations that are typically part of a broader "ruling apparatus" (Smith 1987). These are locations that have also been labeled "contradictory" (Wright 1979), or as constituting a distinct class antagonistic to both capitalist and working classes (Ehrenreich and Ehrenreich 1979).

class—I have assumed that class is more accurately assigned to households than to individuals: the point is not that a woman (or man) simply shares the position of a spouse, but that households are the actual units that mediate the family experiences associated with class (Rapp 1982).[9]

My aim in identifying these groups and sorting households among them is not to draw distinct boundaries or argue for inevitable effects of class membership, but to provide a basis for exploring the implications for family life of different sorts of involvement in relations of production. Keeping in mind the contradictory aspects of many class situations, and the effects of income levels that are not always correlated with occupational class,[10] I attend both to the effects of cash income on feeding work (in chapter 7), and also to the ways in which the social organization of class both requires and depends on different kinds of family work (in chapter 8).

Half of the women studied worked outside the home for pay (about the same proportion as among mothers in the population as a whole), and they were nearly equally represented among the different class groups. Three of these women had part-time jobs: one was a poor woman who did not want to lose her welfare payment because of full-time work, and two were affluent women who liked the flexibility of part-time work. Two women were part-time students, and another had established a small business in her home.

9. Feminist scholars of the early 1970s criticized the assumption, in traditional stratification and class analysis research, that a woman's status was derived solely from that of her spouse, and argued for taking account of women's own involvements in class relations (Acker 1973; Oakley 1974). My analytic strategy here—taking the family/household as the unit of analysis—should not be taken to imply that women are not themselves connected to relations of production outside the home, or that class-related family experiences are undifferentiated for all those in any household. For more detailed discussion of these and related issues, see Sokoloff (1980), Hartmann (1981a), Smith (1985), and Acker (1988).

10. The median household income of study participants was $25,000 per year (close to the median income for the year in the Chicago SMSA), with a range from $6,000 to over $100,000. The incomes of poor households in the study were all lower than $9,000, with a median of $6,850; medians for working-class/white-collar and professional/managerial households were $24,000 and $35,000, respectively. Not surprisingly, there was considerable overlap in the household incomes of these two groups, due mostly to the higher combined incomes of dual-earner families in the working-class group and the lower incomes of professional/managerial households in which women did not work for pay. Except for the poorest households, the families' incomes seemed to be derived almost entirely from wages, although a few of the wealthier interviewees mentioned some stock holdings and a few others spoke of relatively small payments from other sources.

The women at home, caring for children, had usually worked for pay before becoming mothers, mostly in clerical or semi-professional jobs. Most seemed to have chosen to be at home, at least at the time I interviewed them. However, two women reported that they had "tried to work," but had not been able to negotiate the conditions of their work with their partners and arrange for adequate child care.

Figure 1 provides a graphic representation of the sample, arrayed in class groups and along an income axis. This chart combines much of the background information summarized above, and shows how the characteristics discussed as discrete variables combine to produce distinctive household configurations in different class groups. The figure shows, for example, the extent of income overlap between professional/managerial and working-class/white-collar groups, the greater dispersion of professional/managerial incomes as compared with a relatively narrow income range in the working-class/white-collar group, the effects on income of women's wage work, the distribution of different race groups, and the larger family sizes at lower income levels, especially among the minority families.

This study was conducted during a period of change in women's work and household activity, at a time when feminist ideas about women's equality had been circulating for some time in mainstream media as well as social movement circles.[11] Indeed, it was my involvement in feminism that provided the impetus for a study of housework. My focus, however, was not so much on attitudes toward housework or women's roles as on the character of the work itself. When I introduced the study to interviewees, I explained that I was interested in women's work and especially in the kinds of work that are not often recognized; I believe this statement provided an introduction that was neutral with respect to explicit feminism. As our talk proceeded, I was open to discussion of feminist issues, but did not initiate it, and very few informants talked spontaneously about feminist ideas or the women's movement as such. Still, there was ample evidence that these individuals were struggling with social changes associated with feminism. Many expressed a general awareness of these issues, and varying degrees of concern, approval, and sometimes defensiveness about changing expectations for women's and men's activities. A very few

11. Freeman (1975), for example, suggests that feminism began to receive extensive media coverage in 1970.

women identified themselves as feminists, and a few expressed strong adherence to traditional views. Most fell somewhere between these extremes, accommodating their lives and beliefs to changing cultural ideals without completely abandoning familiar patterns. Many made reference to some concept of "fairness" as they discussed their household division of labor, suggesting an interest in some version of egalitarianism in marriage. Some talked about more specific ideas that might be identified as loosely related to feminist thought, and these more specific themes tended to be distributed among the sample in interesting ways. Working-class women with paid jobs emphasized the economic trends that have pulled more women into the labor force and the resulting changes (or at least strain) in traditional family patterns. Professional/managerial women who had chosen to stay home with children often adopted a metaphor with feminist undertones to underline the importance of child care, referring to mothering as their work, equivalent to a job. In both cases, these themes might be understood as justifications for choices already made rather than as ideological commitments; still, individuals in both cases are drawing on discourses that bring women's work into view, and recognize that the "naturalness" of traditional family patterns might be questioned.[12]

Their responses to social change meant that for some couples, the division of household labor between spouses was a matter for negotiation and adjustment. These issues will be discussed more fully in chapter 4, but a brief note here will help to put the entire study in perspective. About half of the couples studied expressed some level of commitment to sharing household and family work. At the same time, the presence of children in all of these households had the effect of pushing them toward more conservative patterns. The added work burden of child-rearing was most often taken up by wives. One reason for this choice could be the typically lower salaries of employed women, which might make it more likely that mothers will curtail their wage work than fathers. However, though this economic rationale is often cited, many women seem to have simply taken for granted that child-rearing will be their responsibility. Further, "sharing the work" does not necessarily mean sharing all of the work, or sharing equally. For a variety

12. This study provides a "snapshot" of these family/households in the early 1980s. Time will tell whether their lives and beliefs represent a brief stage in a transition toward new family patterns, or a more enduring adjustment to a "stalled revolution" (Hochschild 1989) in family life.

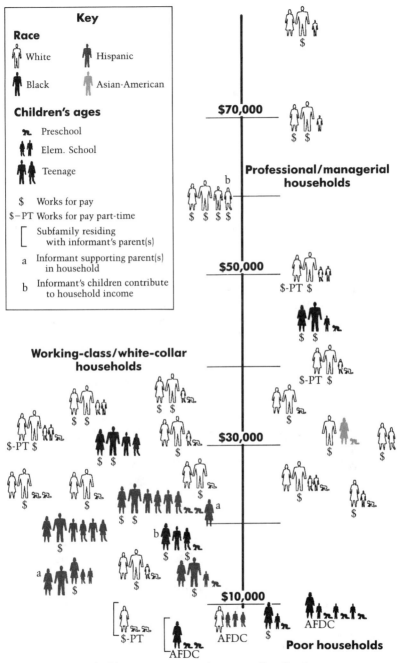

Figure 1 Household composition and income distribution
for families in the study

of reasons, feeding the family remains an activity conducted mostly by women, even for many couples whose talk emphasizes shared responsibility.

The interviews. My aim in conducting the interviews was to explore with these individuals the contours of "ordinary" experience in a range of household settings. I told interviewees that I wanted to talk with them about "all the housework that has to do with food: cooking, planning, shopping, cleaning up." Although I organized the interviews around several quite general questions (e.g. "Tell me about a typical day's eating."), I indicated through my more detailed responses to informants that they should talk very specifically: "Who gets up first?" "What kind of cereal?" and so on. In spite of the ambiguity of our "topic," these interviews were remarkably easy to conduct. Almost everyone—those who loved to cook and those who disliked and resented the work—spoke easily and naturally. Looking back, I can see that I identified, at least in outline, a category that made sense to these people because it was a category that organized their day-to-day activity. For those who do the work, feeding is a central task and takes considerable time. Strategizing about how to do it leads to the development of routines, to frequent rearrangements and improvisations, and to pride in the "little tricks" that make the work easier. It is a topic easily referenced by those who do the work. Furthermore, our talk happened in a way that I and my informants knew and were comfortable with, because everyday conversations among women are often settings for discussing this kind of work. Chatting about the details of household routines provides opportunities for finding out what someone else does, reflecting on one's own practice, getting and sharing ideas or solutions to common problems. Most interviews were one to two hours long. I tape-recorded and personally transcribed them nearly verbatim.[13]

In the analysis of these interviews, I treat the people I talked with as "expert practitioners" of household caring work, a term used by ethnomethodologists to refer to the ordinary social competences of members of social groups—their "seen" but typically "unnoticed" understandings (Garfinkel 1967). Those who live and work in a particular setting are the ones who understand its organization, precisely because they must coordinate their activities with those of others in the setting. Their words, alone, do not pro-

---

13. I summarized in the transcripts some material that seemed marginal to my concerns, but retained the tape recordings so that I could review that material when necessary.

vide a sociological analysis of the setting's organization. But their words provide powerful clues for the analyst. They speak in particular ways not because they see the social organization of their setting, but because they know how to conduct the work of the setting. Thus, their vocabulary, the taken-for-granted concepts that organize their talk, the structure of their accounts, all serve as features of the talk that express the social organization of the work.[14]

I use the data from these open-ended interviews, focused very concretely on everyday routines, to develop a view of the everyday work of feeding a family. One of my aims is to describe the conduct of the work in considerable detail, so as to get beyond conventional assumptions like the common disclaimer: "I don't really do much housework." Sometimes I treat the interview data as reports of actual activity. But the disclaimer itself is of interest, as part of the line of fault in experience, signalling a gap in expression and knowledge. Problems of expression—when people complain that "it's hard to explain"—provide similar pointers. These linguistic indicators of disjuncture are essential to the dual project of recovering experience and exposing the ideological forms that have obscured it for so long. I have included in this book a great deal of talk about rather ordinary, mundane matters, and some readers may find this talk "trivial" or somewhat boring. However, my analysis is driven by respect and appreciation for such talk and the activity it refers to, and I urge readers to study it respectfully as well. The particularities of these accounts of household routine, the mundane details of practice, reveal the diversities of life in different households, as well as pointing toward the more general social organization of "family." I have assigned fictitious names to about half of the interviewees, whose situations I discuss in some detail, so that readers can follow these individuals as they appear throughout the text (and the Appendix provides brief profiles of these named informants). In some cases, I have changed informants' specific occupations or other details of their situations in order to protect their anonymity.

My intention, in the analysis that follows, is to explore the territory around the line of fault I have begun to excavate in this chap-

14. My approach follows Smith's discussion of how social organization appears in talk (1987:187–89). It is also related, though more loosely, to other sociological approaches that focus explicitly on talk or discourse as the object of analysis (e.g. Paget 1983; Mishler 1986; Todd and Fisher 1988). For a more detailed discussion of my treatment of these interview data, see M. DeVault (1990).

ter. Though based on analysis of people's accounts of the day-to-day work of feeding their families, this exploration will go beyond the everyday. It will show that this line of fault is part of a larger structure of social relations of caring and power. In its organization, this book moves from its beginning in "women's experience" toward a recognition of the ways that the discursive construction of women's "place" in social organization obscures the diversity of lived experience in material settings. In Part 1, I develop the concept of feeding as "family work," not just because it is done within the family, but also because the work actually constitutes a social group as "family" from day to day. I wish to make possible for readers a kind of "seeing" of the work of feeding that includes its usually invisible parts and begins to reveal its organization. In Parts 2 and 3, I explore the gender and class organization of feeding. In Part 2, I show how feeding is "women's work," and how by doing the work, women are drawn into relations of service to others, subordination of self, and deference toward male partners. I also examine the character and limits of several men's attempts to share feeding work. In Part 3, I look behind the ostensibly class-neutral character of "women's work," and show how strongly the material differences of particular settings condition the conduct and meaning of "care." In this section, I attend more specifically to the discourses that organize family life, obscuring class differences and simultaneously recruiting women into the project of perpetuating them.

Part One

The Work of "Feeding a Family"

1 Doing Family Meals

Eating, apparently a biological matter, is actually profoundly social. What we eat, where we get it, how it is prepared, when we eat and with whom, what it means to us—all these depend on social arrangements. Food sustains social and emotional life as well as physiological being, through the cultural rituals of serving and eating. The work required to feed a family is partly determined by the material situations of household groups: the organization of markets, supply and distribution of energy, and typical arrangement and accoutrements of dwellings. But the work of feeding others is also shaped by, and in turn expresses, beliefs and customs of the society at a particular time. More than just the provision of edibles, feeding work means staging the rather complex social events that we label meals.

In this chapter, I begin an analysis of the work of feeding that makes visible these essential, social aspects of food provision, by examining the production of family meals. But eating practices in contemporary households should be seen against a backdrop of larger economic and technological changes. Even a few generations ago, when more households were agricultural ones, and when work was usually closer to home, families were more likely to eat together, three times daily. They had little choice, because there were few other places to be fed. Cooking for an entire household was time-consuming and heavy work. Technological developments—new products and appliances—have made the material tasks of cooking much easier than in our grandmothers'

A portion of this chapter first appeared in *Families and Work*, edited by Naomi Gerstel and Harriet Engel Gross, pp. 178–191. © 1987 by Temple University. Reprinted by permission of Temple University Press.

time, and more and more of the arduous work of processing foods has been transferred from home to market. These very real changes have affected the way that most people think about housework, so that housework sometimes seems to have practically disappeared. Susan Strasser (1982) charts the history of technological development in terms of the activities that are no longer necessary—"By 1870, most people could buy soap and candles; by 1920, they could afford to purchase most of their clothes"—and claims that, "by 1970, they could stop cooking."

In fact, it is not clear that these technological changes have significantly reduced the amount of time people spend on housework. Rather, most analysts agree that social and technological developments have brought shifts in the types of housework required to support families rather than in the total work burden (Cowan 1983). Between the 1920s and the 1960s, for example, time spent on food preparation itself decreased somewhat, but additional time spent on shopping more than made up for the decline (Vanek 1974). And although the "convenience foods" introduced after World War II have been widely touted as time-savers for women, Joan Gussow (1987) argues that there is little evidence of any significant savings, and that advertisers have sold an illusion of time savings in order to promote new products.

While the total time spent on housework may not be very different, the form of feeding and eating has changed dramatically since the turn of the century. Now, family members who work for a wage often leave home early and work far away. They may do shift work that takes them from home at different times. Many children are at school or day care all day. In addition, cooking itself has become less and less necessary. Many technical skills have been marketized: new products incorporate much of the work of food processing formerly done at home, and the growth of the restaurant trade and tremendous expansion of fast-food franchising provide new options for purchasing meals. Food industry analysts claim that we now live in a "grazing society" (*Advertising Age*, cited in Strasser 1982:297), where individuals no longer come together for meals, but grab quick snacks here and there during the day. It is hard to say whether this claim accurately describes many family/households containing children.[1] But the kernel of truth be-

1. Despite much concern and public discussion, it is difficult to evaluate the significance of an expanding food service industry for family eating. While the share of food expenditures for "away-from-home eating" is increasing rapidly (e.g. from thirty percent in 1965 to forty-five percent in 1988), these are dollar figures that reflect

hind this popular image is the fact that most people in modern industrial societies are no longer compelled to return to a household to be fed. Family meals have become less necessary and more a volitional social form.

Typically, in contemporary households, work and school schedules cut into meal times so that very few families eat even two meals together each day. Breakfast and lunch, especially, barely survive. In the households I studied, men and women who work outside their homes eat breakfast quickly, often before the rest of the household awakens. Some purchase food on the way to work and eat on the job. Even when the entire family is awake, the pressure of various schedules makes an elaborate meal unlikely. In almost half of the households I studied, children are fed quickly in the morning while their parents are busy with other work. At lunchtime, almost a third of these households are empty; in several others, women are home alone. Even when women are home with children, and prepare lunch, the meal is an attenuated ritual. In some households, women sit down to eat with their children, but in an equal number, they feed the children alone and either skip lunch or eat later by themselves. Dinner is more consistently arranged as a well-defined meal, but can also be disrupted by the scheduling of outside activities. One man leaves the house for his night shift at 6:30, less than an hour after his wife returns from her secretarial job. Another, a professional worker, arrives home late in the evening, just as his children are going to bed. Evening activities—going to school or the gym, bowling or playing pool, working in church or community groups—may mean that men or women and their children miss dinner several times a week.

In the context of such changes, with more and more activities pulling individuals away from their households, bringing a family together for any kind of regular meal requires a new kind of effort. Still, the parents I interviewed were concerned about establishing

---

more precipitous increases in restaurant than in grocery prices (Blaylock, Elitzak, and Manchester 1989). Further, these figures do not indicate who eats away from home or how often. Average per-person weekly expenditures for food away from home are greatest in single-person households, somewhat less for two-person households, and still less for larger household groups (U.S. Department of Agriculture 1987b). This pattern suggests that family groups may be less influenced by the trend toward eating out than single persons and childless couples. Informants in this study did talk of eating away from home and purchasing take-out food items, but they discussed these practices as occasional treats or conveniences rather than as replacing family meals.

patterns of regular meals. They talked of strategizing about routines, and their comments revealed the importance of the concept "meal" as an organizer of family life. For example, the mother of an infant talked about pulling her daughter's high chair up to the table so that they can eat together "as a family," and a single working mother explained that she has continued to cook every evening for her teenaged daughter so as to provide "a dinner made by her mother." In addition, people arrange meals to mark the rhythms of family life, with regular dinners for extended family, or "special" Sunday dinners designed "to enrich our family life."

The work of feeding a family has changed, then, in ways that we are just beginning to understand. Most writers focus on the work that has disappeared. Strasser, for instance, concludes:

> Hardly any modern families get together for all their meals, and restaurants and supermarkets provide options for buying food that somebody else has cooked. Cooking remains the central ritual of housekeeping, but like the rest of the housekeeping routine, that ritual endures only in truncated form. The work itself, performed with gas and electric stoves, devices that do the chopping and mixing, and utensils requiring little care, bears little relation to the time-consuming, hazardous, heavy work of the colonial hearth. (1982:48)

Strasser shows how the traditional skills of housework—the heavy work of cooking, for example—have been transferred from home to market. In this book, I will focus on a different aspect of this change, the nature of the work that remains. Though its character has changed profoundly, feeding remains a "central ritual," not only in housekeeping, as Strasser notes, but in the production of family life itself.

One thing that has not changed is that the work of feeding a family goes on and on; food must be provided again and again, every day. One woman I talked with complained of "just the everyday, what are we going to have, the drudgery of it, and the demands of it. You know, it's noon, and there are children that need to be fed." Indeed, many people think of cooking, especially everyday cooking for children, as rather tedious but straightforward, simple work. However, the repetitiveness of the work can be deceiving, so that even those who do the work barely recognize how much they do. Far from a purely mechanical task, producing meals requires thoughtful coordination and interpersonal work as well as the concrete tasks of preparation.

The parents who spoke about the importance of family meals recognize that meals do more than provide sustenance; they are also social events that bring family members together. Such rituals provide a basis for establishing and maintaining family culture, and they create a mutual recognition of the family as a group (Bossard and Boll 1950; Charles and Kerr 1988). Indeed, a "family" is not a naturally occurring collection of individuals; its reality is constructed from day to day through activities like eating together. Thus, producing meals—at least in today's U.S. society—has increasingly become work aimed at maintaining the kind of group life we think of as constituting a family. The skills involved in feeding a family are skills of planning and coordination; the work, increasingly, is invisible work. In this chapter I will begin to examine the kinds of work involved in producing meals for a household group. I will make visible the work that women themselves often discount as trivial, and that they reveal only in their detailed accounts of everyday activities.

Planning a Meal

Some women talk of planning meals as "enjoyable," and experience planning as the creative part of their work; for others it is "a hassle." Whatever their feelings about it, planning is an essential part of the work that must be done. Jean's comment highlighted the effort involved:

> My biggest peeve about cooking, preparing three meals a day,
> is trying to figure out what to put on the table. If somebody
> would just send me menus every week, and I could provide
> the mechanics, that would take a lot of the hassle away.
> Because I do—I'll spend time in the morning, thinking,
> about what in the heck I'm going to fix.

Not all women recognize that they "spend time" on meal planning; many claim that they "don't do much planning." But conceiving of a meal requires sensitivity to a variety of concerns, and as they described their cooking routines, all of the people I talked with revealed the thought involved in the work of feeding.

Family meals are prepared for particular people. While "cooking" is work that can be done alone, "feeding" implies a relatedness, a sense of connection with others. Producing meals is about serving family members in a double sense: the food provided for a family cannot be just any food, but must be food that will satisfy them. Other researchers (Luxton 1980; Murcott 1983; Charles and Kerr 1988) have found that women's cooking is strongly influenced by their husband's preferences, and the people I talked with also emphasized foods their families liked. When I asked about typical meals, almost everyone began by drawing the boundaries between foods they would and would not serve, and these accounts were organized with reference to the special tastes of both husbands and children. For example, Donna, a married white woman, reported:

> Like for meats, let's see—he likes so many. Well, he doesn't like pork chops . . . But we usually have meat. And he doesn't like potatoes too well, so I'll usually have stuffing. Or rice-a-roni. Or I'll make like corn fritters or potato pancakes. And you know, the vegetables.

Or, from a black single mother:

> Let's see—well, beans are good. But my children aren't much on eating beans . . . They'll eat meat, but they won't eat a lot of beef—they'll eat like ground beef or something, but like steak is hard to chew. But I cook turkey parts. And lamb, they have these little lambs, I'll buy that and boil it up real nice where it just falls off the bone and they'll consume that. Veal. Liver. They will eat liver. And spinach, they love spinach. And I do push vegetables hard on them, because vegetables are very important. Carrots, and you know, they'll eat mixed vegetables, peas, broccoli and cauliflower, and spinach. But they won't eat greens very much.

Responding to these individual preferences is not a personal favor, but a requirement of the work. Family members may not eat if they don't like what is served, so women usually restrict their planning to items that have been successful in the past.

Mothers are often especially concerned that children eat the foods they need, and work at devising menus that are both appropriate and appealing. Some cook special foods for their children in addition to the family's regular meal, or invent techniques for encouraging children to eat, like Susan, who "disguises" her daughter's meat in mashed potatoes, and cuts cheese into amusing shapes. While not everyone does this kind of double work, the concern for children's tastes that it displays is not at all unusual. Everyone I talked with made some reference to the foods that children would and would not eat.

The ways that women respond to their husbands' tastes are more complicated. Donna, whose husband is "moody," and "a fussy eater," consults him every day before deciding what to have for dinner. He is quite vocal about his preferences, and she caters to his tastes in the same way that many women cater to their children: she will not cook anything he dislikes, and she always prepares foods in the special ways that he prefers. More typically, however, women respond to husbands' preferences out of a combination of duty and pride in their work. They spoke of meals appropriate for a man, and sometimes distinguished between meals they would serve to their children alone, and meals for the entire family. Sometimes these comments referred to men's work and to food as fuel. Susan explained:

> He works hard, he has a physical job, in construction, and he's lean, and his metabolism is not at all like mine, he just burns it off. So I have to give him something with a lot of ballast.

Or, the same thought expressed by Sandra, a white woman married to a professional man:

> I suppose a lot of it is influenced by his day. He is in a very demanding work situation. It's almost as though a decent meal is a reward for getting through a difficult day.

Many women feel that they have succeeded at their work when they have pleased the man in the house. One black working mother, Bertie, explained:

> I like to cook things that make my family happy. I really do. I love to cook things that make my husband lean back in his seat and say, "That was a good dinner, lady." That's very important.

And Laurel, a white woman who described her husband as "incredibly easy to please," explained that, even so:

> He would like it I think if I were more creative in the kitchen, and it was a real gourmet delight every night. So every once in a while I'll, you know, make a salad plate, instead of a big bowl. And I know that that's for him, I know that that's why I'm doing it.

Nickie Charles and Marion Kerr (1988:69) comment on the extent to which women take this aspect of the work for granted, noting that some of their interviewees described themselves as "lucky" because their husbands "like everything."

In order to plan meals that are pleasing, women must know what it is that their husbands and children want, and such knowledge is not so easily gained as we might suppose. While family members can sometimes speak directly about their likes and dislikes, they do not always do so in ways that are helpful. In any case, the actual work of planning is rarely shared by those who only eat. Children will usually respond if given a choice of foods, and many women reported asking them what they want, especially for breakfasts and lunches. Husbands are typically more cryptic. Many women complained that they could not simply ask their husbands what they wanted to eat. For example, Sandra reported:

I'll call at the office and ask, "Is there anything special you'd like for dinner?" And his standard answer is, "Yes, something good."

And Susan explained:

He's a big eater, of something he enjoys. But he doesn't like a lot of choice. You can't ask him, what do you want? I just have to make that decision for him. And if he doesn't want it, he doesn't eat it.

Instead of through direct questioning, women learn what their husbands like "just living with somebody," through "trial and error." They notice what gets eaten and what is left, and which meals are special favorites. One woman reported:

Sometimes it's rather indirect. Like, it's still on your plate, what was wrong with it? You know, that kind of thing.

But the learning process has an active character, which can be seen in another woman's comments: Bertie explained that when she was first married, she had not known what to cook for her husband, so she "started looking for things that he liked better. Up until I saw him starting to get what he really wanted." Eventually, women learn what their husbands like, and take their knowledge for granted. Women who have been married for years experience meal planning as less difficult than those who are younger; they were more likely to report, "I don't get a lot of input; I know what they like."

Husbands' and children's tastes, of course, are often different. Thus, part of the work of planning involves weighing and balancing the contradictory desires of family members. Again, some solve the problem by doing double cooking. Others consider the balance in their longer-range choices. For example, Laurel explained:

> If we've had a particularly good meal one night, and everyone enjoyed it, and everyone ate heartily, and they've eaten well, the next day I might make something that I know everyone—other than Richard and I—they're just not going to give a lick about. And I will try to have something else on the table, that they're going to—not another entree—but a vegetable that they like, or cheese, or something that will fill them up.

Planning, then, means making sure that everyone gets "something that will fill them up."

Those who cook must consider their own tastes as well. However, in contrast to their responsiveness to the tastes of others, most women were scrupulously careful not to give their own preferences any special weight. For example:

> I like spinach and they don't. So every once in a while I'll make spinach, just for me. But I don't make it frequently enough where he would feel that I was being prejudiced one way or the other.

Donna reported more bluntly, "One of us has to compromise, and it's going to end up being me." (The sources for this deferential reasoning will be discussed further in chapter 6.)

If pleasing the family is the first requirement, a meal must do even more; it must also conform to the pattern for a "proper" meal that household members have learned to expect. Within every culture, custom dictates that foods should be prepared and served in particular ways. Anthropologist Mary Douglas illustrates the force of these expectations with a story about her own dilemma as a family cook:

> Sometimes at home, hoping to simplify the cooking, I ask, "Would you like to have just soup for supper tonight? I mean a good thick soup—instead of supper. It's late and you must be hungry. It won't take a minute to serve." Then an argument starts: "Let's have soup now, and supper when you are ready." "No no, to serve two meals would be more work. But if you like, why not start with the soup and fill up with pudding?" "Good heavens! What sort of a meal is that? A beginning and an end and no middle." "Oh, all right then,

have the soup as it's there, and I'll do a Welsh rarebit as well." When they have eaten soup, Welsh rarebit, pudding, and cheese: "What a lot of plates. Why do you make such elaborate suppers?" They proceed to argue that by taking thought I could satisfy the full requirements of a meal with a single, copious dish. Several rounds of this conversation have given me a practical interest in the categories and meanings of food. I needed to know what defines the category of a meal in our home. (1972:61–62)

Douglas proceeds to explore how food patterns are used as markers, expressing the structure of social relations both inside the household and also between household members and outsiders. In her household, for example, as in most, the categories "meals" and "drinks," and the people they are shared with, distinguish between those who are close friends and those who are merely acquaintances. In addition, meals themselves vary, with a differentiation between weekday and weekend meals, for instance, or everyday and special holiday meals, and this kind of variation marks the tempo of household life. Foods and food combinations carry messages about household life. They constitute a code with expressive significance.

For such a code to work, each meal, no matter how simple, must have the system's essential form so that it is recognizable as a part of the code. It must have the basic structure indicating that it is, in fact, a meal. This kind of patterning, of course, is imported from the wider culture into the everyday life of the household. Much of it is ethnically based, learned from shared cultural experience, and signalling membership in a cultural group beyond the household (see Douglas 1984). The forms of meals, then, become part of the social relations of eating: they provide instructions for choices about what to serve and they influence the responses and participation of family members. Most people, of course, are not conscious of food patterns as a coded system, and most cooks are not as introspective or analytical as Douglas about the patterning of their meals. However, it was clear from the way women talked about planning meals that they think about meals in the kind of formal, patterned way that Douglas shows us.

In a study of food practices among families in northern England, Charles and Kerr (1988) found tremendous concern with producing "proper meals." Their sample was relatively homogeneous ethnically, and they report that "proper meals" were understood—in accordance with a "dominant food ideology"—as consisting of meat (or sometimes fish), potatoes, and a vegetable. Informants in the present study, drawn from several different ethnic groups, described different kinds of "adequate" or "proper" meals, but all thought in terms of some cultural standard. Some people talked about a single item that was an essential element in meals for their families (a meat entree, for example, or beans and tortillas). In addition, when asked to describe a typical dinner, most people talked in terms of the several categories of foods that make a meal. For example:

> I try to have a salad and one or two vegetables, some kind of starch—potato or maybe some kind of bread—and then some entree—maybe meat or some sort of casserole.

They also spoke of rules for the kinds of combinations they can make:

> We Mexicans usually have rice with pork. And if you have steak, we would have, like, any kind of soup, with broth.

The importance of such categories can be seen by the fact that people referred to them as a sort of standard even when they described meals that deviated from the form that was typical for them. For example, Laurel's description of a somewhat unusual dinner shows how she thinks of the meal as a set of "slots" to be filled:

> Richard had been out for a business lunch, so I knew he wasn't going to be real hungry, and I'm on another diet, so I wasn't going to be eating the regular meal, so I didn't make, like, that slot that holds potatoes or noodles or something like that.

These cultural codes also extend beyond daily eating, with special meals to mark weekends, birthdays, and holidays. Charles and Kerr (1988) describe their informants' "festive" meals in some detail; I spoke with people about day-to-day cooking, but many of them also made reference to important "special" meals (and see Counihan 1988; Sered 1988).

Family members respond to meals in terms of such patterns, insisting on habits such as "meat and potatoes," rice with every meal, or special holiday menus. Some women reported that they were trying to change their families' ideas about meals, to encourage them to eat less meat, or more vegetables, for instance. But they could only succeed if they were sensitive to household members' own ideas about what a meal should be. Susan reported that when she served a quiche, her husband told her, yes, it was very good, but he did not want "breakfast for dinner." Even though others respond to cultural patterns, those who are served are undoubtedly not as conscious of these codes as the women who actually work at designing meals. Ed, who had just begun to cook for his family, explained some of the requirements of planning meals, and his problem:

> There has to be a vegetable. And not two starches. The trouble is, I don't know what a starch is, I can't remember what a starch is, so sometimes I end up with two starches, sometimes I don't.

He knows that the meal should be patterned, but he is still learning to construct the patterns himself.

The kind of responsiveness to family members I have described above implies that women who cook will select foods primarily from the set of things that have been successful in the past. The importance of food as a code implies that meals conform to particular patterns. However, these aspects of meal planning are combined with a third important concern—that meals should be varied—and the people I talked with also emphasized their efforts to make meals different and interesting.

Variety is more important in some households than in others, and it means different things in different households, but some notion of variation was fundamental to meal planning. At the simplest level, for example, a Puerto Rican woman reported:

> When I go shopping, I buy different kinds of meat, something different for each day.

In addition, when they told how they make decisions about particular meals, the women I interviewed described a process in which they take account of a series of meals from previous days: "I wanted to fix a Chinese meal, I kind of felt like we hadn't had it for a while." Or: "Yesterday I decided it was time to have fish again." The same kind of consideration applies to the selection of side dishes:

> I try to sort of get a variety . . . I sort of look in the freezer, and then just take out a vegetable that goes with it, that we haven't had yesterday or something.

People's concern with varied menus comes partly from contemporary U.S. health discourse, which links variety and nutrition. Food producers and nutritional scientists have promoted the idea that the safest and healthiest diet is a varied one. All of these informants reported that they were concerned about cooking nutritious meals, but their understandings of nutrition were often very general. (Those who followed media nutrition reports in more detail were predominantly informants in professional households, and will be discussed in chapter 8.) Many people summarized "good eating habits" with formulas like, "keep the variety up, and keep the sweets to a minimum." However, women also talked of variety as a part of their craft, important to producing meals that are not just adequate but interesting as well. Many expressed concern about "getting into a rut":

> It's kind of boring to have the same thing over and over and over and over again.

Or:

> You get to the place sometime where you think, now what am I going to cook, you know? And you've cooked everything, you've cooked around, and you want to think of something different, something I haven't cooked in a long time.

This woman's talk of having "cooked around" conveys the character of the process: she relies on a set of relatively standard food items, but she selects from among them to produce a series of interesting meals. Women search for new ideas, and many reported that they talk with friends about how to produce different meals:

> It seems like when you're going through a rut so is your friend . . . [At these times they'll talk.] . . . Like, oh gosh, what am I going to do with the potato? There's only so many things you can do with it.

Such conversation has typically been regarded as trivial, as one of the unremarkable ways that women "pass time" when they get together. In fact, new ideas are important for each woman's work, and their talk provides one of the ways that they can learn about the essentially private household practices of their peers.

Planning a meal is rarely recognized as the kind of intellectual problem it actually is. The process is like solving a puzzle. There are special requirements stemming from individuals' tastes and preferences, and relationships within the household, but variety is also important, so that the puzzle must be solved in relatively novel ways each day. The intersection of these different, sometimes contradictory concerns means that planning requires continual monitoring and adjustment. Planning is based on the overall form of each meal, and also the way it fits into a pattern of surrounding meals. By solving this puzzle each day, the person who cooks for a family is continually creating one part of the reality of household life. At the same time, she (or much more rarely, he) is constructing her own place within the family, as one who provides for the needs of others.

Meal planning is not a simple matter of decision making as conventionally understood. The intersection of several different kinds of requirements generates a holistic approach to the problem. Those who do the work are only partly aware of its principles. They can articulate some, but not all of their methods. They are like musicians and theater people, who choose to play particular notes because "it swings," or to do a scene in a particular way because "it works" (Becker 1982:199). The fact that the principles underlying this kind of knowledge are seldom articulated can make the work appear somewhat mysterious, or even mystical. For example, a man who has just begun to cook attributes his wife's superior planning abilities not only to experience, but also to "personality." And Bertie, who has been married and cooking for over twenty years, maintains that skills come automatically:

> When you become a housewife, some of these things just—
> if one cares at all—they come almost automatic . . .
> Instinct, it's sort of like instinct.

The activities of feeding a family are of course not really instinctual; they are socially organized and their logic is learned. However, comments like these emerge from actual practice. They point to real characteristics of the work of feeding: its invisibility, its improvisational character, and its basis in a tacit, rather than fully articulated kind of knowledge.

The Meal as Event

The details of everyday meals—the times and places that families typically eat, the formal and informal rules that govern their behavior, and the kinds of interaction that are part of the meal—vary from one household to another. But most people's thoughts about meals reflect idealized versions of family life. Laurel described her family's typical hurried breakfast and explained apologetically, "It's not a Walton family breakfast, by any means." Even though actual events fall short of the ideals suggested by television families such as the Waltons, people work at making their meals particular kinds of events. Those I interviewed reported that they tried to make meal time "a calm time," "a very social thing," or "an important getting together time." Such goals can only be accomplished through attention to the meal, and efforts to orchestrate the event.

Talk is considered an important part of most families' meals, and is something that people reported working at. For example, an Asian-American woman, married to a white professional man, reported:

> At dinner we usually talk about the kind of day that Mark and I had. You know, you try to relate what cute thing, cute and wonderful thing the child did, and things of that nature. We try to talk during dinner.

Sometimes, these norms are even more explicit:

> My son will sometimes be very grumpy and grouchy, because "The whole day went wrong," and he's told that that's simply not an excuse for not talking.

One affluent mother with five children, worried that they might not all have enough of a chance to participate in the dinner talk, had tried to get each child to read a news item each day and report on it at the table. The system did not work, she reported, but the story does reveal this mother's concern for her family's mealtime conversation. Such concern with organizing talk at the meal seemed to be somewhat class-specific. Though informants in all class groups talked about meals as events of coming together, middle-class and especially professional women were more explicit about the effort they put into organizing talk. In a few working-class households, talk at the dinner table was an item of contention between taciturn husbands and their wives, who were striving to construct the meal as a particular kind of social occasion. One of these women argued with her husband over his dinner-table behavior, while another simply gave in on the issue; she explained, "If I sit and start talking, he'll say, 'What the heck, can't you ever shut up?'" These comments suggest that at least some working-class women, but fewer working-class men, share the more middle-class expectation that meals should be times for family interaction.

In all households, children's behavior at the table must be monitored and controlled. Sometimes this is relatively simple:

> Now they're getting older they aggravate each other at the table. You know, "She did this," "She's doing that." So I have to sit there and kind of watch.

In more difficult situations, when children are problem eaters, managing the meal can become a "project." Laurel explained:

> There's a lot of nights when it's, you know, "Either sit up and eat or leave the table." And you know, then the whole meal is ruined, it's just an aggravating situation. So the two of us are working on just not letting that happen. We give her real small portions, and just try to encourage her, and praise her when she is cleaning her plate. It's a project for Richard and I to get going on.

Most parents monitor their own behavior at the table, since their children learn from them; mealtime is time for "setting an example." One woman talked about how her daughter was learning to use a cup by mimicking the others at the table. Another, highlighting her own active role in this kind of imitative learning, explained:

> I really have changed my way of eating. Like I will always take the vegetable, even though I'm not much of a vegetable eater. I don't make a big deal about it, but so that they at least see that that sort of thing is eaten.

This kind of interpersonal work may be directed toward the needs of adults as well as children. For example, a South American woman whose elderly parents live in the household explained how the whole family has helped her father adjust to health-related dietary restrictions:

> We love coffee because we come from a country that's very rich in coffee. But we aren't drinking it so much now, mainly because of my father. It's not fair, if we are drinking and drinking coffee every time, and he's just watching us, it's terrible. Now we are very familiar with these herbal teas.

Her comment highlights the fact that the social experience of eating something together may be more important than the food itself. And both examples show how social interactions, and even one's own eating, become part of the work that contributes to the production of a family meal.

Most people do not think of themselves as working when they sit down to eat with family. Often (though not always), they are enjoying eating themselves, and enjoying the companionship of the others in their households. They engage in habitual behaviors that seem natural, that they often described as simply "what everybody does." But the difficulties that may arise, especially for parents who have other work as well, provide occasions when the effort required at mealtimes becomes visible. With the family so seldom together during the day, the meal becomes critically important. Laurel again, who was running a small business at home, explained:

> It's a real hard situation. By the end of the day, I'm tired,
> Richard's tired, the kids are either wound up or tired. And
> it's a real volatile situation. It can either be just great, a real
> pleasant experience, or it can be a real bummer.

She does not talk about the problem in terms of work that must be done, but her comment suggests it. She and her husband are often too tired; they have trouble making the effort required to control a "volatile" situation.

In an observation of one family's dinner, I was able to see how Ed, the black professional man who organized it, thought of this work of interaction as the essential activity defining the meal as event. After the family finished eating, the older son was to load the dishwasher; Ed remained at the table, supervising him in this task. A younger son brought his book to the table, and they looked through it, discussing each picture. When they had finished, when Ed had sent his older son off to do homework and was finally left alone in the kitchen, he turned to me and announced, "Well, that's dinner at our house." There was clearly more work to do—food left out on counters and stove—and he went on to do it, but when the children left the room he felt the closure that marked the end of "dinner" as an interpersonal event.

The time and effort required to orchestrate family meals comes into focus even more clearly when we examine the households in which family members have difficulties coming together for regular family meals. All of the women who reported that they rarely sat down to dinner as a group were women working outside their homes (although some working women did manage to organize regular family meals). Conversely, of the women who are at home rather than working for pay, only two reported that they sometimes did not eat as a family group. Bertie, who works full-time as well as going to school, whose husband has two jobs, and whose teenaged children are involved in their own activities, commented that sitting down to dinner every day is "just one of those luxuries that we have to give up." Thus, part of the reason for eliminating the dinner as a regular family event is the difficulty of coordinating multiple work schedules instead of just one. However, it is also clear that arranging for family meals is work that takes time and energy, and that it is most easily accomplished when there is someone at home with time and energy to devote to the task.

Rick and Robin, a young white couple who both worked full-time (he as a delivery truck driver and she as a clerical worker), talked eloquently about this problem. Their two children were seven years and seven months old at the time of the interview. Both had been working full-time throughout their marriage, though their jobs had changed frequently because of cutbacks and layoffs. Robin was going to school at night, and they hoped that soon she could earn enough that Rick could stay home as a househusband. For the present, though, they described their routine as a "helter skelter" one, with no "set patterns." She is usually late because of school or overtime work, so they often eat at different times. In any case, supper is in the living room, in front of the TV. She talked of how different their life seems from the way she grew up, and of her regrets:

> My mom was home. And it really makes a world of difference. She always had good meals on the table . . . It was more of a family thing. You know, my dad got home at a certain time, and we always ate dinner after he got home. And then we'd watch TV. On Saturday nights it was like a regular routine. We'd always have hamburgers and watch Science Fiction Theater. I mean, it was great.
>
> Now it's like a helter skelter routine. If we're all home fine, if we're not then we just work around it. I don't think Kate would know what it's like to sit down and have a formal meal with the family. It's such a rare occurrence. The only time we really do that is the holidays.

There are a lot of times when I really regret it. I regret not having a family routine. It feels like, you know, your kids are being shuffled around, and you're being shuffled around.

And there are times when I get this real craving to stay home, stay home and play housewife. But then you know that there's no way in hell that you could afford it. It's a matter of economics. You have to do it, in order to survive.

It is a real problem for her, the one thing she would like to change about their eating habits, and something that she says they talk about "all the time." Rick seemed more resigned to the situation, though he talked about their routine in much the same way:

We don't have any set patterns like I was raised up with. It's just, you know, the food's here, there it is, eat. It's not, you know, the table's going to be cleared off, and there's going to be four place settings around the table, and the whole schmear like I was raised up with.

When I asked him why they didn't have "set patterns," his answer was ambiguous, but ultimately reflected the time and effort involved in arranging for meals:

It doesn't make any difference. Well, it does. But you're so damn tired. It's not the time, because you could do it if you wanted to. It just gets to where you're so tired, and fed up with the way the money situation is, and you just say, the hell with it.

Many working parents feel frustrated and defeated when they cannot arrange family meals of the sort they remember. Their comments often reveal the complexity of meanings they attach to family meals, and provide clues to the reasons that they feel so bad when they do not conduct them successfully. Jean, a married woman who works as a legal secretary, reported real distress because of her inability to arrange the kind of meals she wants, and discussed the reasons for her concern:

If you have a real discussion at the dinner table, like we used to when I was a kid, you can give a person a chance to let you in on their life. What they were doing all day when they weren't with you. You can find out more about that person. That doesn't happen in our house at all . . . It's time when you can show that you really care about that person in more than just a caretaking role. I mean, I'm their mother, so I attend to certain needs for them. But that doesn't mean I really know them.

Providing food is a way of "attending to needs." But Jean's comment makes clear how the work of relating to others is an even more essential part of producing a "family meal" than the provision of food.

In professional households, parents were more often able to arrange regular family meals, even if both were employed. However, in these households, almost all of the women who worked outside the home worked part-time instead of full-time, and they usually had jobs with flexible schedules, so that they had considerable control over their own activities. They had fewer obstacles to overcome in arranging a regular mealtime routine, and more time to devote to this work.

Single mothers in this sample were somewhat less likely than married women to eat with their children (though other researchers have found no such differences [Wynn and Bowering 1987]). Some of these women reported that they arranged and supervised regular meals for their children, but they themselves ate alone, at another time. For example, a mother with six children, who is home all day, explained, "I'd rather wait until it's quiet." And a single woman who works all day as a receptionist said:

> We usually sit down and eat. Or I have them in here and
> I'll—because, you know, I've been working all day, and I
> might go in and sit in the living room so I'll be by myself for
> a while.

In such situations, there is only one person to do all of the family work, and no one to provide any relief, or even help in sustaining a conversation. Like the working couples described above, these women need some respite. They find that it is simply too much to keep working during their own mealtimes.

The "breaks" that these single mothers allow themselves highlight the continuous nature of the interpersonal work that organizes a family meal. The meal is part of the ongoing process that constitutes the life of the household. Whatever its particular features, a "family" has a problematic existence: it is a socially constructed group, continually brought into being through the activities of individuals. Repeated activities—and especially routines and rituals like those of family mealtimes—sustain the reality of a family. Thus, when people talk about the work of feeding a family, we sometimes hear hints of an interweaving of the rather mundane business of the food itself with more fundamental aspects of group life. One woman explained:

> The initial drudgery is what you dislike. Actually going shopping, doing all the planning, chopping, cutting, what have you. And of course cleaning up. But you do it for the good parts, you know, you get enough of the good part to keep doing it. And of course, you have to survive.

"Doing" a meal, then, can be a complex and tiring project, but also one that holds promise for the rewards of good family times. It is a matter of survival, but also a matter of the "good parts," beyond survival, which are harder to label and discuss.

Invisible Work

Most everyone would count "meal preparation" as an important kind of household work, but we seldom stop to think about the activity that produces a meal. Most would assume that "meal preparation" refers to the discrete tasks of cooking. Meals, however, depend on more than food alone. They come into being as socially organized events, with recognizable form and tempo. "Doing a meal," then, requires more than just cooking; it takes thoughtful foresight, simultaneous attention to several different aspects of the project, and a continuing openness to ongoing events and interaction. These kinds of effort must be considered part of the work of feeding a family, but they are seldom identified as work: they remain invisible even as they are done.

Researchers who study household work often rely on commonsense assumptions about the content of the work, asking interviewees to report on tasks such as "cleaning," "cooking," and "ironing" (Oakley 1974) or to estimate the time they spend on "home chores" or "taking care of children" (Pleck 1985). In another approach, respondents log their household activities in time diaries, and researchers assign these activities to categories such as "after-meal clean-up" and "marketing" (Walker and Woods 1976). These studies are useful: they call attention to the amount of time devoted to housework, the greater share of housework done by women, and the work "overload" (Pleck 1985) and consequent "leisure gap" (Hochschild 1989) experienced by women who work for pay as well as at home. But the expanded view of feeding work put forward here suggests that time studies, or those based on commonsense understandings, capture only a fraction of women's household effort. While such studies document the performance of physical tasks, they miss most of the planning and coordination involved in household work, as well as the constant juggling and strategizing behind the physical tasks.

We find clues to the invisible work of feeding in people's accounts, as they refer to their planning toward family meals. Though preparation time is bounded, the strategizing that supports preparation extends throughout the day. As Bertie explained, "The antennas are always out." Those who will cook later spend time considering their plans, strategizing about how to make the meal better, or prepare it more quickly. This thought work is often squeezed into the interstices of other activities. Barbara, the busy mother of two-year-old twins, explained:

> As soon as I get up in the morning or before I go to bed, I'm thinking of what we're going to eat tomorrow. Even though I know, but do I have this, and is this ready, and this ready?

And another woman, though not so pressured, reported:

> I turn the alarm off and I have about ten minutes of kind of free time while I'm lying there in bed. And during that time, I usually try to think of what I'm going to put in Brad's lunch. So that when I get up, I don't have to stand there and say, "Whoa, what am I going to make for him?" I have it in my head already.

At their paid jobs, or in odd moments, people think about what to have for dinner, what they need from the store, or how to fit all of the activities of food preparation into the time available.

This work of planning, and the kind of interpersonal work I have described in this chapter, are essential parts of the work of feeding a family, but they are invisible activities. Most analysts of women's "invisible work" have meant work that women are not given credit for, like volunteer work, work on a husband's career, or behind-the-scenes work in organizations (e.g. Kahn-Hut, Daniels, and Colvard 1982:137–143; Daniels 1987). The kinds of work I have been discussing can be thought of as unacknowledged work in this sense; however, they are also literally invisible: much of the time, they cannot be seen. Planning is largely mental work, spread over time and mixed in with other activities. In addition, these tasks can look like other activities: managing a meal looks like simply enjoying the companionship of one's family—and of course, is partly so—and learning about food prices can look like reading the newspaper. The work is noticeable when it is not completed (when the milk is all gone, for example, or when the meal is not ready on time), but cannot be seen when it is done well.

The invisibility of this thought work, along with the way it combines with physical tasks, can hide this part of housework even from those who do it. There are few words for this kind of effort, and a pervasive trivialization of the work of managing meals. Thus, many of the women who talked in detail about the kinds of activities I have described here also told me that they did not do any "planning." They dismissed the thinking involved in what they did with words like these:

> It's just routine to me. It's just all up there, you know. Just what comes natural. It's just a part of—just like, my work.

In fact, this woman's sense of the "natural" character of her activity reveals the extent to which thought work is at the heart of what she does. It is "just all up there," "just routine." But keeping track of the routine, keeping it "all up there," is in fact the heart of her work.

2 Provisioning

The family meals discussed in the last chapter are made from grocery items obtained outside the home, and part of the work of feeding a family involves keeping the household supplied with products used in the day-to-day routine. Much of this work is included in the activity usually called shopping, although some people also garden, or trade food items with relatives and friends. I refer to the work as provisioning rather than shopping because I intend to provide an expanded view of the work: to indicate that there is more to it than we can see inside a store, and to emphasize its embeddedness in a socially organized household practice.

In the past, farm families grew much of their own food, and some, though many fewer, still do today. Most households now, especially in urban areas, depend on food that is produced elsewhere and purchased for home use. This shift to mass production and distribution of food developed as part of a turn-of-the-century reorganization of the economy that produced today's largely urban, industrial society. Increasingly, part of the work of feeding—production and distribution—has been done collectively, by large corporations for large numbers of people. Preparing and serving food are also more widely offered as market services than in the past, but these activities are still more often conducted as "housework"—in private homes for household groups. Much of the older work of feeding a family, then, is now done socially, through the market. This change has given new importance to a gap between market and household which must be bridged: supplies must be funneled from relatively few large organizations with standardized products to a great many small and particular private homes. As mass production and national-scale retailing have developed, consumption has become an increasingly important part of the economy.

Some writers have noted that these shifts produce an expanded sphere of work for women as shopping becomes more extensive and more necessary. Nona Glazer (1987), for example, shows how retail organizations draw women into doing the work of shopping and benefit from their unpaid labor (see also Willis 1972; Weinbaum and Bridges 1976). Like these analysts, I am concerned with shopping as work activity. However, rather than considering the work as a piece of the economy, I begin in the home, with the everyday activity of shopping and its significance for individuals living their lives in family households. From this perspective, shopping for food can be seen as a complex, artful activity that supports the production of meaningful patterns of household life by negotiating connections between household and market. The activity is shaped in many ways by the economic context in which it is done (and shopping can be a cruel task, fraught with anxiety and frustration, especially for those with inadequate resources), but the market is also a terrain in which many shoppers learn to maneuver in their own interests quite skillfully. They use the market to obtain the products they need if they are to continue to "do family."

There are many different ways to do the physical work of provisioning. Some people shop for food once a month while others shop almost daily. Some go to a single store while others alternate, or make the rounds of several shops in a single day. Some of these differences arise from the strongly class-related constraints of neighborhoods and resources (the availability of stores, transportation, and home storage space, for example); others are based on individual preferences and inclinations. Differences in specific situations meant that some of the women I talked with had more autonomy than others in planning these routines. Poor and working-class women worried often about prices and "making ends meet," while more affluent shoppers felt freer to make choices on the basis of preference or convenience. In addition, the physical work of provisioning was generally easier for those with more resources. These differences will be discussed in chapter 7. Here, I will examine common features of the process through which people develop and carry out strategies for provisioning their households. As in the previous chapter, I will display the character of the work required, and point to the skills of coordination and adjustment developed by those who do it. In addition, I will begin to display the significance of household work in constructing a distinction between "public" and "private." The work of provisioning involves social relations that are both public and private, as we typically understand these terms. The work connects "public" and "private" realms, but since it is largely invisible, the connections go unnoticed. Instead, people do shopping, and use their purchases, to produce "personal life" and thus, actually to construct the boundary between home and market.

The Household as Context

Shopping for groceries is more than a simple matter of buying a few things that one needs, because "needs" grow out of an everyday routine that takes shape over time. Teresa, a Chicana woman married to a white-collar worker, laughed when she remembered going shopping when newly married:

> I remember when I first got married telling my husband, "Well, we have to go out grocery shopping, because the pantry's empty." And I thought to myself, "Oh, no, grocery shopping! What do I get?"

Not everyone is so bewildered when they start the work of feeding a family. However, everyone develops a plan for provisioning over time, in part consciously and in part as a result of routine and habit. The plan comes to be expressed in choices about the stock of foods to be kept on hand. Replenishing the stock of foods periodically makes it possible to carry on the everyday routine.

When the people I talked with explained how they did their shopping, they referred to the organizing power of a conceptualized standard stock of foods, though they did not explicitly label it as such. For example:

> I just buy things that I know we're going to use . . . And I know—I usually buy the same cuts, even though I don't make the same thing out of it.

Since the set of items to be purchased remains fairly constant, preparing for shopping is relatively simple:

> I go around and I check, in the refrigerator, and I check the cupboards and I check the bathroom to see what I might have missed. And I make the list.

The question is not so much what to get as how often, and how much:

You buy the same things every week, you know, you really
do, every two weeks, whenever you go. It's just do you have
enough of it.

From such comments, provisioning appears to be highly routinized. However, the story is more complex. While shoppers describe their activity as "routine," they do not actually do the same
things each time they go shopping. Instead, shoppers make different specific purchases within repeated categories that provide instructions for deciding on individual items. For example, a grocery
list might include the instruction to buy "treats" for children,
without specifying a particular treat. The shopper describes herself
as buying the same thing each time (some kind of treat), but she
actually chooses a specific item at the last moment in the store
(Lave, Murtaugh, and de la Rocha 1984). This observation suggests
a modification of the commonsense view of "routine" activity as
mechanically repetitive. The routine character of shopping does
not come from the sameness of every trip to the supermarket, but
from the way that shopping fits with a parallel "routine" in the
household, the way that habitual purchases become the constituents of "standard" family meals.

Shoppers must consider the economic resources of their households, attempting to balance taste and economy as they decide
how much to spend. The people I talked with had varying incomes:
some were quite wealthy, while others received public aid and food
stamps to supplement minimal income. Surprisingly, however,
none emphasized money when they reported on their shopping.
All could estimate what they spent for food, and though some had
quite limited resources, all reported that they "managed" to get
what they needed. Shopping practices were often influenced by the
way that money flowed into the household: many people planned
shopping trips to coincide with paydays, especially in working-
class households. But how much to spend seemed an old decision,
and one that was taken for granted. Since so many decisions were
based on habitual practice, staying within a budget did not seem to
require special effort:

We just have an idea of the categories of things we ought to
have, and what we can afford.

This is not to say that shoppers are unconcerned about money.
Many reported worrying about the price of food, and almost all
shoppers try to economize in various ways. (Their reports will be
discussed in chapter 7.) But when people described their shopping

strategies, none except the poorest informants organized their accounts around issues of budget; most referred to cash resources only indirectly, as taken-for-granted background for their strategizing.

Decisions about stocking up on supplies are related to the kinds of meals that people want to produce. For example:

> A few of the things we buy might be for the immediate week. Other things are kind of general categories. Like if you've got pot roast around you can make beef stew, or beef teriyaki. Chicken, whatever, you can do something with chicken. Hamburger, you can make some kind of spaghetti.

Sometimes, family members assert their preferences, and complain about foods they do not like. Jean reported:

> There are all different kinds of rice-a-roni, I mean brands that you can buy. But my family only likes one kind, so it doesn't make any sense for me to buy something that they aren't going to like and eat.

The one who does the shopping must discover which of the many products on the market are acceptable. Mostly, the process is one of trial and error. However, Janice explained why she makes a point of encouraging her teenaged children to go shopping with her occasionally:

> Then they get what they want, and not what I want. And I also get their idea of what they like. Would you rather this brand or that brand? Or they don't like particular kinds of cheese . . . That kind of thing, where you've got to sort of get to know your kids, and the people you're working with.

Her account shows her need for such information, though, like many shoppers, she probably learns less from such questioning than from her occasional mistakes, when her son "gets hysterical" about foods he considers unhealthy.

Keeping the household stocked with food supplies has become especially important given the growing tendency of family members to eat separately, on their own schedules. Although some family members prepare their own meals (especially breakfasts and lunches), they can only do so if the ingredients they need are available. Sandra explained her role in providing for her husband's breakfast as follows:

> He fixes his own breakfast—a standard fried egg and toast. And he's got it timed so that he puts down the fork,

grabs the briefcase, and is out the door and just makes the
7:48 train. So I make sure that there's breakfast stuff on hand
for him.

"Breakfast stuff" is one of the categories that organize this
woman's shopping; by making sure the "stuff" is "on hand," she
provides for her husband to carry out his own routine for getting off
to work.

An extended example, from a somewhat unusual household,
will show clearly how a household routine can structure shopping
practices, and conversely, how shopping in a particular way can facilitate a routine. Janice shops for her husband and two adult
children who live in the household. She works as a nurse, a position she achieved a few years before our interview, after working in
a lower-level position and attending college while her children
were growing up. During that busy time, she was often away from
home and her children learned to take care of themselves:

If anybody wanted to eat, you had to feed yourself. You had
to find a way to do it. And they were—not taught, but I told
them how to cook.

Now, family members are quite independent. Though Janice's husband does not cook, the three children, in their early twenties, contribute financially to the household and also share housework
responsibilities. Janice herself participates in evening sports and
the children are often involved in their own activities; they rarely
plan for meals, and sometimes eat dinner—singly or in twos and
threes—at a neighborhood restaurant. Still, meals are often family
events, prepared and eaten at home together. Janice or the children
decide on the spur of the moment whether or not to cook, and
"whoever is home sits down and eats it." Janice's shopping is what
makes this kind of independence possible:

What I do is provide enough food in the house for anybody
who wants to eat. And then whoever is home, makes that
meal, if they want it.

Janice's son is a vegetarian, and a daughter and her boyfriend prefer
not to eat red meat, so menus are limited in complex ways. Again,
Janice has a principle that guides her efforts: she expects the
children to do their own special cooking, but she takes responsibility for providing the special ingredients they might need. She explained that her son might make himself a quiche for dinner, and
described the process in terms of the division of labor they have
negotiated:

He wants it, so he builds it himself. I mean, I provide the milk, I provide the cheese, I provide the eggs, the pie shell. He builds it.

Janice is pleased with the household routine. She talks with pride about how the children take care of themselves and she thinks of their system as a cooperative one:

It's like anybody in society. You try to make things mesh together. It doesn't always work. This happens to work.

Still, it is very clear that this routine does not just "happen" to work: Janice herself spends considerable time and effort to make this system work. She explains that she can ask the others to do shopping, "if I say that I just don't have time." But she also reports, matter-of-factly:

You need to get food in the house, you spend Saturday morning doing grocery shopping. And when I don't, we end up somewhere around Sunday night saying, why isn't there any bread for breakfast tomorrow, or for lunches tomorrow.

Her transition from the most general of observations, applicable to anyone ("You need to get food . . . "), to a very different statement of the real consequences when *she* doesn't shop, reveals the extent to which supplying the household remains her job. (Of course, the comment also hints at how her weekend time—leisure time for other family members—is taken up with attending to household needs.)

Janice, like other shoppers, pays attention to her family's preferences, noticing what gets used and what does not. For example:

I have two or three things of jello in there, and they've been there for ten years. And nobody's going to make them, unless I do. If I put pudding in there—regular chocolate pudding—it might be gone tomorrow.

The comment refers to the fact that, in this household, there are several cooks, whose different demands make shopping a more complex endeavor. Janice's method of preparing for shopping involves other family members more than is typical in other households:

OK, what I do is I take out an envelope. Whatever came in Wednesday or Thursday's mail, and is still sitting around. I take an envelope. I will write down whatever I get from the newspaper [i.e. sale items], and then I'll yell, what do you want? What do we need? Because I'm not in the kitchen, you know, all the time. I mean, I don't go through, and I'm not doing all the cooking. So I say, what do we need? And somebody'll tell me that we need baking soda, or that we need something, we're out of coffee, or we're out of bread, or I didn't have something for breakfast this morning that I wanted. And I'll put that on the list.

For Janice, the point is to find a division of labor that is both reasonable and effective. She sets limits on what she herself can do:

I cannot run an eight-room house by myself. I cannot take care of five people's needs, by myself . . . If there's something that needs to be done, you have to tell me about it. If we're out of shampoo, or we're out of laundry detergent, you have to tell me.

Still, Janice does attend to five people's needs, and her language associates the routine chores of grocery shopping with care and sensitivity:

I'm aware of other people around me, and their needs, and I know that it'll have to be purchased.

In spite of the considerable effort that Janice spends on provisioning, her routine does provide flexibility and allows her to give up the preparation of an inexorable series of dinners which her grown-up children may not even be home to eat. But Janice continues to shop for family members, in spite of their considerable independence, and in doing so, continues to care for them in ways they have come to depend on. Janice's routine is somewhat unusual because the household is unusual—it is organized to promote independence while maintaining some sociability. However, its atypicality makes it an especially effective illustration of the strategizing that ties provisioning to the particular needs of a specific household group.

The Market as Context

Shopping as everyday activity is done for a particular household; it is experienced by those who do it as a search for the items that will be used by a group of individuals with idiosyncratic needs and preferences. The items needed must be found in one or more of the many kinds of food stores available in any city, from small mom-

and-pop groceries and ethnic or gourmet specialty stores to huge self-service supermarkets. Within each of these stores, the products offered for sale are those that the retailer has procured from distributors, and the products available from distributors are those produced by the complex network of food producers and processers, increasingly multinational, mega-corporations. The "market" provides a context for provisioning, then, in two senses. In an immediate and concrete way, specific stores are the places to which people go to buy foods, the settings for their shopping activities. More generally, the features of these specific stores are produced by much larger economic processes.

The activity of grocery shopping is carried on in a dialectical interaction with the specific store as a setting for activity. That is, shoppers enter a structured environment and respond to it, but they do so in ways that aim at carrying out their own intentions: they use the store in ways that will allow them to get the things needed in their own households. In the same way that the household stock of supplies provides the basis for a routine for food preparation, the store as setting becomes part of a regular shopping routine. People learn what is available in a favorite store and where frequently purchased items are stocked, so that the store becomes a setting with particular meanings for individual shoppers. Those who have no need for certain items (pet food, for instance) can bypass whole sections of the store, so that "some aisles in the supermarket do not exist for a given shopper" (Lave, Murtaugh, and de la Rocha 1984:71), while other areas may be filled with items that are relevant because they are often selected.

I will treat shopping as one part of an extended course of action that also includes learning about the options available and making decisions about when and where to shop, and how often. The market context for the activity, conceived in this way, includes all the stores available to shoppers, and the various organizational features of these stores.

There are, obviously, many food stores in urban areas like the one where my informants live. Most of them, however, did their shopping regularly in a few favorite stores. The choice of a store is a primary decision, so that when I asked about shopping, many people began by telling me where they typically go, and why. The convenience of stores near home is often a decisive consideration, and when people reported that they went farther than the nearest store, they usually explained why. When shoppers own cars, they can make choices that balance cost, convenience, and the features of particular stores. One woman rejected the store closest to her house because she did not like the layout of its parking lot, and Barbara, with her two-year-old twins, chose to shop at the store whose employees would help her carry groceries and children to her car. Women without transportation must work harder at getting to stores, and find it more difficult to strategize about the best, and especially the cheapest, places to shop. When I asked about shopping, a poor single mother, living in a neighborhood with few stores or services, responded by talking first about transportation:

> Now that's the big job. It's not really—you know, it wouldn't
> be such a big job, it's just such a big job because there's one
> single parent . . . I can't do shopping with all my children.
> I've even tried shopping with just the twins, and it's very,
> very chaotic . . . Usually I'll call my sister to watch the
> children, maybe take them over on a weekend . . . [When she
> has the opportunity], I try to go to the most difficult place,
> the most distant place that I can't get around to fast. And a
> lot of places they do have delivery service and stuff. So it's
> really a matter of me struggling to get on over there . . . I
> may not get there when I want to. You know, it depends on
> when I can get my sister. Sometimes I'll say, "Can you take
> me here?" "Well, I can't do it this week, I can do it next
> week." You know. And then it's if I feel like spending the
> extra money to go out and get a delivery service or
> something to bring the food here.

This kind of problem is compounded by the fact that, historically, stores in poor neighborhoods have taken advantage of their captive clientele to charge more than stores elsewhere (Caplovitz 1967).

Most people use several stores for different purposes. Some make regular trips to two or more stores, to take advantage of sale prices. But even when people get most of their groceries at a single favorite supermarket, there are usually small nearby stores where they stop for an item forgotten on a previous trip, or special stores where they purchase items that cannot be bought elsewhere:

> If I run out of stuff during the middle of the week, which I
> hate to do, but you know, sometimes you do, everybody
> does—there's a store on the way home that I'll stop at.

Some people use supermarkets for canned goods and pet food, and get meats or produce at small markets they think have better food, and most of the Mexican and Puerto Rican women I talked with shop regularly at small stores in their neighborhoods for tortillas or vegetables that are unavailable in the larger stores. The stores people know constitute a kind of repertoire for variations on the shopping routine—the places one might go or not. Decisions to shop or not, at particular places and times, are part of a larger strategy for managing to fit necessary shopping chores—that is, those that support a household routine—in among the other activities of everyday life.

Within the store, shoppers encounter a distinctive setting. The most common form of retail food store now is the self-service supermarket, a store in which shoppers select their purchases from an array of thousands of different products. These are packaged and displayed amidst a wealth of printed information designed to do the "selling." The products available, and the print that tells about them, are tied to processes of production, marketing, advertising, and state regulation of these activities. Most of the items for sale are brand-name products, known nationally because of their mass-media advertising. Indeed, much of the information that surrounds the shopper in the supermarket consists of ads and displays provided by large food companies or the central offices of supermarket chains.

Shoppers must decide which of these thousands of products they need. Some fraction of the information available in the store is relevant to their concerns, and the rest, as people are well aware, is designed to encourage them to buy more and spend more. Shoppers, interested in getting what they need as quickly as possible, try to routinize their decisions, choosing mainly familiar items that they've already identified as "good buys." But there is always the possibility that new or unfamiliar products may be better or cheaper, and this possibility encourages attention to product labels and displays. The context requires that shoppers constantly sort through the information available, screening what is irrelevant, taking and using just what they need.

The "context" for shopping, in this sense, extends beyond a particular store, and so does the activity. As they read the newspaper or watch television, shoppers notice prices, new products, stores and their offerings. They learn, in a general way, what to expect in a store, how to recognize a bargain, which kinds of products to look for. Some rely heavily on traditional practices and what they have learned directly from familiar people, while others notice advertising, study product labels, and pay attention to specific features of the items they want. For example:

> I always wait to see what somebody else has to say about things and then I'll try it.

But, to illustrate the latter strategy:

> We read labels. What comes first. Is there more sugar than anything else, is there more starch than anything else, are there a lot of additives? Things like making sure that you're not getting a drink, that you're getting 100% juice.

One can see in this comment the way that merchandising and advertising set a context for this kind of learning. Reading labels is a special skill: when this woman explains that she looks to see what comes first, she assumes that we share her knowledge that ingredients are listed in order, indicating their proportionate share in a product's composition. And when she speaks of making sure she does not buy a "drink," she has adopted legal, advertising terminology that distinguishes pure juices from those that are diluted.

These two comments also illustrate a general concern with selecting food that is healthful, and the rather different ways that general concern is expressed. Virtually all those I talked with emphasized that they chose foods they believed were nutritionally beneficial for their families, and most made some reference to widely disseminated nutritional principles emphasizing the importance of a varied, low-fat diet. But some put these principles into practice in a vague and general manner—talking about nutrition simply in terms of "getting the basics," for example—while others, like the second shopper quoted above, selected products on the basis of very specific nutrition-related criteria and the kind of specialized knowledge this woman displays. I argue in chapter 8 that such differences arise from the tendency for individuals in different class situations to draw from a health and nutrition discourse in different ways. In this chapter, these different approaches can sometimes be seen, as here, in the particular ways people describe their shopping practices.

As shoppers try to find the items needed to provision their families, they must deal with the fact that the range and character of products on the market are determined by corporate decisions, which are only partly based on any notion of household needs. Defenders of capitalism point to demand, and claim that the "consumer is king," and ultimately gets what "he" wants (in strangely inaccurate language for retailers who are keenly aware that most shoppers are women). But critics argue, more convincingly, that needs are learned, and that retailers force consumers to buy what is available while providing the illusion of choice through minute and mostly insignificant differences among the products on the market. Charles and Kerr (1988) point out that the decisions that most influence quality of diet are made at the levels of public policy and corporate strategy, rather than by consumers simply choosing healthy foods. And Batya Weinbaum and Amy Bridges (1976) have shown how it is the shopper's responsibility, through "consumption work," to reconcile private production of commodities like food with socially determined household needs. When the products available do not fit with everyday needs, consumption can be difficult and frustrating, as shoppers struggle to translate the material goods they can afford into "nurturance." The shoppers I talked with were certainly aware of the economic forces shaping the market. They strategized about which products were worth buying for their households, and what the alternatives might be, and they developed methods for dealing with products they did not want as well as those they did:

> My kids want this cereal, or Choco-this, or Froot Loops, and
> I just tell them flatly, "No, I will not buy it." I just give them
> such an emphatic no that they know what to expect now.

Such comments hint at the ways that stores are inadequate, but few people think much about these problems. They have mostly found "good enough" strategies, and their own work accomplishes the reconciliation that is necessary: by doing provisioning, they minimize any lack of fit between their needs and the market. In the "unusual" situation—recession, poverty, an illness that calls for a special diet—shoppers become more aware of the market as an adversary and sometimes become more militant. But typically, shoppers are absorbed in the everyday work of *making* the market suffice.

In fact, when shoppers engage the market as context, they do enter a kind of struggle. They must deal with a superfluity of products and information about them, and with essentially antagonistic marketing techniques designed to disrupt their routines and induce them to buy new products. In this context, the screening and sorting that shoppers do is a specific kind of skilled practice, but one that goes relatively unnoticed. It is essential to the operation of a market economy, but it is experienced—if noticed at all—as activity conducted privately, for the family. Shoppers enter stores with their own plans foremost in their minds, use the market in

the way they have decided is best for their purposes, and then go
home to their families.

Monitoring and Improvisation

Routines for provisioning evolve gradually out of decisions that are
linked to the resources and characteristics of particular households and to features of the market. The routine is made to work
through monitoring activities that fit the regularly occurring
categories of routine to specific events from one day to another.
Monitoring also provides a continual testing of typical practices.
This testing occurs as shoppers keep track of changes on both sides
of the relation: household needs and the products available.

Monitoring on the household side means watching for the needs
and preferences of household members and keeping track of supplies. People learn to notice supplies and sometimes make notes
about which items they will need. They describe the process as
simple, but their comments also belie this simplicity with an
awareness that they do not always get it right:

Even though it's the same thing, I still make a list. Because
I'll forget what we have and what we don't have. Like we
may have enough juice one week, the next week we don't,
and I have to write it down, otherwise I'll think we have
enough juice, you know, and we don't.

In addition to keeping track of supplies, monitoring means paying
attention to new or evolving needs. Sometimes provisioning becomes a topic of conversation. Gloria explained:

Sometimes he'll come home with something I don't like,
and I'll mention it to him and we'll talk about it. Or
sometimes it'll come from him.

This kind of negotiation seems to occur most often in households
where both adults participate in the shopping, perhaps because it is
only in these situations that both are aware of the options available
and the choices that are being made through provisioning. When
one person does all of the keeping track, this kind of monitoring
may simply mean noticing that conditions or requirements are
changing.

Monitoring is especially critical when the household routine is
a difficult one and mistakes can be costly. Barbara, for example, a
former school teacher, now spends her days taking care of her two-

year-old twins who have been diagnosed as slightly hyperactive. It is very demanding work (as I discovered while we talked), and her household routine is built around managing the children. She plans carefully for her weekly shopping trip—deciding on a menu for each dinner and writing down "everything we're going to eat for seven meals"—since a trip to the store for something forgotten is no simple matter. Still, she has to go out every few days for milk, and she is constantly aware of what they will be needing:

> I always have to be thinking ahead, like how many gallons do I have at home. Or if I do sneak out, am I running low on this, or am I running low on that, or will I make it between Thursday and Friday of next week. So as soon as I get up in the morning or before I go to bed, I'm thinking of what we're going to eat tomorrow. Even though I know, but do I have this, and is this ready and this ready? And then it's like, three, four o'clock, can I get them down in their chairs so I can get dinner going, if I don't, we're really behind schedule. And having these guys hungry—Thinking, you know, do we have bananas in the house, for fresh fruit for them.

It is interesting to note the "shorthand" she uses to talk about her monitoring. Gallons, of course, are of milk, and Thursday or Friday is her regular shopping time, and she speaks of them in our interview in the familiar way she is used to. She does not think of explaining these details, because, typically, she is the only one who needs to understand.

In addition to monitoring the household, shoppers must monitor the market, so that they know what is available and where to get it. Much of this learning, too, is accomplished through trial and error, but there are many more formal sources of information about products as well. As they sort through terminology, products, and prices, shoppers work hard at devising routines to reduce the amount of decision making they have to do. Most people reported that at times, they have studied prices carefully, but that once they have decided on "best buys," they tend not to re-examine their decisions.

Routines, however, are always subject to revision. Various changes—a move to a new neighborhood, the closing of a favorite store, advice from a friend about products or places to shop—may be occasions for revising these choices. People pay attention to new products and consider whether they will be better than old standbys. Often, time spent in the supermarket is partly time for learning what is available. Teresa explained:

> I read labels sometimes, just if it catches my eye, and I think, "Gee, I haven't tried this." Then I'll read what it is, what's in it, how to prepare it. It's just curiosity more than anything.

This kind of casual study seems like curiosity to her because it does not solve an immediate problem; however, it is one of the activities that provide the general information about the market she needs in order to continue to do provisioning for her household.

Routinization makes the work manageable; it means that choices do not have to be newly made with each trip to the store. However, the benefits of routinization are balanced by the need to attend to shifting circumstances; consequently shopping, like the design and management of meals, has an active and improvisational character. One aspect of this dimension of shopping is the way that purchasing becomes part of the process of planning meals. The items that are chosen, and the variation within an established pattern, are thought of as part of an overall design. Sometimes the planning involved is relatively routine:

> Most of the time, I kind of plan when I'm at the store, you know? Like OK, we have chicken Monday, pork chops Tuesday—I be kind of, you know, figuring out in my mind, as I shop, what's what.

For others, this planning involves a more contingent kind of thinking:

> I saw a spaghetti squash at the grocery store the other day and it was cheap and I thought—well, I automatically organized things in my mind because I knew I had to cook the spaghetti squash fairly soon and I'd be eating it for several days, so, you know, that took care of that.

In both cases, part of the work of shopping is an active organization of the possibilities of using the things that are purchased. Even when they did not explicitly describe such a process, the comments of some women provided hints of this rather subtle mental dimension of shopping. For example, Donna explained why she would prefer that her husband not accompany her to the store:

> My husband likes to just get in and out, and then that's it.
> Whereas me, I like to look around, and just think, you
> know?

She has no clear vocabulary for the organizing that she does mentally while in the store, but she has noticed its consequences. She knows that it takes time to consider what she needs.

In addition to this kind of planning at the supermarket, shopping includes an improvisational element that involves changing the routine to adapt to particular circumstances, or take advantage of especially appealing items:

> I'll probably get two or three things that aren't on the list,
> that will just catch my eye, and I'll say, hmm, that's an idea,
> I could make that instead of this, depending on whether it's
> on sale, or whatever.

For those with less money to spend, improvisation is usually a response to price variation; in higher-income households it may also mean taking advantage of the availability of special items that cannot always be found or items of particularly good quality. In both cases, however, it requires an on-the-spot rearrangement of plans, an ability to shift from the regular routine to a variation of it and to make adjustments for the unusual purchase. This kind of constantly shifting routine is at the heart of the work of provisioning, which must be based on multiple criteria for choices, a mental inventory of supplies at home, and a long-range but flexible plan for using them. The holistic nature of the process explains this woman's comments about using a shopping list:

> I find a prepared list almost dulls my memory rather than
> sharpens it. If I have time enough—it's not even time—if
> I'm concentrating enough, since I do it so often, I can go to
> the store and walk down the aisle and be inspired by, oh yes,
> we're missing that. And pick it up.

Many shoppers do use lists; however, like this woman, they keep much of the information relevant to provisioning in their heads, so that they can adapt and adjust to changing circumstances.

"Public" and "Private"

Shoppers go to the supermarket looking for the materials they need in order to put plans (though they are often barely articulated as plans) into practice. They must use the stores and services they find in their neighborhoods, with whatever advantages and limitations they have, to fulfill the needs of their own households as well as possible. Products are standardized, designed for a mass market. Thus, part of the work of provisioning is a kind of strategizing directed toward using the market to suit particular needs. Choices about provisioning, like those involved in planning and managing meals, are based on strategies about household life. They are guided not only by the contingencies of decisions about price and quality, but also by the tacit, improvisational skills of feeding a family in the broader sense: the skills that exploit the possibilities of material objects in order to produce family life within a specific household.

Like planning and managing meals, the work of provisioning is partly invisible. An observer can see someone going to the store, gathering up purchases, paying for them, taking them home and putting them away. But the ongoing strategic parts of the work—the planning, monitoring, remembering—cannot be seen. Family members who do not share the provisioning work often do not understand it. Janice explained:

> They're sort of amazed when I walk in with something. And
> they look at me and say, "How'd you know I needed that?"
> But I did know they were going to need it. I mean, if not
> instinctively, at least I had taken a look to see whether it
> was gone or not.

Since monitoring is only partly conscious, and choices are made improvisationally, the work is taken for granted even by those who do it. For Janice, knowing what is needed seems almost "instinctive"—though she realizes as she speaks that actually she had "taken a look."

As more and more options for purchasing prepared foods have become available, the technical work of cooking has become less necessary. Now, the coordinative work of supplying family members as they "flow" through the household is at the heart of feeding work. The work of provisioning links the household with the distributive network outside, and thus serves a family group within a market society. Those who do provisioning are involved in social relations both within the household and also outside. They match the needs of a particular household group with the standardized products on the market.

The activities of provisioning knit together the ragged edges of household life and the larger society. This knitting together consists of a continual process of adapting and adjusting. On one side, there is the market in the broadest sense: not just stores and services, but also institutions like schools, the media, and state and legal arrangements. These are organizations that operate on the basis of abstract, conceptual categories designed to be applicable in a broad range of situations. On the other side are a multiplicity of households, each a local and particular setting inhabited by a unique combination of specific individuals. In this context, making any single household work properly takes a particular kind of knowledge and effort. It means knowing both the local and abstracted settings, searching the market, making selections from among the alternatives available, and delivering the "goods"— again, broadly defined—to the home. These processes are at the heart of provisioning, and of other aspects of the work of feeding the family as well. The one who does this work is located precisely at the point of connection between home and the world, and is pulled in two directions, responding and adjusting both to internal family dynamics and also to the world outside.

3 Constructing the Family

The form of family found in modern Western societies has developed over time. As productive work moved out of the home, the family began to be thought of as a bounded unit, "associated with property, self-sufficiency, with affect and a sphere 'inside' the home" (Collier, Rosaldo, and Yanagisako 1982:32). As this kind of family developed, its day-to-day construction came to be part of the work to be done within a household, and as the physical tasks of maintenance have become less arduous, the work of constructing a particular type of household life has received increasing emphasis. Leonore Davidoff, in an analysis of middle- and upper-class households in nineteenth-century England, points out that we can see this activity emerging clearly in those households where servants did the routine work of maintenance and wives could devote themselves to supervising the construction of a special sort of place:

> The ultimate nineteenth-century ideal became the creation
> of a perfectly orderly setting of punctually served and
> elaborate meals, clean and tidy and warmed rooms, clean
> pressed and aired clothes and bed linen . . . there was to
> be a complete absence of all disturbing or threatening
> interruptions to orderly existence which could be caused
> either by the intractability, and ultimate disintegration, of
> things or by the emotional disturbance of people. (1976:130)

Obviously, such standards could be met in only a very few households. Still, they served to define a model which was becoming the basis for a developing form of family life. Davidoff's analysis led her to define housework as a project of "boundary maintenance":

> Housework is concerned with creating and maintaining
> order in the immediate environment, making meaningful
> patterns of activities, people and materials. (1976:124)

The ideals have changed—hardly any contemporary wives or
mothers even aim for "perfect order"—but housework is still a
project of "making meaningful patterns." Feeding the family is
work that makes use of food to organize people and activities. It is
work that negotiates a balance between the sociability of group life
and the concern for individuality that we have come to associate
with modern family life.

Sociability

Meals are social events. They can provide occasions when household members come together as a group, but they do not do this
"naturally" or automatically. If household members are to come
together for dinner, someone must organize the meal so that it becomes a part of several different sequences of events. Family members are involved in various individual activities throughout the
day, mostly outside the household. Their paths do not necessarily
cross, and points of intersection must be planned. Since routines
are often customary, they seem natural, like "what everybody
does." But those who organize meals work at developing these patterns, and understand that they have significance for family relations; they talk about their choices as pieces of a consciously
crafted structure of family life. The times of coming together that
result are thought of—though not entirely consciously—as making a family.

The intentional quality in the plans that produce these activities, apparently so simple and natural, can be seen in women's
accounts of the details of their everyday routines. Susan, a white
woman whose husband is a construction worker, quit her job as a
nurse when her two-year-old daughter was born; now she works at
taking care of her child and house. Though she has been married for
five years, her daughter's relatively recent arrival signalled the beginning of a new kind of family. When I asked how the mealtime
routines had changed, she explained:

> Our mealtimes are at a certain time. And I have an idea of
> what I'm going to have. Whereas before, it was, whatever, it
> was very casual. We didn't have the responsibility.

The responsibility she speaks of is not merely responsibility for
providing food. As she elaborates, we can see that she organizes the

mealtime routine so that the three individuals in her household will come together "as a family." She said:

> I'll pull her high chair up so that she can be part of the family . . . I think she was six months old when she started eating as part of the family—breakfast, lunch and dinner. We adjusted our schedule a little bit to her schedule. And it worked out really well. Now, everything is as a family.

Part of the intention behind producing the meal is to produce "home" and "family." In a study of mealtimes in Welsh working-class families, Anne Murcott (1983) found that women thought of the evening meal as a kind of marker for their husbands, signifying the end of work and return to the family. They talked of a "cooked dinner" in terms of associations with home and well-being. But the significance of the meal is not just that it represents, or is associated with the idea of family; indeed, the meal comes to be thought of in this way because it involves household members in the actual day-to-day activities that constitute family relations over time. Furthermore, the linkage between food and family depends on women's work. Susan spoke of how she produces a homecoming for her husband:

> If it's real ugly outside and I know that my husband's going to want a hot meal—which is all the time—and I want the house to warm up and smell good, I'll make stew. Or I'll bake a cake.

As she thinks ahead toward the evening meal, she plans to produce an experience: the return to a warm and pleasant house.

Susan's comments also show how activities like baking can be fit into a larger scheme for producing a particular kind of everyday life. When she spoke of baking a cake, she added:

> I usually end up freezing half of it, because we don't usually eat that much of it. It's just something to do. Or now that my daughter's helpful, we bake a cake. And we make cookies. That's an all-day affair.

Cooking is a way that she and her daughter can spend time together, and a way that her two-year-old learns, through participation, the special work of producing home and family, anticipating a dinner together.

Scheduling a meal requires attention to the various schedules of individuals in the family, and a process of adjustment that reconciles family events with their separate needs and projects. For Susan, this process is relatively simple: her husband's work schedule is fixed, and she must adapt to it; and she has developed a schedule for her daughter; but her own activities are quite flexible. She uses this flexibility to preserve the routines of others. For example, she explained:

> Routine is really good for kids. They know what's expected of them . . . I don't like to stray too much from my routine. Because then she's going to get confused.
>
> But dinner time, though, I can probably stretch, if my husband's going to be home late, or whatever. I can stretch within an hour. But if it looks like too much, I'll feed her, first. But she likes to be part of the family supper.

Susan is the one who keeps track of the activities of other family members. When her husband takes more time than usual coming home, she must consider the consequences of this change for her daughter, and for the "family supper." Part of her work is to monitor schedules, and eventually, to make a judgment as to whether it will be possible to have a meal together. In order to make it possible, she changes her own activities, "stretching" the dinner hour as far as she can.

Susan adapts to her daughter's schedule throughout the day as well. She explained that she can easily complete her household chores by noon, and added, "Then I have the rest of the day to spend with her." She has observed that her daughter is especially cranky while she is preparing dinner, and she organizes her work routine to minimize this time:

> Usually what I try to do, if I know what I'm going to prepare, and it's going to take time away from her—a lot of time, like chopping vegetables or whatever—I'll do it while she's sleeping, her nap. And I'll have everything ready. If it's something like breaded pork chops, I'll bread them before, put them in a pan, and put them in the refrigerator. So all I have to do is put them in the oven. Or even like a salad, I'll put everything in but the tomatoes. And I'll do it when she's not around, so she doesn't feel rejected.

Again, Susan considers the consequences of different ways of organizing her work. She plans her work activities to produce a particular kind of everyday household life for her child.

Susan likes the way she does things, and seems to do them easily. She explained that she is a very disciplined person, and that she thinks about organizing her household work as part of an overall strategy for managing her home. She is "big on rules," and explained that, "It's just a lot easier if you're organized. If you know where to put things, you know where to find them." The work of adaptation and reconciliation that produces Susan's family is relatively easy; she has fewer material constraints and competing demands than most women. The family is small, and Susan's daughter is too young to be involved in independent activities. Though Susan enjoyed working as a nurse before her daughter was born, she has decided since then that she is "more needed at home." She does not need to work outside the home because her husband's wage is adequate for the family's support. She has plenty of time to devote to the work of constructing a family life.

For other women, the work of scheduling is much more complicated and difficult. But the process is similar: the task is one of adjustment and reconciliation in order to create points of intersection among diverse sets of activities. Jean, for example, is a white woman who works as a legal secretary, whose husband works at night as a security officer. Her two children are in elementary school. She must plan meals to fit with several different schedules outside the home, and she has little time to plan and prepare meals. Like Susan, though, she works at combining different schedules, and using the resources she has, to produce points of intersection among diverging paths. The process can be seen in her detailed account as she thinks out loud about how she will manage one evening meal, which she must prepare and serve in the time between her own arrival home and her husband's departure for work an hour later. She explained:

> Tonight has to be a real rushed dinner, because the kids are going ice-skating and they're getting picked up at 6:00, so there's a package of smoky links in the refrigerator and they're going to have that. And David will probably either have that, or—well, we had friends over last night, actually I did, because he was gone—and it was a potluck dinner, but I was lucky because since it was at my house I got all the leftovers. So tonight—this isn't a good night to ask about, but—so the kids will—it'll be three different things. The kids'll probably have the smoky links, and David will probably have—well, see there's still a little hunk of ham left, and there's still—what's the other thing? We have

something else left over, plus we have the things from last night.

I asked what the children would have with their smoky links:

> They'll have—if I have time, I'll make macaroni and cheese to go with it, because that's one of their favorite dinners. They'll have that. And if I can get them to, they'll probably have an apple, for dessert, or I think I'll get them to eat a tomato, I don't know. It won't be real balanced.

And her husband?

> Given the choice, given the fact that—I don't know what he'll have. I tend to think he'll have the very last bit of that ham that's left. I could be wrong, he might have smoky links. I don't think he'll have what we had for dinner last night because I think it's something he doesn't like.
>
> If he has the smoky links he'll probably just have it in a sandwich, because he doesn't like macaroni and cheese— see he's not big on pasta, he doesn't like spaghetti either. He would probably just have a sandwich. I might be able to get him to eat some sliced tomatoes too, but that would probably be it.
>
> If he has the ham, he'll probably slice it up, and I would imagine that it'll be fried with some eggs, or I'll make an omelette for him, something like that.
>
> And if I have the leftovers, I'll have the leftovers and probably a sliced tomato. That'll be it. There are some brownies left, I'm sure I'll have a brownie [laughing].

The meal that Jean imagines will be produced at the intersection of several sequences of events. She has to keep interrupting herself in order to explain to me why she has various things on hand, and as she thinks prospectively toward the meal, she can see that much depends on her husband's choice among the several options she will offer him, so that she must think of several alternative plans. The previous days' meals, the children's plans for the evening, and the preferences and choices of family members (which I will say more about later)—all these are part of the reasoning behind the choices she makes. With all of these things in mind, in the time that is available, Jean will provide a meal that fits into her husband's and children's lives. When she thinks of having a brownie at the end of it all, one cannot help feeling that she will certainly deserve it.

Jean must organize her family's eating in the context of a very difficult set of schedules. She works all day; she has only the evening with her children, and only an hour or so before her husband must leave for work. Still, like Susan, when she organizes her time and work, she aims at producing the kind of household life she wants for her family. She explained:

> So much of the way I manage my time is affected by my children . . . Really that whole chunk of time, from 5:30 or 6 at night until bedtime, is theirs.
>
> During that chunk of time of course I do make dinner. And sometimes do the dishes. Usually I wait and do the dishes—I mean I really have this worked out into some sort of weird system of my own. I watch the news, you know, at 10:00. And when the sports comes on, I really could care less about sports, I go back to the kitchen and I do my dishes. And then depending on what I have left to do . . . It's all just sandwiched in.

Jean gets everyone in her family fed, but she is not usually able to produce the kind of regular family dinners that Susan talked about. Jean worries that her family rarely sits down together and talks, because she believes that such encounters constitute "quality family time":

> If you have a real discussion at the dinner table, like we used to have when I was a kid, you can give a person a chance to let you in on their life. What they were doing all day when they weren't with you. You can find out more about that person.

When she was a child, she explained:

> We'd sit down and everybody would tell what they had done that day. And my father, when the main meal was over, you know, like if there was dessert or something, that was time for Daddy to give us quizzes on world capitals or something like that.

Jean works at creating such family times, seizing the few opportunities available in her busy weeks. For some time, she made a special effort to get the family together for Saturday night dinner. On those evenings, she explained:

> There were some rules for that. I mean, there were self-imposed rules. That it be a good meal, not—not hamburger,

not hot dogs, but something decent. You know, a really nice meal that I really took some time to create and prepare. The kids would set the table. Yeah, there would be rules about what would be served and how it would be served and it would be a more formal thing.

These attempts were frustrating, though, partly because she did not get the help she needed from her husband, who doesn't share her ideas about "family time." She reported:

Lately what's been happening—we hardly ever all eat together—but lately David gets up and leaves before the rest of us, and that really makes me angry. Because I think that's a rotten example he's setting.

Part of Jean's work, then, is to struggle with her husband (she called it "hammering away") about the activities that constitute family life. He seems not to share her understanding of how specific activities contribute to the construction of a group life. His reluctance makes her efforts to produce "family times" stand out in sharp relief.

He said, "What do you want me to do?" And I said, "You've got to give us at least two Saturdays a month, that are just ours."
So this Saturday, we'll see, we're supposed to go bowling. And while we're bowling, I'm supposed to have something cooking so that when we're done we can come home and eat it together.

This kind of event is conceived as a time for being together, when family members can share a pleasurable activity. But there is work involved in producing such an event. Jean, like most women, is the worker behind the scenes, as well as a guest at the party. Somehow, while they are bowling, she is to "have something cooking." It is her work that brings their time together into being.

Both Susan and Jean are doing more than just cooking. In addition to producing meals, they organize their cooking so as to produce a group life for their families. They adjust to work and school schedules, and as they make decisions about managing their work, they weave together the paths of household members. Their efforts are directed toward creating patterns of joint activity out of the otherwise separate lives of family members.

Individuality

Feeding the individuals who live in a household makes them a group, as shown above, by reconciling their different activities in order to produce a common life; but feeding is also done so as to produce a particular kind of group, one that is intimate and personal. The work involves special attention to the individuality of each household member. To some extent, this kind of attention to preference is necessary: children, especially, may not eat at all if they dislike what is served, and in many households, individuals have health problems that require special diets. However, the personal attention that is part of feeding work has a family character that goes beyond necessity. The family is a place where people expect to be treated in a unique, personally specific way instead of anonymously, as they are often treated outside. Part of the work of feeding is to give this kind of individual attention, and doing so constitutes a particular household group as the kind of place we expect a "family" to be.

All of the women I talked with reported planning meals around the tastes of family members. They select and serve foods that will be eaten enthusiastically. But the personal service I refer to here is more meaningful than this feature of planning suggests. It involves attention to the specific, often idiosyncratic tastes of individuals within the family group, and decisions about which of these desires will be satisfied and which not. Often, it involves making distinctions among individuals in the family, and personalizing their meals. Distinctions can be quite simple or rather elaborate. For example, a Puerto Rican woman whose second husband is from Guatemala does extra cooking almost every night in order to satisfy his different tastes. Her mother cooks a standard meal for the rest of the family, and she adapts it for her husband. She gave some examples:

> If I know that she's making, say, rice and black beans and
> steak in a sauce with lots of onions and green pepper, then I
> know that for that day what I'll do is I'll take the black beans
> and I'll mash them in a special little machine that I have and
> then I'll refry them, because that's what he likes, the refried
> beans. So that the rest of us will eat the beans whole and
> he'll eat them refried.
>
> For the next day, if there's steak left over then what I do is
> I chop it up real fine, and I'll buy the large Mexican green
> peppers that are hot, and I stuff them with this and then I

beat eggs and I fry those peppers for him. And I'll use some canned stewed tomatoes for a sauce over it. So that this way I'm kind of satisfying both tastes.

In other cases, adjustments are much simpler. For example, I watched while Ed served his family a dinner that was standard for the household: beans and rice. But I saw that each of the two children had a unique way of eating this standard meal. As he served one son, Ed asked him, "Now do you want your beans right next to your rice?" And as he served the other only rice, "You're going to have your beans later, right?" Each boy had established his own routine. Their father had learned to take these preferences into account, as a small but important part of the negotiation required to insure that each child would eat his meal.

This kind of personal attention is unique to feeding at home. When we eat with friends, we usually take what is offered (though friends often care for special guests by serving favorite foods). When we eat in restaurants, we can choose what to eat, but only from a standard set of foods (though the most expensive restaurants may offer customized service, and some wives continue to attend to husbands by helping them order their meals). In most settings outside the home, then, we learn not to expect meals tailored to our individual tastes; we select from the items that are offered. Consider, for example, a family's dinner in a fast-food restaurant: I watched a father ask his son what he wanted, and heard the boy answer, "Double cheese, large fry, large coke." A pause, and then, "No—medium coke." Clearly, this child knew the categories, and could use them. At home, however, there is no standard set of categories, and family members can be quite picky.

The women I talked with take many individual preferences into account as they work at feeding their families, but they do not think of themselves as controlled by individuals' whims. Rather, they understand that preferences are part of what constitutes individuality. They pay attention to preferences and they consider how best to satisfy divergent tastes. As they do so, they evaluate the boundaries of legitimate preference, and make decisions that simultaneously define both arenas for the self-assertion of family members and also the women's own roles as caretakers.

Most analysts of housework point out that women's decisions are often influenced by husbands' preferences (Oakley 1974; Murcott 1983; Charles and Kerr 1988). Studies consistently demonstrate that husbands' needs dominate, and that women's own needs generally come last. Meg Luxton (1980:50), while noting this pattern, also suggests that women are not "powerless," and that a woman will often "get him to do things her way." These writers sometimes imply that the issue is a rather straightforward one of autonomy versus constraint. I would argue that the phenomenon is somewhat more complex. Certainly, the behavior of many women suggests a trained unwillingness to be forthright about their own needs. But my informants' accounts show that personal attention is only partially the result of pressure from others; it also makes sense to these women. It is part of the logic organizing their work, a way of caring for others well that is central to the social contribution they make through their work.

The women I talked with did not think of themselves as "catering" to family members. They distinguished themselves from others who they think do "unreasonable" amounts of work. Still, they insist that some attention to personal taste—quite a lot in some cases—is "reasonable," and, in a quite straightforward way, part of the craft of feeding. Janice, for example, told about her complex shopping routine: she buys special foods for her adult children, who are vegetarians, and particular cuts of meat and brands of canned foods for her husband. Then she added:

> It's not a hassle. I mean, I don't think it's outrageous. It's not—there's nothing eccentric about it. I mean, you know, everybody has food preferences.

She is aware that some would criticize her care with the shopping as unnecessarily burdensome, and she responds to the possible criticism in my questions about the influence of individuals' tastes. She begins by asserting that what she does is no "hassle"; then, apparently not quite comfortable with that statement, she starts again and explains what she means: attending to preference is a normal part of the work, and she expects to do it.

"Everybody has food preferences": the statement provides an understanding of human nature that sets conditions for the work of feeding. Part of the work is to understand the character of taste, and how it operates for the individuals in a particular household. When women talk about taking account of special requests, they rely on rudimentary theories about eating, which they develop partly from the knowledge of their own food preferences. For example:

> I'm sure—I remember quite clearly as a child, and even to a certain extent now—texture of food is very important as to

how you like it. And I would assume she doesn't like the texture of rice, because she likes noodles, and they slide down.

Again, her understanding makes this preference a "reasonable" pickiness.

The issue, then, is not whether, but which special tastes should be allowed. Laurel, whose children are young, reported that she does not do much catering to their preferences, but then added:

I'm sure there'll be a time when that'll be necessary. Just because of legitimate taste differences.

Ultimately, women must decide which of their family's requests are "legitimate." As they make these decisions about what they will and will not do, they operationalize unspoken conceptions of the family, and the extent to which individuality will be accepted as legitimate within it. Some foods, for example, are defined as beyond the bounds of family life. Susan reported:

He really likes lobster. But he'll never see it here. We go out for stuff like that. I mean, certain things I don't make, because I know I can't compete with the restaurant. He can take me out for it if he wants it.

In the same way, family members must be made to understand that they cannot always have what they particularly want. Annie explained that she sometimes mixes corn with rice; her boyfriend likes the combination, but her son does not:

He'll eat it, though. Because I tell him, if he doesn't eat that, he's not eating anything. But sometimes he'll ask, if I'll leave the corn out. And sometimes I do. But I tell him, if I do it that way just for him, he'll think he's in a restaurant.

Her account not only shows that she is in charge of deciding how often to satisfy the tastes of each family member; in addition, her own language draws on the contrast between family eating and the abstracted provision of service in a restaurant setting. Family members cannot be independent, as they would be outside the home, but must adjust their demands to allow for the needs of others.

Women's comments about whose needs they would attend to also reveal strong connections between feeding and family life, and can often be understood as indicators of the boundaries of their concepts of family. People were ambivalent, for example, about pets. Janice, who does quite a lot of special shopping for her family, explained that she refuses to do that kind of shopping for the dog, which belongs to her husband and son:

> Sometimes I'll buy a couple of cans of food to tide them over, but I'm not going to go about the business of hauling home a bag of food, I'm not going to spend a lot of time and energy buying dog food.

Another woman finished her account of special tastes by reporting wryly, "We don't do a lot of special shopping for the dog." And then added, "But when we were overseas, that did figure into the shopping, we had to get horse meat for the dog and make dog food."

The connection between special cooking and the boundaries of family life can be seen even more clearly in households that do not conform to their members' ideas of what a family should be. For example, Phyllis, a white single mother, cooks only to please her daughter, and not for her male friend who lives with them. She explained:

> I usually cook a real dinner. But only for Marilyn. Because when Marilyn isn't home, if I know it ahead of time, I won't cook at all . . . I only make it for her, really, so anything she doesn't like I wouldn't make.

When I asked if she considered her friend's tastes, she laughed and answered, "He's lucky to get what he gets."

Margaret, another white single mother, was living with her children in her parents' household when I interviewed her. She was recently separated, as was her sister, also living in the house, and their parents were considering a separation as well. Margaret's job was to cook for the young children; she would also do special cooking for her father, and she would cook for her brother and sisters as well, but only if they got to dinner on time:

> If they're here, they're here. If they eat, they eat, if they don't eat, they don't eat. I'm not cooking later on. Except I'll cook for my dad when he gets home, around 11:00.

Margaret defined her stay in her parents' home as a temporary one. She explained that, because of the disruptions in all of their lives, things were "on edge," and that "nobody really does for each other as they should." The members of this household did not make up what she thought of as a proper family. When I asked if people's preferences had much influence on her cooking, she replied:

> With my father, I more or less know that he won't eat
> tomatoey stuff and spicy stuff, because he's got an ulcer, it
> disagrees. And that's what it does to me, so I kind of
> remember that way. Then with my brother, the only
> vegetable he likes is corn, so that's easy to remember. And
> you know, stuff like, if I was to make chicken soup, I'd know
> he wouldn't eat it, because he's fourteen years old, he's more
> into hot dogs and corn and stuff like that. But I don't really
> get into it so much because I won't be here that long. So
> except for cereal, I stick with—I don't really go deep into it.

She has decided on a minimal level of attention to individuality in this transitory situation; she doesn't "go deep into it" as she might in a family she defined as more legitimate.

The family, then, is a setting in which wives and mothers learn to attend to quite particular needs, and others learn to expect such attention. Women contribute to this expectation when they organize their work to provide personal attention. However, there are boundaries to the kinds of attention considered appropriate. As women do the work of feeding, they make decisions about what they will and will not do, and these decisions are based on a conception of "family" defined in terms of a balance between group life and individuality. As they act in accord with such a conception, these women constitute particular household groups as personal "family" spaces for household members.

Feeding Produces "Family"

An analysis of family work from the standpoint of those who do it shows that the work joins material and interpersonal tasks: the organization of maintenance work emerges from a conception of family life, and the ongoing accomplishment of the work, day by day, produces interpersonal relations through specific activities. Feeding work, for example, reconciles the diverse schedules and projects of individuals so as to produce points of intersection when they come together for group events. Within the group that this kind of scheduling creates, attention to individual needs and preferences establishes the family as a social space that is personalized.

These household activities are organized through shared understandings of family life, communicated in a variety of ways. As women talk about their work, they refer to the practices of mothers. They also reason about the needs of family members, and how to manage the work with the time and resources available. They talk with friends about how to feed their families better, or more easily. This strategizing has an ideological component: women, mothers, friends, and family members have all learned about feeding and family life partly from literature and the media, from advertising, and from professionals in social services and health care. As they do the work of feeding, these women draw from a discourse with a history, which both reflects and organizes concepts of "family." They apologize, like Laurel in chapter 1, for not producing a "Walton family breakfast." But they integrate such media images with more idiosyncratic, largely unarticulated ideas that develop from their own experience. From a variety of sources, then, these women develop routines appropriate for particular household groups. Through day-to-day activities, each produces a version of "family" in a particular local setting: adjusting, filling in, and repairing social relations to produce—quite literally—this form of household life. The households they live in rarely fit the pattern of some ideal "family." Instead, households are quite varied, homes for motley groups of actual individuals with their particular quirks and idiosyncracies. Both inclination and necessity produce variation in daily activities within and among households. But the work of "feeding the family" tends to collect these unruly individuals and tame their centrifugal moves, cajoling them into some version of the activity that constitutes family. Because this work of social construction is largely invisible, such efforts simultaneously produce the illusion that this form of life is a "natural" one.

Part Two

Organization of the Work

4 Feeding as "Women's Work"

My aim in the previous three chapters has been to describe the work process of "feeding a family," bringing into view the mostly invisible coordinative work that produces "family life" for a household group. In this chapter and the next two, I begin to explore the organization of this family work—that is, the material and ideological contexts that give the work of feeding its distinctive shape. I argue, in this chapter, that the work is strongly gendered. I draw on an approach that treats gender as an ongoing interactional accomplishment (Connell 1987; West and Zimmerman 1987), and I argue that the activities involved in feeding family members are understood as "womanly" activities, and therefore contribute to the ongoing production of gender in families. In the following chapters, I show how the character and organization of the work give to women virtually limitless responsibility for the family's well-being, and how practices and expectations associated with the family setting organize feeding as a project of "womanly" service for men.

The claim that housework is women's work hides a more complex reality. The home as an arena that requires women's domestic activity was actively constructed during the nineteenth century, partly in tandem with larger projects aimed at consolidating men's power (Hartmann 1981b; Smith 1985), and partly by women reformers who aimed to develop the home as a site of power and influence for women (Rothman 1978). Actual practice, of course, has been far less uniform than the cultural ideals created during this period would suggest. In particular, the middle-class pattern of specialization in domesticity has rarely been an option for poor and minority women. Especially in working-class and minority families, the exigencies of survival have often required that all family members, regardless of gender, cooperate in maintaining households (Tilly and Scott 1978; Dill 1986). But the broad pattern of women taking responsibility for care at home has been pervasive and powerful. For feminists, women's responsibility for domestic life has been key to understanding women's subordination, and an important item on any agenda for change. Whether they have argued that women's domestic work must be acknowledged and compensated (e.g. Edmond and Fleming 1975), shared with men (e.g. Chodorow 1978; Hochschild 1989), or fundamentally reorganized (Hayden 1981), feminists have been concerned with understanding the processes of choice and enforcement through which women's responsibility for domestic life has been maintained.

In most households in this study, food work was done mostly by women. However, few of these households looked much like the "ideal home" of the nineteenth century—or even the "typical family" of the 1950s—and many of these women resisted the idea of domesticity as unquestioned fate. Although most of these women were doing most of the work of feeding their families, they did not necessarily do so automatically, without thought or negotiation. Some professed a desire to share the work of caring for children with their husbands, and had attempted to do so, with more or less success. Some actively resisted complete responsibility, and struggled to convince husbands to do more. But even couples who shared egalitarian ideals faced difficulties in developing equitable arrangements that in most cases pushed them toward more traditional patterns in actual practice. Further, both the material interests of women who might want to reduce their household work and the egalitarian ideals of sharing were undermined by the power of the socially organized practice and discourse of mothering. As these women grew up, they learned, both from their own mothers and from more general ideas about what mothers *should* be, to participate in the social relations that organize the family work of feeding. They also learned a skill or capacity—for attention to others—that allowed them as adults to see the responsibilities that arise out of the needs of others and of a group. I discuss one source for this kind of learning—participation in gendered activities, first as children observing mothers and female kin, and later as mothers themselves. There are, no doubt, other ways that women are recruited into the work of care. However, the influences of mothers and mothering were especially prominent in these accounts, and may be especially influential with respect to food work.

In this chapter, I first examine the actual patterns of activity that obtained in the thirty households I studied, attending to the ways in which considerable diversity in actual household practice must still be understood in terms of women's responsibility. Then I examine women's accounts of learning about food work, and discuss some of the activities that contribute to the construction of feeding as women's work.

Who's Cooking?

One might expect that as more women do paid work outside the home, men would contribute more to family work, but research findings suggest that more typically, working women reduce their housework time without much change in their husbands' contributions (Hartmann 1981a). During the last decade, men have begun to do more housework than in the past, though most analysts agree that any increase has been relatively small (Berk 1985; Coverman 1985; Pleck 1985). Still, increasing labor force participation by women has produced new contingencies for decisions about housework, requiring adaptations of traditional patterns, and has changed the discursive context for these decisions, providing a powerful rationale for some kind of change.

The accounts of these informants reveal considerable diversity in household divisions of labor, produced by ongoing processes of reflective (though not necessarily fully articulated) decision making, adaptive response to material circumstance, and negotiation within the family. I began each interview by asking the interviewee to tell me about the people living in the household, and who was responsible for housework. As the interviews proceeded, and we talked about day-to-day routines, informants gave more detailed accounts of decisions about the allocation of tasks, and of the processes involved in negotiating a division of labor. In the discussion that follows, my intent is to display the gender structuring of their work—in its diverse forms—and to identify practices that organize feeding as women's work. Although I discuss differences among these households, I do not claim to identify causes for different kinds of arrangements; still, these stories do provide some insight into the processes through which so many women end up doing so much of the feeding work in their families, and also the conditions under which more equitable routines seem to develop.

Married-couple households in the study are arrayed in table 2 to show the extent of male participation in the work of feeding. (I consider single-mother households, briefly, later in this chapter.) Since some husbands participated in shopping or cooking but not both, their contributions to these activities have been accounted sepa-

Table 2. Division of Feeding Labor in Married-Couple Households

	A. Husbands' Participation in Everyday Cooking			
	Almost never cooks	Occasionally cooks (e.g. some weekend meals)	Cooks almost half of the time (2–4 times per week)	Almost always cooks
Professional/ managerial households	Sandra[lf-pt, y] PK[lf-pt, y] SB	BL[y] RT[y] YM[y]	Gloria & Ed[lf, y] MK & LK[lf]	
Working-class/ white-collar households	Janice[lf] Jean[lf, y] Bertie[lf] AM[lf, y] Teresa[y] VG	Barbara[y] Donna[y] Laurel[y] Susan[y] CF[y] JR[y]		Robin & Rick[lf, y]

	B. Husbands' Participation in Provisioning			
	Almost never shops for food	Occasionally shops for food	About half of food shopping	Almost always shops for food
Professional/ managerial households	Sandra[lf-pt, y] RT[y] YM[y] SB	PK[lf-pt, y]	Gloria & Ed[lf, y]	BL[y] MK & LK[lf]
Working-class/ white-collar households	Bertie[lf] Janice[lf] Jean[lf, y] AM[lf, y] Barbara[y] Donna[y] Susan[y]	Teresa[y] JR[y] VG	CF[y]	Robin & Rick[lf, y] Laurel[y]

Households are identified by name(s) or initials of interviewee(s).
lf = Women in labor force (pt = part-time)
y = Households with young children present (preschool and/or early elementary)

rately. The table shows that in most of these households, husbands never or only occasionally share the work of cooking and provisioning; wives take primary responsibility for these tasks. Although the table is organized to identify households by class group, by wives' labor force participation, and by children's ages, none of these factors serves to clearly divide households into those in which wives have major responsibility for feeding and those where husbands make significant contributions. (The pattern of women having primary responsibility, with fathers contributing occasional help when they are home, is especially characteristic of couples with young children, especially when wives do not work outside the home, and this relation will be discussed below. The presence of young children by itself does not seem to dictate such an arrangement, however, since other couples with young children developed routines involving either more or less sharing of household tasks.) Examining the stories these people tell about household routines, we see that they have developed compromises over time, working to construct arrangements that suit their inclinations to the extent that material circumstance and their spouses permit.

In a significant group of these families (at least eight of the twenty-one couples), wives do virtually all the work of feeding. This group includes some couples who share traditional views about the obligations of husbands and wives, in which women apparently choose to do the housework themselves, and some couples in which husbands insist on the male prerogative not to do housework and impose this responsibility on their wives. Teresa and her husband serve as an example of the first case: both seem to have assumed from the beginning of their marriage that he will be the primary breadwinner and that she will do family work. She talks quite straightforwardly about the fact that she does not enjoy cooking, but she does not complain about doing it; instead she cooks simple meals so that she can "get it over with." Her husband does the shopping for meats, and Teresa explains that he does so because he knows more about meat and can negotiate more successfully with the neighborhood butcher. When Teresa works for pay, her husband feels "kind of guilty" and they go out for dinner more; he also helps more with the shopping when she is pregnant. Thus, his responses to her childbearing and episodes of wage work seem to reinforce their mutual understandings about a division of responsibility. The strength of gender as an element in Teresa's construction of family responsibilities can also be seen in her relations with other kin. On the day of the interview, a sister-in-law whose family had just arrived from another state was cooking for the household, and Teresa explained, "It's her turn, so that's why I'm taking it easy."

In some of these families, women resist total responsibility, and their husbands' lack of participation appears to be the result of their refusal to do housework. The four women in such marriages seemed to object to doing all the housework at least in part because they all worked outside the home for pay as well, and all referred to their paid work as explicit rationale for resisting total responsibility. One of these four (Jean) reported that the household division of labor was an ongoing point of contention in the marriage, and another (Bertie) described an earlier period of conflict, since resolved. (These women's experiences of conflict will be discussed in chapter 6.) The other two (Janice and another woman, from a more affluent, professional household) referred with rather oblique frustration to their husbands' lack of participation, but seemed not to have contested the division of labor overtly. By the time I interviewed them, three of these four women (all except Jean) had reached accommodations in their household routines that they described as relatively satisfactory.

The women who found themselves in such positions adopted several strategies to ease their accommodation to spouses. One affluent white woman works only part-time, as well as curtailing her household effort somewhat. She seems to accept her husband's lack of participation in family work, but as she has become more involved in her own career, food has become "rather secondary." She also reported that she has arranged the kitchen so that her children can feed themselves during the day, explaining, "They can get it themselves. I don't like to wait on people." The option of part-time work—and to some extent the kind of choices about interior design that facilitate children's independence—is not usually available to lower-income women, but the strategy of training children to help with household work is more widespread. In several households, the manner in which children took up household responsibilities served to buffer wives from their husbands' refusal either to contribute to family work or to accept simpler routines. For example, Janice's cooperative household routine, discussed earlier, allowed her to reduce her work effort but did not increase the work demands for her husband. And Bertie explained that her husband himself took an active role in arranging a substitution for the labor she withdrew from the household: "When I started my thing of going back to school my husband decided he did not want to cook. So he taught my daughter to cook."

Much less commonly (in four or five households at most), informants attempted to establish relatively egalitarian household arrangements, and made conscious, sustained, and at least partly successful efforts to share household work or distribute it in nontraditional ways. (The three families in which this was most true were those in which I interviewed husbands as well as wives.) These people usually talked about their atypical division of labor in terms of the exigencies of women's paid work, as well as their personal goals and preferences. In the three households where husbands made the most substantial contributions to household work, all the wives worked for pay, all expressed a high level of commitment to paid work, and—most important for differentiating them from others—all had husbands who supported their work outside the family. In the one case where a husband and wife— Robin and Rick—had almost reversed traditional roles so that he did most of the everyday cooking, both explained that they preferred such an arrangement and he commented that there is "no stereotyping" in their household. The strategies adopted by these relatively egalitarian couples, and the limits to their success at achieving an equitable division of labor, will be discussed in more detail in chapter 6. Considered alongside the families in which women do all the housework, these couples help to show the strong effect of husbands' preferences on the household division of labor. Some women in both groups were committed to activities outside the family, and resisted total responsibility for feeding; what determined the actual division of labor for each couple was that some of their husbands were willing to take on part of the burden of family work, while others simply refused.

Finally, a substantial number of couples (about nine) adopted strategies somewhere in between these two extremes, with women taking primary responsibility for feeding, and men making secondary contributions to the work. Virtually all the women in this group had withdrawn from paid work, and all had young children. Thus, they help to illustrate the processes through which child care and feeding activities connect and develop in tandem. There seem to be two routes to this sort of division of labor. Some couples share the same belief in women's responsibility for housework that, in other families, produces a near-total separation between men's and women's activity. But husbands in this group choose to do certain types of cooking, at certain times. Donna's husband provides the clearest example. Although she takes responsibility for all the day-to-day cooking, she also reports that he "helps a lot"; as she talks in more detail, it is clear that he helps on his own terms. He wants favorite dishes cooked in particular ways, and he cooks these items so that they will be exactly as he prefers. Sometimes they cook "together": usually, this means that she prepares ingredients and he combines them and adds seasoning. Though she repeatedly interpreted these reports in terms of his "help," she also laughed ruefully as she referred to the injustice of this kind of participation: "When I make potato pancakes . . . I do all the grating and that, and he puts the stuff in and then he gets all the credit." More typically, husbands in these couples participate in occasional cooking defined as appropriate for fathers: summer barbequeing or preparing weekend breakfasts for the family. Susan and her husband illustrate this pattern well, and her comments show the limits to this sort of male participation. She reported that her husband "pitches in," especially when she is pregnant or "in a pinch." But his cooking is quite minimal: when they barbeque, she reports, "I prepare it, and he sits there with a beer," and when he prepares breakfast on the weekend, it is "usually frozen waffles or dry cereal." Susan is satisfied with their arrangements. Like many wives in such marriages (see e.g. Charles and Kerr 1988:50), she does not expect to share feeding work, and as a result, she makes much of her husband's limited contributions.

A number of other couples espoused more egalitarian intentions, but developed quite similar arrangements based on women's specialization in feeding activity. In these households, cooking is, at least in part, activity that comes along with mothering a young child. These wives had decided to devote their time to child care at home rather than to paid work. I did not ask them to talk in detail about that decision, or how it was made, but their accounts showed clearly that once the decision is made, women become primary food workers. Some of them continue to speak about sharing the household work, and some do report that their husbands make significant contributions. But these couples' strategies for accommodating men's work schedules and child care combine to limit the men's contributions, and especially their contributions to feeding work. As a practical matter, these women are at home during the day while their husbands are not—indeed, husbands sometimes increase their time spent on paid work as children are born in order to support larger families without their wives' wages. When they describe their routines, then, these women talk about their cooking as a matter of simple convenience, explaining that they prepare all the meals during the week because they are home and can arrange time for the activity.

These couples adopt a rhetoric of sharing family work, but usually without attending to the extent of sharing or the distribution of tasks between spouses. Thus, seemingly unnoticed asymmetries are obscured by an espoused egalitarianism. Laurel, for example, reported that she and her husband "really try to keep a clean house, sex-wise, in terms of apportioning the work," and that they were dismayed when their five-year-old son announced one day that "Mommy's supposed to do the cooking." Close examination of her report shows how the textures of both egalitarianism and asymmetry can be woven into the household arrangements of these reflective, "humanistic" parents. Laurel and her husband do share some kinds of housework, and he does virtually all of the shopping for the household. But she is the one who spends the entire day at home and who—during the week, at least—prepares every breakfast, every lunch, and every dinner. Thus, it is not so surprising that the children are unaware of their father's role in feeding the family. Even his shopping is relatively invisible to them: since he usually shops on his lunch hour, he often runs out of time and leaves the groceries on the back porch for his wife to unpack.

Husbands of this sort do participate in family life, and in some parts of the work of feeding the family. Several of their wives reported that these men were especially concerned about the conduct of the meal, and especially energetic in organizing mealtime conversation and supervising children's eating. One woman reported, as an example: "Something like, 'Do you know where curry comes from?'—in an effort to get them to try it. [He] loves to give these little nutrition lectures." But because they are so often away from home, while wives spend most of their time there, these men typically cook in limited, "extra" sorts of ways. Thus, even though these couples intend to share feeding duties, the effect of their decisions of "convenience" is to produce a pattern that looks much like that of the patriarch who presides over a meal cooked by his wife. Some of these couples do attempt quite consciously to arrange for more participation by husbands, but the occasional character of these men's cooking makes their participation in feeding work atypical, set apart from the everyday responsibility that still belongs with the women of these households.

The demands of child care, and efforts to share that work, seem to exacerbate this effect. Among couples who wish to share family work, men often spend time with children while women cook. Several women reported that both partners prefer this arrangement. It provides a chance for fathers who have been away to spend time with their children. And it also provides a respite for these women, who spend most of their time with children and enjoy the chance to work alone in the kitchen. Barbara explained, "I'd rather fix breakfast than get them out of bed and change diapers. And this way he gets to spend some time with them in the morning." And another woman reported, "Chopping onions is wonderful sometimes, compared to dealing with my child." Again, these women talk in terms of preference and convenience, apparently intending to claim that gender is irrelevant. But again, what their decisions produce is a distinction between mother's and father's activity, and a strong association between "mothering" and the preparation of food.

Finally, in some of these families, the compromises developed are uneasy ones, and wives negotiate—either explicitly or in unspoken ways—for more male participation. In these households, as in others, husbands seem to have considerable power to define their own contributions to housework. For example, one woman home caring for a young child and married to a professional man reported that their division of labor was "worked out after a great deal of discussing, and searching, and various decision-making processes." Though she does not emphasize conflict over these issues, her account suggests some resistance from her husband, and also the extent to which he was able to negotiate a routine he preferred. He does the shopping, she explains, because "it was one of those things that he doesn't mind doing. He prefers that to say, cleaning the bathrooms. So I've been more than happy to give it over to him." This woman's account suggests subdued conflict and subtle accommodation. She may well prefer cleaning the bathrooms, but her account is constructed in terms of her husband's preference, not her own. She also explained that her husband cooks when they have Italian food, because he prepares it so well; then she added, "You know, in some ways you refuse to learn because you don't want to get into it, you don't want to offer to do it." Her refusal to learn serves as a kind of resistance to housework, though it is difficult to know how clearly she thinks of it as part of an ongoing negotiation.[1]

In virtually all of these married-couple households, then, two kinds of gender organization seem to underlie quite disparate patterns. First, men seem able to refuse to participate in family work, or to limit sharply the nature and extent of their participation. Doing housework is understood as exceptional rather than "natural" for them, and they are rarely held accountable for doing it. Thus, only a few men opt to work with their wives toward symmetrical routines. In addition, both the large and small decisions surrounding child care—from who should stay home with children to who should watch them while dinner is prepared—seem often to have the effect of defining feeding as women's work even among couples who think of such decisions as matters of simple convenience.

So far, this discussion has been concerned only with married-couple households. The single-mother households in the study illustrate yet another version of women's responsibility for feeding: in these households, women have nearly total responsibility by virtue of their status as sole caretakers, but, ironically, they also experience the gendered character of feeding work as somewhat less constraining than many married women. Although single mothers do all the work of feeding, they experience less pressure to elaborate the work for male partners. In addition, they are somewhat more likely to recruit children to help them with housework. Both of these features of their experience will be discussed further in chapters 6 and 7.

This examination of married couples' various solutions to the problem of dividing the labor of feeding suggests that the connection between women and feeding work is not inherent in women's nature, or even primarily psychological. Instead, it is a connection that is jointly constructed by women and other household members, through experiment and negotiation, in response to recurrent features of household organization and the ways households are connected to other institutions. These experiments and negotiations are conducted within an ideological context. As women and men respond to social organizational contingencies—considering

1. Hochschild (1989) discusses "incompetence" and sickness as strategies used unconsciously by some traditional women in order to obtain their husbands' help without having to ask for it explicitly. Here, this woman seems to construct her "incompetence" more deliberately as an aid to maintaining the nontraditional division of labor she and her husband have agreed they will pursue.

who will work for pay, how child care should be organized, what kinds of household routines are most efficient or pleasant—they refer to shared, historically constituted understandings of the practices of family life, and especially of mothering. The next sections of this chapter consider how the activities of mothers and mothering appear in women's accounts of feeding work, and how these historically specific practices both reflect and sustain the character of feeding as women's work.

Learning from Mothers: Responsibility

For most girls, learning about housework begins early. And one of the lessons that most women learn is that housework is "womanly" activity. More than a few of the informants in this study made some reference to fathers, as well as mothers, who cooked—especially in working-class families—and two reported that their fathers had done most of the cooking in their families when they were growing up. However, they also referred to these patterns as atypical, discounting the evidence of their own families in favor of assumptions about daily activities in other households. And while references to fathers' cooking were rather brief, many interviewees spoke at length about learning from mothers. As we talked, these women grew thoughtful and speculative; they knew they had learned from their mothers, but they were seldom very sure just what or how they had learned:

> She never sat down and said, "OK, this is how you do such and such." She may have done that with something like baking cookies, but not everyday meals . . . So I think if I picked things up at all it would be through osmosis. And then kind of adapting, you know, things that I remember her cooking. That kind of thing.

The comment displays an effort to talk about learning this woman has rarely thought about: learning that is powerful, but informal and unsystematic.

Within households, or small networks of related households, much of the knowledge underlying the work of feeding is transmitted through activities that link women across generations. When families get together, for holiday meals, for instance, or in some everyday situations, the women of families work together at cooking tasks. For example, Susan's parents come to her house to eat every week, and she explains:

Everyone gets involved, like washing the pots and stuff. It gives a chance for the women to get together.

Her comment is striking because it reveals the taken-for-granted character of the division of labor by gender. Though she begins by claiming that "everyone" is involved in the work, her next sentence reveals that she means "every woman"; the men of the family are exempt from consideration and disappear from her remark (as they do, literally, on these Sunday afternoons, one imagines). A Puerto Rican woman goes shopping on Saturdays with her mother; they go to several stores, and it takes a long time, but she says, "We also have fun on the way." Little girls often participate in these womanly projects. One woman told me, "I have these fond memories of shelling beans, on the front porch with my aunt." And Gloria explained:

I used to watch my mother cook. And help her out. I was the one who cleaned the silver, I was the one who set the table . . . I don't know if she would ask me to help her, or if I would just hang around the kitchen and help her indirectly, or just watch her and pick up a lot of things. I think a lot of it was just visual.

Women whose mothers live with them, or nearby, may continue to rely on their help with the work of feeding. In two Hispanic households I studied, grandmothers do much of the cooking. And Teresa, a Chicana woman whose mother lives next door, pools resources and effort with her mother. When she worked as a secretary, for example, her mother would help with her cooking:

If it was something that was going to take a lot of time, I'd leave it for my mother to do. I'd say, "Ma, why don't you do this, because it takes so long." So she'd start it off for me and then I'd come home and finish it up.

Women who visited their parents to eat talked about bringing home leftovers, and one even incorporated them into her planning. Susan reported:

And Monday and Tuesday—Monday we're going out at my mother's, and I'm begging for a leftover, [laughing] so we might skimp on Tuesday.

Even when informants did not see their relatives so often, their remarks occasionally suggested that women in their families were connected through feeding activities. For example, one working-class white woman, whose husband and children refuse to eat the kinds of food she likes best, explained:

> It's mostly holidays, when his aunts come over, that we have
> the things that I really like, the sauerkraut and stuff.
> Because they make it—they know that I like it and they
> bring it over.

This kind of active network of women helping one another means that, consciously or not, many little girls learn that feeding is women's work. Robin, remembering her family's holiday dinners, commented on her "blissful ignorance" of the work involved in such events:

> It was always the smell of all the food cooking, this is the
> kind of thing you think back on. You would play with all the
> cousins. And then they would call you when the food was
> ready. You just never gave a thought to anything else.

Now that she is grown, however, she feels responsible for such work: she is the one who works at preparing this kind of meal, even though her husband does almost all of the everyday cooking for their immediate family. She explained:

> I love doing that, I love laying out a big meal. You know,
> roast beef, and ham, and potatoes, and you know, salad and
> dessert and the whole thing. I love doing that.
>   He likes to be in there too, because he thinks it's his
> kitchen. But he usually does more of the, being a good host.
> Making sure everybody's got drinks and stuff, while I'm in
> the kitchen.

Others, too, see learning about food as a way of continuing family traditions, and understand this guardianship as a particularly womanly responsibility. Susan, who had asked her mother for a "lesson" on gefilte fish, explained why:

> Saturday I'm going over there for one of my ethnic cooking
> lessons. She's making food that I've had my whole life, that I
> don't know how to prepare. And I should . . . My mother's
> not really old. But there's the possibility that this might be
> our last holiday together—she might be retiring to Florida.
> So I said, someone has to make the fish. Someone has to
> learn how to do it.

Her comment reveals the powerful effect of observing throughout childhood that feeding is done mostly by women. The force of the idea that "someone has to do it"—a phrase that appeared in other women's talk as well—lies in the assumption (often not unfounded) that no one else will. And it is clear from the context for such remarks that "someone" actually means that "some woman" must do the work.

Often, the things that women have learned from mothers seem natural, because they are "just there":

I was lucky enough to grow up with lots of fresh vegetables.
And no one ever preached about it. Because it was just there,
it was sort of an ingrained value.

In fact, the "naturalness" of this kind of learning seems more an element in the accounts people give than in the experience itself. Women cannot simply imitate their mothers, since the methods and standards for housework change from one generation to another, and the work varies from one household to another. But they often interpret their conduct of household work as making them, quite "naturally," like their mothers. For example, a young black woman whose mother was a domestic worker explained how she learned about cooking:

I've always been with her, on all of her jobs, when I was
growing up—she took me with her, because I went to school
where she worked at—so I just learned how to cook by
nature, it was something I had to do. I had to learn how to
clean, you know, because I worked with her, and she taught
me what she knew. So it was from growing up, I grew up in
an environment of cleaning and cooking . . . So I don't know,
it came natural.

Though she describes her recruitment into cleaning and cooking as "natural," the example in fact highlights how varied and contingent the content and organization of housework can be while still producing a powerful sense that "womanliness" lies behind the variation. In this case, a black mother performed domestic work for pay, in someone else's household. Yet her daughter, who now works as a receptionist, still links her own quite differently organized family work to her mother's paid domestic labor.

Though learning about family life is not simply imitative, the privacy of the household does cause people to learn, initially at least, quite particular household routines. Households tend to be relatively closed groups, and people rarely know much about what others do inside them. From glimpses into other homes, and no doubt from the media as well, individuals compare, evaluate, and reflect on the practices they have observed in their family homes. For example, Jean talked nostalgically about the meals she had been served as a child, meals planned "with great care" by both of her parents together. Then she commented:

> I didn't realize as a kid, but when I got older and went to other people's houses—you know, you go to someone's house and you'd be served a hot dog and you know, just potato chips, and a glass of milk. And I'd think, "But when is dinner coming?" Because, I mean, hot dogs were never served in my house when I was a kid.

Her own practices are different from her parents', but she retains a strong sense, from childhood, that meals and their conduct are very important. This kind of learning can be especially powerful. The pervasive day-to-day experience of household life can mean that particular practices come to be understood as "standards of excellence." One affluent white woman, for instance, wishes that her husband would recreate the "fatherly" conduct she remembers from childhood:

> It was a matter of pride to my father, to be able to cut the meat just so. And it still is to me. It annoys me that my husband cuts it differently. I mean, he cuts it well, but he cuts it differently, you see. I get annoyed. I mean, there are certain standards of excellence, you know, they can't be expunged.

This kind of learning is implicit, and relatively unquestioned, part of a constructed sense of household "reality" (Berger and Luckmann 1967). More than specific techniques for cooking and serving food, it conveys strongly held beliefs about family, suffused with emotion. When they talked about learning from their mothers, many women spoke of global attitudes: of an "approach to cooking," or a "basic philosophy, of good food, at the expense of other things in some cases."

Perhaps most important, many women seem to learn from their mothers' practices what a meal should be and how it fits into a household routine. For example, when I asked about dinner, Laurel replied:

> Generally it's a full meal. I'm a product of my mother, I mean, I just see myself doing things—I remember as a child wanting so badly to have a soup and sandwich dinner,

because other kids were having soup and sandwiches, which I really loved, but instead I had to eat pork chops, and potatoes, and vegetables, and salad. And I generally aim at that, at least.

Laurel runs a small mail-order business out of her home, and when she is busy with work she serves her family soup and sandwich suppers, but she refers to this as "just sliding," and says, "I feel like that's not really preparing a meal when it's not the full thing. Because my mother thought that."

Laurel does not simply imitate her mother, though she recognizes that this standard has come from childhood. She has reflected on the meaning of her mother's practice for her own life. She recognizes that her mother was "so rigid that she missed out on a lot because of it." But she sees reasons for her mother's behavior: her father was an invalid, and when Laurel reported that "Meals were always served," she added, "I guess that was my mother's effort—to at least keep up the appearance of normalcy." She has thought about her mother's approach to cooking, and has modified it to suit her own needs. She explained, "I got a lot of— which I have toned down for myself—but I got a lot of the right way to do things." What Laurel has learned from her mother, I would argue—though "toned down" for herself—is the importance of regular meals as part of the "right way" to do family life, and the idea that "normalcy" can be produced through this womanly work.

Learning from Mothering: Attention

When women become mothers, their awareness of the importance of feeding, and sense of responsibility for it, are often heightened by the particularly female experiences of pregnancy and childbirth. This heightened awareness does not come automatically. Though pregnancy and childbirth are powerful experiences, uniquely female and biologically based, they are also as fully socially organized as any other activity. Women are taught to attend to their pregnancies, and a strong sense of responsibility for the next generation comes from a multitude of public sources as well as from women's own reflections on the individual physiological and psychological experiences of becoming a mother. I do not mean to suggest that mothering always produces a powerful commitment to feeding or caring work, or that it is the only kind of activity that recruits women into the work.[2] Certainly, women are motivated to take on such work for a variety of reasons, and women without children may be as committed to it as any mother. The discussion here is meant to show how in households such as these, where children are present, the organization of the work of mothering strongly reinforces women's involvement in feeding work.

Many of the women I talked with remembered their pregnancies as times when they became more conscious of food and nutrition and committed themselves to better feeding. Several learned more about food in formal pregnancy preparation courses, but they saw their new knowledge as generalizable beyond pregnancy. As one Puerto Rican woman explained:

> I thought if a pregnant woman has those nutritional needs then you would almost conclude that every human being would have them. The bread, the milk, the vegetables.

In addition to new knowledge, pregnancy provides a special reason for attending to food habits. Teresa, who was pregnant at the time of our interview, explained:

> Now that I'm pregnant I'm trying to have a pretty decent lunch. Before, if I felt like peanut butter and jelly I would have it, not worrying about getting enough vitamins and stuff. Now I'm more conscious about it.

Together, the special attention and new knowledge that come with pregnancy can lead to significant changes. Gloria's comment, below, shows how explicit teaching during pregnancy extends to her practices more generally:

> When I was pregnant, that was an important source of information about food. I learned a lot. And subsequently, although I backslide a little, I made some major changes. I think we're going through a period of backsliding now. But you know, each time I've been pregnant I've gone through a period of very systematically increasing intake of water, eating fresh foods—I've started parboiling the foods, or

2. My claim is that women who mother are likely to develop distinctive perspectives on group life (Ruddick 1980, 1989), but neither the activities nor the perspectives are associated in any simple way with women as a group, or even mothers as an undifferentiated group. Many women never do mothering work and still learn skills and associations like those discussed here from other sources; some men who care for children seem to develop similar perspectives (see e.g. Coltrane 1989; Hochschild 1989).

steaming them, trying to eat more fresh fruits and vegetables rather than canned. Just real basic kinds of changes, that come about primarily through the whole focusing on how you're going to start this newborn kid off.

The physiological experience of pregnancy—and all of the explicit teaching that surrounds it—enforces attention to feeding: a woman learns that she provides, very directly, the nourishment that carries the fetus to term.[3]

Attention to children's sustenance continues as they grow. Even when the physiological connection of pregnancy has ended, mothers are still usually more responsible than fathers for feeding their children. They watch them develop, and consider their responses to food. This relatively affluent white woman's comment shows her awareness that such monitoring and reflection take time:

> I think a full-time mother has got more time to be concerned about diet. You start thinking about it, because you know that that's when children form their basic food habits. You can just observe them and see how they'll eat anything at a certain age, and then their taste buds begin to develop and they start getting real fussy and so forth. It makes you conscious of food, and what you feed them.

Young mothers like this may talk together about what to do. Another reported:

> One of my friends likes to cook and is interested in cooking, and she had children at the same time I did, so we both would kind of compare notes about what was a good thing to do, and what would build strong bodies—how important early nutrition is for your life. You want them to eat good things, so they develop nice strong bodies. And you kind of feel responsible. It's one aspect of parenting.

While these comments come from "full-time mothers," others, too, reported a heightened attention to food after having children. They learn from public sources all around them about their respon-

3. It is important to note, again, that while the processes I describe here are linked to the physiological experience of pregnancy, that experience is strongly conditioned by wider social relations. For example, the account I provide here describes the experience of women who have a network of support during pregnancy, and receive adequate prenatal care. For far too many women in the U.S., these conditions do not obtain.

sibility for another life. Robin, for example, refers obliquely to television advertisements:

> Well, you know, Rick and I, yeah, it's not that important, but for Kate it's very important, because she's in her developing years, as they say, on the commercials for bread and everything.

Though her job does not allow her time for the study and reflection described above, she still feels the pressure of responsibility for the "developing years."

The textual sources from which many women learn about mothering emphasize the gravity of their responsibility for children. These instructions, and mothers' usually quite intense involvement with their children, push women toward thinking about the work of feeding, and encourage them to practice "attention," an activity that supports the work. Attention is a central element in Sara Ruddick's analysis of "maternal thought." Drawing on the philosophies of Iris Murdoch and Simone Weil, Ruddick talks of attention as "an *intellectual* capacity connected even by definition with love, a special kind of 'knowledge of the individual'" (1980:358). She argues that "attentive love, the training to ask, 'What are you going through?' is central to maternal practices" (p. 359), and supports the kind of adaptation to growth and change that successful mothering requires. Her analysis is useful because she begins to identify actual practices and skills that give rise to features of mothering that have more often been seen as arising from emotional or psychological traits attributed to women. As I talked with women about feeding their families, I found that they often reported attending to individuals in their households, and that attention was an essential element in their conceptions of the work they did for others.

At the simplest level, attention involves simply noticing what someone needs. But children's needs for foods, and especially for foods of particular kinds, must be inferred by watching their responses. One woman explained, for example:

> I feel that there's a difference if I give Mark [the baby] something with a lot of sugar in it. I feel that he starts going off the wall. So I will try not to give him a lot of sugary type food.

This kind of knowledge requires monitoring the other's behavior over time and considering its sources. Margaret reported:

Joey, he won't eat eggs. He just won't eat them at all. And
you know, nutrition-wise, he gets that group in other things
that he eats. And I don't like eggs either. I can't tolerate
them, I'm allergic to them, so you know. And he eats french
toast, so when he eats french toast he gets his egg in the
toast.

"I'm allergic to them, so you know," she says, summarizing a train
of unspoken thought: perhaps her son is allergic to eggs too, so that
it may be best not to insist that he eat them.

This kind of attention must be a continuing project, and does
not always have immediate results. Janice, for example, reported
that she believes her teenaged daughter is much too thin, and that
she has been concerned for some time that her daughter might be
anorexic. I asked her what she does to keep track of the situation
and she answered:

Well, that's what mothers are for, isn't it?
[MD: And what's involved in doing that?]
I don't know if there's that much involved, except that I ask
questions and hope to get the right answers. You know.
Where have you been, where are you going, what's
happening, are you going to do this, are you going to do that.
[MD: So what does your daughter say?]
She says, "Get off my back, Ma."

She knows that she cannot force her daughter to eat. Her job, then,
is to pay attention, and to try to advise and help when she can.

Certainly all of these women are responding to some extent to
public, textual sources of information about food and nutrition.
They have received advice from physicians about children's needs,
or have learned from media reports to watch for problems such as
anorexia. But they put such knowledge to use in immediate, everyday ways by practicing attention. They learn, perhaps primarily by
sharing experiences with mothers and peers, to monitor the health
and well-being of family members, and to use whatever public
knowledge they have to locate potential problems.

Paying attention in this way is a skill that these women recognize but often have trouble describing in words. As I talked with
Jean, for example, she gave an example of the kind of strategizing
she does about how to pay attention. But she spoke haltingly, and
with some frustration, emphasizing how difficult it is to describe
her thoughts about the process:

> I guess I see that [keeping track] as one of my roles. But that
> is difficult at times. The tasks—you know they have to be
> done. But—this is very hard to verbalize— One of my
> daughters is a chronic complainer. And the other one never
> complains. So the older one, if she gets a nick, "Oh, I'm
> dying," you know, one of these kind of things. And the little
> one can be getting sicker and sicker by the moment, and I
> don't even notice it. . .
>
> Some nights I sit and listen to [the older one] rant and rave
> about her various health problems, when there are none, and
> other nights I just simply brush her off.
>
> I'm not doing this very well. I'm not saying what I really
> want to say. But I guess that is an area of concern. Because I
> really should pay more attention to the little one, and less to
> the big one. And yet it seems reversed. Because of just the
> way their personalities are.

Attention does not come naturally to mothers; it develops from
both loving concern and the very strong societal prescription that
mothers are responsible for their children's well-being. The concept refers to a set of activities that are not clearly articulated, that
develop in practice through observation of others and in large part
through trial and error, and through the kind of individual musing
that Jean struggles to describe.

Over time, thoughtful attention results in knowledge that is tailored to specific situations. It develops through a woman's individual construction of belief and routine, and women's comments
reveal the personal nature of these understandings. A woman with
formal training in nursing, for example, explained that her education has influenced her household practice, but that she has really
developed her own ideas about what is important. She reported:

> I've actually done with food what I've done with religion,
> which is look around, listen a lot, and come up with my own
> version that I can live with.

This kind of gradual, continuous and personal learning is appropriate to the work of feeding. As Ruddick points out with respect to
mothering, the continuous change associated with both mothering and feeding calls for "a kind of learning in which what one
learns cannot be applied exactly, and often not even by analogy, to a
new situation" (Ruddick 1980:353). The attention underlying
such learning is often unrecognized, just because it is so continuous. According to Murdoch:

> The task of attention goes on all the time and at apparently
> empty and everyday moments we are "looking," making
> those little peering efforts of imagination which have such
> important cumulative results. (cited in Ruddick 1980:358)

Her words were echoed by Bertie, trying to explain just how she had
learned about feeding:

> I believe that a lot of mothering, and homemaking, and
> child-rearing, is acquired—well, naturally acquired by
> experience—but the ability to pick up on that experience
> may be a process of maturation—you know what I mean?
> It's not that it's automatically there, but you know—
> survival. In order to survive you have to learn to do this. And
> for a person who cares about a family, it'll be perfectly
> natural for them to pick up on certain things. And maybe
> not even be aware that they're picking up on things, or
> learning to do certain things.

Because they find themselves responsible for families—because
they have learned from watching the women around them that, as
they say, "If I don't do it, then no one else will"—women pay attention. As they do so, they "pick up on" the knowledge that supports
their work.

Doing Gender

I began this chapter by describing several relatively distinct patterns of household responsibility in the families I studied. Some
women do virtually all the work of feeding their families, while
others share responsibility more equally with partners. Still, I have
argued that feeding is "women's work." This claim, alongside considerable diversity, calls for some discussion of what it means to
label feeding as "gendered activity."

At one level, the claim that feeding work is gendered refers to a
continuing pattern in the allocation of the work: the fact that
women typically do most of the work, and usually do its most important parts. Women continue to feel most responsible for feeding. The British study conducted by Murcott (1983) provides
support for this claim. She found that even when men do some
cooking, wives are the ones who prepare "cooked dinners," which
are associated with home, health, and family. The asymmetry of
men's and women's involvement shows up even more clearly in the
patterns of solitary eating she describes. When either husbands or

wives are home alone, they tend not to cook, but to "pick at" food or "snack" instead. Some—husbands much more often than wives—go to eat with relatives, where they are fed by the women of other families. This alternative is one the men feel entitled to; by contrast, when the women are served by someone else, they talk of "being spoiled."

This example also points to the more fundamental level at which we can refer to the gendered character of feeding activity. It is not just that women do more of the work of feeding, but also that feeding work has become one of the primary ways that women "do" gender. At this level, my approach to the concept of gendered activity draws on the understanding of gender as a product of "social doings" developed by Candace West and Don Zimmerman (1987). They propose that we analyze gender as "a routine, methodical, and recurring accomplishment" (p. 126), that is, as the outcome of people's joint activities in particular settings. In this view, activities like feeding a family are understood by those in families as "properly" women's work, and therefore become resources for the production of gender. By feeding the family, a woman conducts herself as recognizably womanly.

West and Zimmerman view gender as so fundamental to social interaction—at least in contemporary Western societies—that it is virtually always relevant to social conduct. Competent adult members of these societies have learned to view the differentiation between male and female as a fundamental and important one. Thus, much of their activity—virtually all the time, alongside other activities of different sorts—is activity that marks their sex category and identifies that of others. Doing gender, in this approach, is not just an individual performance, but an interactional process, a process of collective production and recognition of "adequate" women and men through concerted activity. West and Zimmerman propose that members of *this* society, at least, are virtually always "doing gender" in this sense—that is, they are conducting interactions, together and collaboratively, so as to mark themselves, and identify others, as acceptable men and women.

Through this ongoing process, activities such as feeding, which members of the society have learned to associate strongly with one gender, come to seem like "natural" expressions of gender. This observation does not imply that all women engage in such activity. Some choose not to do feeding. Others improvise and negotiate, developing idiosyncratic versions of this "womanly" work. And of course, some men do feeding work and remain recognizable men. But as long as feeding is understood, collectively, as somehow more "womanly" than "manly," the work stands as one kind of activity in which "womanliness" may be at issue. Thus, many couples apparently do organize their household activity around shared (or contested) assumptions about gendered activity, their versions of "properly" masculine or feminine behavior. Sarah Fenstermaker Berk (1985:204), using the concept of doing gender to interpret her study of household work, suggests that household tasks often become "occasions" for "reaffirmation of one's *gendered* relation to the work and to the world."

The material in this chapter begins to suggest how members of households learn to associate womanliness and feeding work, and how their later practices can sustain such an association. At an early age, many children observe their mothers at work in the household, and girls are often recruited into womanly activities based on the principles of responsibility and attention; when they become mothers themselves these lessons are reinforced through the urgency and immediacy of infants' needs, as well as through textual instructions for mothers (Griffith and Smith 1987). New mothers are constantly reminded of these principles, and work at putting them into practice; they feel pleased when their efforts seem to succeed, and guilty when their children do not prosper. Fathers, of course, may take the same kinds of responsibility and learn similar skills. When they do so, however, they may be called to account for their "unnatural" conduct (Coltrane 1989). They, too, may have learned caring skills from their mothers (those I talked with suggested that this was so), but they typically have not developed the compelling sense, strongly felt by many women, that care for others is their duty. Women, by contrast, have been trained and encouraged to attend to others and care for them, and to resist these lessons is to risk their "womanly" character. Thus, for many, commitment to the work of caretaking has become an apparently "natural" part of the gendered self.

5 ▪ Never Done

The sense of responsibility for feeding learned by so many young girls and women is attached to a diffuse, vaguely defined set of tasks. Meg Luxton, in a discussion of family life in a Canadian mining town (1980), points out that housework cannot be defined ahistorically, in terms of discrete tasks. Instead, the work must be thought of as "residual," consisting of the tasks to be done at home because they cannot be bought in a particular historical and cultural context. Bread baking, for example, though part of an early rural American routine, is rarely considered necessary in contemporary homes. But, as Ruth Cowan (1983) points out, widespread auto ownership and a more dispersed pattern of living have increased the amount of transportation work required of middle-class mothers. The general point suggests that the definition of housework will even be specific to a particular household. For example, in households with sufficient income, working mothers may purchase prepared foods that reduce the amount of cooking they do. Or, when individuals have food-related health problems, cooking may be organized with these in mind. Routines for housework, then, are quite individual, developed in response to the particular requirements of a specific household group. So how does anyone decide what to do?

In the past, housework was more standardized—at least in similar kinds of households—simply because of the technical demands of the work. Even a generation ago, washing, ironing, cooking, and cleaning were more arduous and physically complex activities than they are today. Families had few of the options for reorganizing work that are now available as a result of new products and services. Now, many of the technical skills of these earlier work processes have been rendered unnecessary by newly available prod-

ucts (permanent press clothing, for example), and services needed
to support family members can often be purchased outside the
home. These changes mean that housework can now be done in
many different ways. Standards and schedules are less traditional
than in the past, and represent intricate adaptations to the circumstances of those in particular households.

Several of the women I talked with had grown up in Polish immigrant families. They described a system their mothers had used for
organizing their housework:

> You wash on Monday, you iron on Tuesday, you mend or
> whatever on Wednesday, Thursday you're free, Friday you
> clean, Saturday if there's any outside work to do you do it.

Susan, who gave this account, has continued to follow a routine
similar to her mother's:

> Because of that, I get up Monday morning and the first load
> of laundry's in by 8:30. And it's great, I don't have to get up
> in the morning and say, should I wash today? You know,
> who'd ever say yes, to a question like that?

This kind of schedule is unusual now, however. In contemporary
urban homes, housework is characterized by variability both in
what is done and how. Since there are few community-based rules
for doing the work, the houseworker is, in some sense at least, her
own boss. However, as Susan points out, this kind of autonomy
creates the additional task of organizing the work: it means saying
yes or no to questions including, but often more complicated than,
"Should I wash today?"

Sociologists who have written about housework have thought of
its organization in contradictory ways. Some have emphasized the
houseworker's autonomy, while others have analyzed how she is
constrained and controlled.[1] These contradictory analyses are
driven by a model of paid work that suggests a dichotomy: workers

---

1. Conventional wisdom says that the housewife is "her own boss," and some
studies of housework have found that women do indeed feel autonomous, and enjoy
making choices about their work (Oakley 1974). Similarly, theorists working in the
microeconomic tradition (e.g. Berk and Berk 1979) think of the household as a "little firm," and assume that family groups choose to allocate their efforts in ways that
optimize their well-being, just as firms seek to increase profit. Writers who emphasize control of the housewife's efforts point to various sources of control. Some imply that husbands are "bosses" for housework (e.g. Delphy 1976), while others argue
that the work is organized by the economy, through institutions like stores and services, so that the housewife has no single boss, but "many antagonists" (Weinbaum
and Bridges 1976).

should be either constrained or autonomous, either "employee" or "boss." In fact, housework is organized quite differently. House-work tasks are not clearly defined; indeed, many are invisible, based on a tacit understanding of the work and unacknowledged even by those who do them. Rewards are uncertain: the house-worker works partly for herself and partly for others, who compel through implicit as well as explicit demands, and who may or may not acknowledge her efforts. Standards and routines for work with-in the family are not externally given, as they would be if the work were done for pay. Nor are work routines simply shared among households. Individuals grow up in families that are idiosyncratic in many ways, and although they learn cultural images of family life, they have few windows into the actual family lives of others. Thus, part of the work for the houseworker is to determine just what is required and how much to do. Those who do housework are neither bosses nor workers, but actors organizing their own efforts in concert with the projects of others, guided by the demands and preferences of others, by a concept of family life, and by the limits of material possibility.

What to Do

The routines that people describe are schemes for facilitating the activities of household members. In their accounts, women re-ferred to these others' needs and activities as fixed conditions for their work. The houseworker's responsibility is to plan her efforts so as to support these others. Sandra, for example, had developed a system that involved cooking two meals each evening. She has a professional degree, and does consulting work somewhat spo-radically on a free-lance basis, as well as all of the household work; her husband is in an especially demanding professional position that requires long hours away from home every day. Her descrip-tion displays the experienced reality of her decisions about family work: she takes for granted that the work should be done and that she will do it; she recognizes that it is difficult, but also insists on the perfectly normal character of her efforts. Her tone suggests common knowledge, that any middle-class suburban mother would tell a similar story. She explained:

> During the week, things get a tad crazy. Two days a week I
> bring home a three-year-old friend of Jan's [her daughter],
> that I feed here. They get home about 5:30 or so, and of
> course they're starving. And they're in the stage now where

they like macaroni and cheese, and hot dogs, and all that kind of stuff. So I end up really cooking two evening meals a day. One for the kids, and one for Ward [her husband] and me. Because of course, Ward does not like macaroni and cheese. So it gets a little crazy at times. And often he doesn't get home until 10:00 at night. And since he puts in such a long day, I don't feel that I can just say, get yourself a sandwich. I mean, his schedule is really too much for that.

As we talked, she explained how the routine had to be tailored to the activities of each day of the week as well:

What I often do is say, "All right, it's Monday night, I'm going to have three children. What do I have on hand? What do they like?" Tuesday nights I have two children, my own. Wednesday nights we have dancing lessons right after Jan's school, at quarter to six, and Kathy doesn't get back from hers 'til 7:30. So that's our treat. That's usually the run to McDonald's. In two shifts. Jan goes to her dancing lesson and I take Kathy to McDonald's—it's only three blocks away— then I take Kathy to her dancing lesson—because of course they're in different classes—and then I take Jan to McDonald's, come home, and another parent brings Kathy home.

She recognizes that her schedule is "a tad crazy," but she describes this craziness in a breezy tone that conveys the assumption that her responsibilities include accommodating a professional husband who works hard and children who study ballet—at different times, "of course." She is not unaware of the effort involved in this kind of support work—she cooperates with other parents to share the work when she can—but she also works at defining her accommodations as easy, and even fun: the dash back and forth between ballet class and a fast-food restaurant becomes their "treat."

The problem, for a houseworker like Sandra, is not that a particular task must be done in a particular standard way, but rather that schedules, resources, and the demands and preferences of several individuals produce a web of conditions that set requirements for the work. Decisions about what to do refer to many of these conditions simultaneously, and represent judgments about what is possible in the time available. Phyllis, a single mother, described one afternoon's dilemma in terms that highlight the compelling character of the conditions for her work:

Like today, the goddamn word processor messed me up, right? And Marilyn had to be at a rehearsal at six, and it was 4:15. And I knew there was chicken marinating, and I had to get home to put it in the oven. And she wanted—she asked me also would I pick her up some Nexus shampoo. So I wasn't—you know, I had this terrible anxiety, that I get home, and get the dinner going, and make everything right and you know, get it done before she had to leave.

No one tells her what to cook or when, but she knows that somehow her cooking must fit around work and shopping (for the particular brand of shampoo that her daughter prefers). She must dance through this maze of requirements in order to "make everything right." And even the planning that she has done ahead—marinating the chicken—becomes a condition that requires a particular kind of work.

Closer examination of Sandra's account shows that her language, too, reflects the force of such conditions. Her description is organized around statements of necessity, referring to the absolutes that must be considered, around which she weaves the pattern of her work:

Of course they're starving.
They're in the stage now where they like . . .
Of course, Ward does not like . . .
His schedule is really too much for that.
It's Monday night, I'm going to have three children.
Wednesday nights we have dancing lessons.
Of course they're in different classes.

These key statements in the account report on aspects of these people's lives that Sandra takes as given and that set the conditions for her work. Her language is that of facticity: her talk is repeatedly and emphatically punctuated with the phrase "of course," or pegged to the unquestionable, inevitable course of the calendar ("It's Monday night, I'm going to have three children"). Rather than simply telling what the children like, she attributes their preferences to a "stage," and when she explains why she cooks a late meal for her husband, she insists that his work is "really" too hard for a sandwich to suffice. She implies that these conditions are the givens: they require a particular routine.

Sandra's schedule seems especially complicated because of her children's lessons and her husband's long professional work day.

However, this kind of account is not so unusual, nor limited to professional households. Rick, the working-class man who does the cooking for his household, described a startlingly similar routine, and in the same matter-of-fact way. He prefaced his statement with a reminder of what anyone would have to remember:

> You gotta remember you've got a seven-year-old. She comes home, and her last meal was at lunch. So she had from 12:00 until—I usually pick her up about 5:00 or a quarter after five. And maybe they might have had a snack at school. Maybe not—that's very rare. So she comes home, "I'm hungry." Well, I'll start preparing—I'll start hers first. Because I'll usually wait for Robin [his wife]. Unless I'm really hungry [laughing]. Then I'll fix everybody's, and I'll warm up Robin's in the microwave.

Sometimes Robin works late, or goes to her evening class, and then he has to decide how to adapt to her schedule:

> If she's going to be working late, I usually get Kerry [the baby] fed first, then I'll start whatever it happens to be. If it's a quick something, I'll make Kate's and I'll wait for Robin. If it's something that's going to take an extremely long time, or something that when Robin comes home she doesn't want to be waiting around for, I'll make everything up and then warm it up in the microwave.

His laughter is revealing: "I'll usually wait for Robin. Unless I'm really hungry [laughing]." He laughs as he refers to his own eating, a bit embarrassed about considering his own needs. He has learned that the work is to be organized by adjustment to others; his own preferences do not have the compelling character of others' needs, but are supposed to be deferred while he considers how best to serve others. (His report here is quite similar to those given by women in the study, suggesting that the activities of feeding give rise to distinctive capacities and attitudes, no matter who does it. In the next chapter, however, I discuss some limits to these similarities.)

This kind of routine is a plan encompassing the events of a day rather than a string of discrete tasks to be completed; the routine takes on a coherent shape as it forms around the daily activities of the household. Tasks are necessary because they have places within the routine. Since the very definition of the work is so contingent, it often changes as circumstances change. For example, from Teresa, who had just quit a full-time secretarial job to stay home during the final months of her third pregnancy:

> I haven't been able to stick to a schedule yet. Everything's new to me. I don't know when to do groceries yet, I don't know how much to buy. I'm still experimenting a lot.

Her language is revealing. She says "everything's new," yet she lives in the same house as before with the same husband and children, and shops in the same stores. Still, because she has so much time at home, and because, with only one paycheck, she plans to economize more, there is a sense in which her routine feels totally new. When she reports that she "doesn't know yet" when and how to shop, what she means is that she has not yet decided how to organize a routine. She must adjust to new conditions. Others indicated that routines are always temporary; even before things change, people are conscious of the fact that they will need new routines. Robin, who had two children, explained that the baby was still eating "jar food," and commented:

> So it's no big deal. Not yet. When he starts on table foods then we'll have to start the whole routine, probably have to develop a whole new scheme.

A "whole new scheme" is necessary because the routine is designed to solve many problems at once. When a new requirement emerges, the existing compromise may fall short. Together, the language of a "whole new scheme" and this characteristically matter-of-fact tone convey two features of the organization of family work: the interrelatedness of household tasks and the fact that revision and adjustment are not exceptional responses to crisis, but thoroughly ordinary parts of the everyday work.

Ambiguity and Its Consequences

Most people are not accustomed to articulating standards for housework tasks. When I asked women which parts of their feeding work they do best, and which they have trouble with, many seemed surprised by the question, and puzzled about how to evaluate their efforts. They had to pause to consider the question, and they often responded with some uncertainty. Donna, for example, commented:

> I don't know. It seems to me that it goes by pretty good. I don't really have any complaints about it.

As long as things "go by pretty good," it seems, people do not need to make standards explicit. But individuals are constantly making day-to-day decisions about how to proceed. As they do so, they develop principles to guide their work by combining and revising "rules" received from a variety of sources: mothers, friends, family members, the media. Over time, decisions evolve into standards and routines adapted to particular households. When they talk of particular aspects of their practice, women describe quite specific, individually formulated "rules" representing compromises of various sorts. For example, Janice said of the dinners she prepares:

> Maybe it's not gorgeous, but it's healthy. It always at least has some protein in it, and it always at least has some vegetables in it. In some form. I mean, even if it's just spaghetti and meat sauce, half of that sauce is onions and mushrooms. If it's tuna salad, it's tuna salad with two or three stalks of celery and some onions, it's not just tuna with a little dab of pickle and some mayonnaise.

When I asked what she meant by "not gorgeous," she explained:

> Well, maybe it isn't colorful, you know, like you see some of these beautiful dishes. I mean, if you take a bowl of spaghetti sauce, and you put it on the table with a bowl of spaghetti, that's not gorgeous. It's just food. And that's what it is.

She is aware that some think meals should be "gorgeous," but in her household, no such standard obtains; "just food" suffices. But of course, even "just food" is a concept that she has defined for herself, in terms of the components of an acceptably "healthy" meal.

Among decisions about work routines are decisions about houseworkers' own efforts. They pace their own activities and decide when to work harder or not. The loosely structured nature of household work, and ambiguity about which parts of the work are essential and exactly how it should be done, mean that many such judgments must be made. Each becomes part of an overall plan, another in a series of compromises with ideals. For example, a black single mother who had just started a new job explained how the change had influenced her breakfast routine:

> When I wasn't working then usually in the morning, in the wintertime, I got up and I would make sausage and eggs and biscuits, you know, some mornings—but since I started

working all I do is something simple. Cereal, or hot cereal, the instant kind. I'll stay real simple.

Another woman, at home all day caring for her child, explained that she usually cooks something special for her infant son, a picky eater, but then added, "Or he might just have cottage cheese and fruit, it depends on how energetic I am."

In the same way, individuals make many decisions about their efforts to economize. A rather wealthy white woman, for example, saves coupons but refuses to spend time waiting in line at the cheaper supermarket in her neighborhood. Others buy brand name products, but spend time watching for sales and make special shopping trips in order to stock up. Strategies differ; what these people have in common is the process of weighing alternative practices and choosing strategies with implications for their own efforts: deciding how much work, of what sort, is enough. These kinds of decisions are made in the context of local circumstances. Specific material conditions—the number of people in the household and the income available for supporting them, the variety of stores and services in the neighborhood, and so on—are given. Within this frame, houseworkers treat their own efforts—and decisions about when to work harder and when not—as the variable factors over which they have some control.

This feature of the organization of family work is quite different from the expectations governing paid jobs, where workers have only limited opportunities to regulate their own efforts. Paid employees are expected to work on the job no matter how "energetic" they feel, and they do not have the right to adjust work standards in order to make their jobs easier. They can make some decisions about the character of their own efforts, or they can resist the conditions of their work, but they do so within the bounds of a situation defined somewhere else. Standards and incentives are established externally; others make the decisions about workers' activities.

The houseworker both plans and executes her own work process (though always within a network of conditions and constraints). To a much greater extent than in a paid job, she defines her own standards and regulates her own effort. This kind of flexibility makes it possible for a single person to take responsibility for a variety of tasks, conserving effort for use where it is most necessary. Barbara, with her two-year-old twins, for example, adjusts her standards for evening meals so that she can cope with their demands. She explained:

> Usually on Fridays I try to make something easy because it's
> my hardest day of the week. It's just that—try being with
> these two Monday through Friday—it's really hard. So I'll
> make a casserole, or chicken kievs you buy from the store.
> Something that you just, you know, put in. Last Friday we
> had omelettes, cheese omelettes, something that's real easy
> for me. Because I'm the one that has to clean up the kitchen,
> and if I'm tired I don't want to do that either.

Her comment contains a clue to the way such flexibility works: she plans meals that are easier to prepare not just to make her cooking work less arduous, but, perhaps more importantly, so that she will have the energy to clean up the kitchen as well.

The fact that "what to do" is always up for grabs produces an open-ended sense of the possibilities for improving family life through more work. Many people spoke of "plans" for the future in a way that I came to recognize as a peculiar variety of "wishful thinking" that illustrates the significance of everyday household practice. In one interview, for example, I asked what the evening meal was like. The reply was a long one; we had been talking about this woman's own parents and how they ate, and her answer gave information about her own childhood as well as the patterns she and her husband have developed. Eventually, I asked her to explain how their "family style" meals were different from those of her childhood. Again, her answer was long and specific and moved beyond the question. Her husband serves the meat, but not as well as her grandfather and her father did; this bothers her sometimes. Then she went on:

> And the service is important. You know, how the table is set
> and so forth. We probably, again when I was growing up we
> never had paper napkins except when my dad was out of
> town. We do now, have paper napkins, although we have
> cloth napkins and I like it. What I would like—maybe I will
> but probably not—but at one point where we lived we had
> cloth napkins and everybody had their own napkin ring, and
> that way you didn't have to keep changing the napkins.

She went on to talk about other things, but I was haunted by a fragment of this excerpt: "What I would like—maybe I will, but probably not—," which struck me immediately with its offhand poignancy. As I thought about the context that might produce such a remark, I began to see how this woman was doing her work as we talked; she was, momentarily, musing and strategizing about the kind of meal she wished to produce for her family. Telling about her family routine, she mentions napkin rings, and thinks that she would like to use them again. Her wistful, automatic thought that she will do something different (again, not quite planning, but something akin to it) reveals her sense of how the material trappings of meals can become foundations for more emotional aspects of family life. And her brief comment also contains clues to the fate of her own preferences and desires: she plans and wishes, but she also recognizes that she alone is responsible for doing the work, and that in the end she will have limited time and make choices that reflect the priorities of others.

As I thought about this remark, I remembered the time in my own life when I thought I might save my marriage by making better salads. And once I began to look, I found this kind of thinking in the comments of others as well. Food is so central to family life that it can easily become a focus for more diffuse dissatisfactions, and cooking differently can seem like a solution to larger problems. Ivy, an unemployed single mother, for example, was quite depressed when we talked and spoke of the difficulties she was having organizing her cooking. (I will discuss her situation in more detail in chapter 7.) She thought frequently about "getting organized" so that her family's meals could be "more delightful":

> If I get a chance I would like to learn. Maybe take up
> cooking, learn more, learn how to fix it more—more
> delightful, more, you know, variety.

Her thinking seemed a curious mix of specific ideas and vague, unfocused fantasy: there are plenty of specific models for cooking to be collected from the media, and she speculates that perhaps a new recipe will solve larger problems:

> But I saw a new idea for chicken on the TV, they were saying
> you can use that Heinz 57 sauce and honey, you know, I've
> never tried that, maybe I'll try it. That's an idea.

Similarly, when I interviewed Rick, his work hours had just been cut by one day per week, and he expressed the hope that this extra time would mean "better nutrition" for his family. When I asked how, he answered:

Well, maybe I shouldn't say better nutrition. It's money-wise, and—days that you feel like crap when you come home, I might just make cheese sandwiches and french fried potatoes, and that'd be it. [With the extra time] I think I can do a little bit better planning on nutritional eating habits. Maybe we can sit around the table and eat, in the dining room.

He is not "planning" in any concrete sense, but his comment reveals an aspiration toward planning as well as his sense that, somehow, his time might be devoted to producing something "better" for the family.

This kind of talk was most common among the poor, who were less able than others to feed their families as they wished. But many of those with more resources also felt dismayed by the sense that there was always more that could be done:

You know, I always have trouble. At the end of the day I still have sixteen things I wanted to get done.

And:

Really, like most people probably, I'll start out with all these grandiose plans, and you know, oftentimes, more than not, they'll go.

Some women recognize that they do housework in an effort to control other parts of their lives. For example, Gloria, who works full-time and tries to do much of the cooking during the weekend, observed:

Every once in a while I'll get too ambitious, and I'll set up an agenda for myself that's just too much . . . If I spend six hours in the kitchen—which I have done—cooking and putting stuff in the freezer, then it gets a little bit much. But then again, the fact that I'm doing that much is more an index of tension about things outside than something that produces the tension.

Her schedule is always a demanding one, but she does have some control over how to do the cooking. She knows that doing more work on a Saturday will make the week's activities easier. But the difficulty is to decide how much more she can reasonably do. Her comment illustrates that strategizing about the decision is itself a part of the work that takes continual attention.

Ambiguity in the definition of housework tasks also leaves much room for women to doubt their own performance of the work. In comments throughout these interviews, women revealed worries about their practice. Sometimes, their talk referred to particular problems. Ivy, for example, has been told by doctors and teachers that her children do not eat enough, and has received professional advice while in the hospital and again as part of a federal nutrition assistance program. But she is unsure about how to change her everyday practice, and simply reiterated throughout our talk that she must "find more ways" of doing the work. Others, without such acute difficulties, also wonder if they should do things differently. For example, a black working-class mother who wondered whether she should cook more varied meals explained why:

> Because like, you don't expose your children to it, you know, you don't give them a chance to find if they like things like that. You know, if you're brought up not liking okry, then you don't cook it, and your children never really know anything about okry. When it's for them to say, well, I don't like this, and I like that.

Similarly, Jean reported:

> Probably the one area we're all lacking in is fruit, vitamin C. But we all, well we do eat, we drink a lot of orange juice. [Laughing] Frozen canned orange juice. Yeah. But fruit is the one thing that we probably don't eat enough of.

The comment, and especially her laughter, reveal her uncertainty about whether she has a problem, and a bit of embarrassment when she feels that she may be revealing inadequate performance of her duties. They do eat a kind of fruit, but perhaps it is not enough, or the wrong kind—"frozen" and "canned" rather than, by implication, fresh and healthful.

Even though most of these were households in which there was enough money for an adequate diet, many women worried about whether they should work harder at economizing. They made many decisions, some taken for granted as right and necessary, and some that they later questioned. Doubts were often stimulated as they told me about their aims and then reflected on particular practices. Jean, for example, described this common dilemma:

> I suppose if you bought all your—like what do you call it, you know, the stuff besides meat and produce, what do you call that, the stock? the staples, yeah—If you could buy all that in generic, I suppose you could save money. But I don't

think I'd be a happy person. I don't think my family would
be happy.
So I guess I wish that I could think of a way to save more,
spend less. I mean, I'll go to the check-out counter and cry—
I mean, not cry, but literally, I get a sick feeling in my
stomach. And then I'll suddenly think, "Do I really need all
this food?" And the answer is yes. I don't feel that I buy
unnecessary things. I'm not that kind of buyer.

Even for someone who believes she does well enough at economizing, the "sick feeling" at the check-out counter is almost inevitable. Jean went on to tell about one purchase that loomed so large
that her worry about it has been "killing":

I'll spend more for certain things because I like them, but I
won't buy things that are extravagant, really. Well, that
ham—but I don't think that was so extravagant. I've been
killing myself—I've been thinking about that for a week.
You know, did I really need to buy that?

What makes this sort of worry so troublesome is in part a problem
of uncertainty: it is quite difficult to know just how much one can
do about high prices for food. As Margaret, a single mother with an
even lower income, reported:

Sometimes I buy something I shouldn't, I don't know why I
do that. But usually, you know, you just have to, because the
prices are too high—it's just that things are too high.

Most people believe that their work makes a difference—that they
can save money by economizing (comparison shopping, planning
in order to take advantage of sale prices, collecting and using
coupons, and so on); they recognize at the same time that there are
limits to what they can accomplish through their own activity.
Since there are so many different ways to organize the work of
shopping and cooking, these limits are quite difficult to determine.
Such ambiguity leaves people prey to anxieties about doing enough
and gives rise to the undertones of guilt in their talk. Sometimes,
the anxiety and guilt are counterproductive. Margaret, for example, works hard at shopping for bargains and is proud of her ability
to stretch a meager income; however, she went on to explain:

Sometimes I blow it, but after a penny here, a penny there—
after so long—I say the hell with it, I'm going to buy this. I
regret it afterwards.

Her comment reveals not only the phenomenon of the occasional lapse, but also a tone of judgment—"sometimes I blow it"—which appears in the talk of others as well. As women talked about their work, they often referred to the compromises with standards as evidence of "laziness." Laurel, who spent much of her time on her home business, told me that she often planned "easy" meals, and then apologized, "I really am stingy with my time." And a single mother with six children, who likes to save her own dinner until they are in bed, observed, "That's a bad habit I have, I like peace and quiet."

This kind of uncertainty and unfocused guilt is a characteristic aspect of women's experience of family work, and can be seen in other studies based on mothers' own talk about their work. Molly Ladd-Taylor's (1986) collection of letters written to the U.S. Children's Bureau, for example, reveals the poignant anxieties of mothers in rural areas who had few opportunities to seek advice from others. Similarly, Ann Oakley (1981) reports that one difficulty she faced in conducting a study of pregnant women's experiences was deciding how she should respond to the many questions they asked her. Though standard "scientific" prescriptions for interviewing call for the interviewer to assume a distanced stance, many of the women in Oakley's study came to her with requests for information and advice they needed but were reluctant to seek from their mostly male and often rather forbidding doctors. Alison Griffith and Dorothy Smith (1987), researching the work of mothering in relation to children's schooling, also reported that some mothers used the interview as an occasion to request advice about their interactions with teachers and school administrators, checking the decisions they had made and strategizing about various courses of action. And Griffith and Smith, single mothers themselves, found that doing the interviewing for their study could stimulate their own anxieties about being good mothers, even though their children were grown by then and their worries about mothering presumably past. These characteristic ways of thinking about household work are rooted in the social expectations that organize it, in the notion that the houseworker should be available to respond to whatever problems arise, that her responsibility, indeed, is virtually limitless.

The Construction of Responsibility and Guilt

Since housework is conducted in very specific household contexts, it is at heart an enterprise of making do with what is available. Talk of "adjusting" is common, though it may refer to very different kinds of adjustment. What women in quite different situations have in common is that they each face the constraints of a particular situation, and find ways to deal with those constraints. For example, the concept of adjustment appears in Sandra's talk about her shopping:

> I'm really hampered in the space I've got, so I can't shop way ahead for things. And also with the arthritis, I don't like carrying a lot of bags. For me, if I can do a two- or three-bag trip, that's good. You just learn to adjust your lifestyle to what you can do.

The term appears as well in the talk of a welfare mother who confronts her difficulties with far fewer resources:

> My friends are always, "I don't know how you manage to do it, with six children! And still keep your sanity! How do you manage?" And I say—you know, I do believe in God, to some extent, you know—and I'll say, "Well, the Lord don't put no more on you than you can stand. So I guess I'm able to cope with this." And I have been, you know, I've been adjusting pretty good, I think.

Both of these women talk of adjusting. They intend to say that their work is manageable, that they are succeeding, or at least getting along. However, their stories show that "adjustment" does not refer to some easy, automatic coincidence of need and activity, but to specific activity that calls for effort and struggle. Adjustment refers to a difficult practice of using the means at hand—and sometimes they are meager—to make the specific circumstances of a household yield the things required for day-to-day sustenance.

The historical roots of this notion of adjustment can be seen in the writings of Catharine Beecher, spokeswoman for a new style of domesticity developing in the mid-nineteenth century, when new relations between home and economy were being forged. Beecher and other advocates of the "science" of home management counseled a careful attention to the variety of tasks that were seen as contributing to a "proper" home. But they also recognized the limits imposed by material conditions and the strength of a woman managing her household alone. Beecher, for example, includes chapters on "The Preservation of Good Temper in the Housekeeper" and "Comfort for a Discouraged Housekeeper" in *Miss Beecher's Housekeeper and Healthkeeper*, her final book of domestic advice. She suggests that women decide which of their tasks are most important, and adds, "Then make up your mind that all the rest must go along as they do, until you get more time, strength, and experience" (cited in Strasser 1982:194). The idea that the vitally important work of home management can sometimes be ignored is an apparent contradiction: after so much attention to defining what the houseworker should do, what is the reader to make of this idea that part of the work could just as well be abandoned? But when just one person is to do the work, this sort of calculation provides for the only kind of adjustment possible. Thus, the advice supports an approach to household work: goals that seem possible, but are infinitely expandable. Such an outlook allows virtually endless adaptation to the changing and highly variable needs of particular households. Since work and management are combined, the houseworker has both autonomy and responsibility: a mother paces her own work, but she alone is held responsible for determining what work is essential and getting it done, to use Janice's words, "in some form."

Much of the anxiety that individuals feel about family work arises from the distinctive way that housework is structured from outside the home. The work is not managed directly; rather, discourses of family, health, and child development construct ideal conceptions of family life, and these serve as points of reference for those within the family. Beginning early in this century and continuing to the present, experts and advertisers have instructed wives and mothers through a discourse that plays on the peculiar organization of housework through open-ended suggestion. The media provide a plethora of technical suggestions for doing housework more efficiently, suggesting it is always possible to do more work and thereby contribute to the family's well-being. Mothers are held responsible for producing wholesome, healthful families, and they are taught to believe that their husbands' and children's problems result from inadequate performance of household duties. In this context, a degree of ambiguity about precisely what should be done reinforces this sense of responsibility, and helps to obscure the fact that many simply do not have the resources to do what others consider essential.

It is a cultural commonplace that women's work is "never done." But here we see more clearly than usual how this is so. Standards for housework are individually negotiated and seldom articulated. In one sense, those who do the work have the autonomy that comes from organizing their own work. However, the other side of this autonomy is the subtle but persistent anxiety that comes from never knowing how much work is enough. Specific definitions of the work of feeding a family—decisions about what to do when—develop as part of a broader project of care for family members. The work is organized so that it becomes part of a set of social relations that constructs a household group as family. Requirements for the work are fluid and contingent. The process of organization is so taken for granted that it seems quite simple until one begins to explain. Bertie, for example, who balances a complicated schedule of paid work, school, and church activities, and whose "antennas are always out," reported, "If I don't have time to do it, I don't do it. That's all." But, then, after a brief pause, she added:

> No, I have to take that back. I do do it sometimes when I
> don't have time to do it.
> [MD: And what makes the difference?]
> The situation. The situation makes the difference.
> [MD: So what are the priorities?]
> People. If it's important to someone else. The importance of
> the situation to someone else. What it will do for them.
> What kind of situation this will create for a person. If a
> person needs to talk, or if a person needs, just to be with
> people.

She insists that although she can "sort of know what's going to happen next week," she cannot have a "planned schedule":

> I'm not that regimented. I have to decide that with the little
> antennas up. When the time comes, and when it happens,
> that gives you the insight to see certain things. And the trick
> is recognizing them. And hopefully, the antennas are always
> out, and see when too much time has been spent here, or too
> much there.

Her explanation emphasizes how futile it would be to think of her work as a set of discrete tasks, and the extent to which she constructs her own standards in an ongoing assessment of situation and need. She makes herself available, using her own time and effort to buffer the unexpected contingencies arising from the projects of others. The work itself is a project of ongoing creation, the construction of social relations from moment to moment.

6   Conflict and Deference

Studies of contemporary couples suggest that equal sharing of family work is quite rare (e.g. Hood 1983; Hertz 1986; Hochschild 1989). In most families, women continue to put family before their paid jobs, and take primary responsibility for housework and child care. Indeed, some studies suggest that husbands require more work than they contribute in families: Heidi Hartmann (1981a) shows that working women with children and husbands spend more time on housework than single mothers, whether their husbands "help" with the work or not. Some analysts suggest that women's responsibility for housework persists because men's careers are typically more lucrative than women's, but Berk's study of the determinants of couples' family work patterns (1985) shows that these decisions do not depend on economics alone. In two-paycheck families, women continue to do more household work than men, even when such a pattern is not economically rational. Berk's explanation is that the "production of gender"—of a sense that husband and wife are acting as "adequate" man and woman—takes precedence over the most economically efficient production of household "commodities." Her conclusion, arrived at through statistical analysis of a large sample of households, is consistent with clues from the speech of informants in this study, who connected cooking with "wife" and asserted the importance of "a meal made by (a) mother."

This chapter explores the effect of these gendered expectations

A portion of this chapter first appeared in "Conflict over Housework: A Problem That (Still) Has No Name," in *Research in Social Movements, Conflicts and Change: A Research Annual*, edited by Louis Kriesberg (Greenwich, CT: JAI Press, 1990), pp. 189–202. Reprinted by permission.

on the expression of conflict and on relations of service and deference. In order to take account of the diversity of families in this
period of change, we must consider several different patterns, ranging from families attempting to share household work to those
where relations of male dominance and female submission are en-
acted and enforced physically, through violence and abuse. I will
suggest that expectations of men's entitlement to service from
women are powerful in most families, that these expectations often thwart attempts to construct truly equitable relationships and
sometimes lead to violence. I do not mean to argue that husbands
are all tyrannical or that marriages aiming at egalitarianism do not
represent significant change. Rather, my aim is to identify the varied but powerful effects of taken-for-granted beliefs and expectations about gender, and to begin to confront these expectations as
barriers to change.

Problems of Sharing

Even when husbands and wives are committed to the idea of sharing household responsibilities, the character of family work contributes to an asymmetry in effort and attention to household
needs. Perhaps because the household routine is such a coherent
whole, it often seems easiest for one person to take responsibility
for its organization, even when others share the actual work. This
person—traditionally, the housewife—is the one who keeps an entire plan in mind. In the households I studied, three men shared
cooking with their wives, and all three reported that for the most
part they take directions from their wives. Ed, a psychologist who
has begun to do more and more cooking for his family, still commented:

> It's not my domain. I have the minute to minute decisions,
> because I'm the one who's here, but she's really the one who
> decides things. I just carry out the decisions. It feels more
> like my domain now, because I've been doing so much more
> than I used to, but she's still in charge. She's the organized
> one.

He perceives her as "organized"; in fact, it is her activity that produces this perception, since even with his increased participation
in carrying out tasks, she is the one who does the organizing. Similarly, Robin, whose husband Rick does virtually all the cooking,
reported that she was "the supervisor":

He handles the greater portion of, you know, taking care of stuff around the house. I tell him. I say, "OK, we need this, this, and this done," and that's what he does. Like I say, "You better go to the store, we need some milk," or "We need the laundry done," and he'll do it. He's the employee, and I'm the supervisor.

Rick agreed. When I asked if "keeping track of things" was a large part of his work, he responded:

You're talking to the wrong person. Robin tells me when I've got to remember stuff. She's—if she could be a computer, she'd have the greatest memory bank in the world. I'm scatterbrained. And I don't remember a lot of things, I'll let things run down and just let things go completely out. . . She'll keep a list in her head for a week.

Though he is quite comfortable and skilled at doing the discrete tasks of cooking, he seems not to have learned the practices associated with responsibility for feeding; she, rather than he, does the work of keeping things in mind.

The fact that standards and plans for housework are typically unarticulated also makes it difficult for husbands and wives to share work in the family. The houseworker defines the work as part of an overall design for the household routine, but this design is only partially conscious. Phyllis, a white single mother, complained, "Once you've got the whole system in your head, it's very hard to translate that into collective work, I think." She has tried to share the work with her daughters, but finds it difficult:

We once made schedules. There was probably something in the paper about that. And I tried to make—you know, we would all take a chore, and write it down and do it. And you know something? When you work all day, and come home, it's almost easier to do it than to have to supervise other people doing something they don't want to do.

Like a manager, Phyllis is responsible for planning and overseeing a range of activities involving others. At first glance, the problem—to get the children to do some of the work—seems similar to the problem of supervision in the workplace. However, a wife or mother lacks the formal authority of a manager. Further, since family work is mostly invisible, household members learn not to expect to share it, and the woman in charge of a household may not even be able to specify fully the tasks to be divided. The invisibility of monitoring, for example, can make it difficult to share the work of provisioning, because one never knows whether another is thinking about what is needed. A woman whose husband shares some housework commented:

> I'll be surprised. Like just the other day, we had just a little
> bit of milk left. And I know he saw that, because he handled
> the milk carton. But he went to the store and he didn't buy
> milk.

Tasks such as planning and managing the sociability of family meals are also invisible, and since maintaining their invisibility is part of doing the work well, people are often unable, or reluctant, to talk explicitly about them.

Serious attempts to share housework require a great deal of communication among household members, because the overall design for the work must be developed, and then continually revised, collectively. Sometimes these attempts at equality provoke conflict over the definition of the work. The problems involved were evident in the comments of a black professional couple, Ed and Gloria, who have been moving slowly toward a more equal division of household work during the course of their marriage. They have had to redefine some activities. Gloria enjoys gardening and yardwork, for example, and used to consider them part of her housework. Her husband Ed is not so interested, and argues that these activities are "hobbies"; he explained, "I say, 'Look, don't be dumping on me because I'm not doing that, because it's not my hobby.'" When they told me about their routine, both of their accounts emphasized that their activities and decisions depended on a variety of factors, and had to be made practically from moment to moment—both kept repeating, "It depends." They must talk about these things, or find some other way of making decisions together. For example, he reported:

> She does more cooking, but every now and then she'll say
> that she wants me to do the cooking. And if I'm really
> uptight, I'll say, "Look, I'll go out and buy it [laughing].
> You're working, we can spend the money." Otherwise I'll go
> ahead and do it.

She described unspoken decisions about cleaning up after dinner:

> That depends on how tired I am or how tired I feel he is. If
> I've had a hard week or a hard day I just leave, and I don't
> care, I just walk out. And either Ed does it or it's there in the

morning. And then it depends on how much time I have. If I
have to go straight out, then I don't know what happens. But
if I have some time then I might clean up some dishes. And
then if I'm feeling up, or if I think he's down, then I'll clean
up after supper.

Making these decisions requires sensitivity, and when there are
problems, explicit talk:

We just feel each other out. We know each other so well that
we can read each other. I know when he's uptight and he
knows when I'm uptight. We don't really talk about it. The
only time we talk is when we're not reading each other very
well, and then one person starts to feel dumped on. Then we
talk, we say "What's going on?" and we try to work it out.

Such comments illustrate the extent to which housework is typically hidden from view. When one person takes responsibility for
the work, others rarely think about it. Even the one who does it—
because so much of her thought about it is never shared—may not
be fully aware of all that is involved. Her work can come to seem
like a natural expression of caring.

When couples begin to share the work of care, its "workful"
unnaturalness—the effort behind care—is necessarily exposed.
The underlying principles of housework must be made visible. The
work must be seen as separable from the one who does it, instead of
in the traditional way as an expression of love and personality.
Some couples do attempt to discuss the effort required to produce
the kind of family life they desire. But as the next section will
show, many people accept with little thought pervasive cultural expectations that connect relations of service with the definitions of
"husband" and "wife," and "mother" and "father."

Husbands and Wives

When I talked with women about their household routines, many
of them spoke of their partners' preferences as especially compelling considerations. In discussions about planning meals, several
women mentioned their husbands' wage work as activity that con-
ferred a right to "good food": "He works hard," or "He is in a very
demanding work situation." (And their more detailed comments
indicate that they use the phrase "good food" here to mean "food
that he likes.") These comments are consistent with the findings
from studies of power within marriage, which suggest that paid

employment brings power and influence within the family (Blood and Wolfe 1960). Family members easily recognize the importance of paid work, and Charles and Kerr (1988) found that many women rationalized their sole responsibility for cooking in terms of their husbands' wage work. However, beliefs about work and domestic service do not operate in the same way for men and women. While men who work are said to deserve service, women who work for pay are (at most) excused from the responsibility of providing that service; they are rarely thought entitled to service themselves (Murcott 1983). Studies of the impact of women's employment on family patterns suggest that men's work at home increases only slightly when their wives take jobs. Employed wives typically manage household tasks by redefining the work and doing less than they would if they were home. I will argue here that women's service for husbands is based on more than the importance of men's paid work. Women's comments about feeding reveal powerful, mostly unspoken beliefs about relations of dominance and subordination between men and women, and especially between husbands and wives. They show that women learn to think of service as a proper form of relation to men, and learn a discipline that defines "appropriate" service for men.

Rhian Ellis (1983) suggests that many incidents of domestic violence are triggered by men's complaints about the preparation and service of meals. She notes, for example, the expectation in some working-class subcultures that a wife will serve her husband a hot meal immediately when he returns from work, and she cites examples from several studies of battered women who report being beaten when they violated this expectation. Typical accounts portray husbands who return home hours late, sometimes in the middle of the night, and still expect to be served well and promptly. In other studies, researchers report that conflict can arise from men's complaints about the amount or quality of food they are served. Some of the researchers who report such incidents remark on the fact that violence can be triggered by such "trivial" concerns, but Ellis suggests that the activities of cooking and serving food in particular ways are in fact quite significant because they signal a wife's acceptance of a subservient domestic role and deference to her husband's wishes. In these situations, men insist on enforcing exaggerated relations of dominance and subordination within the family. We will see below that some of the patterns taken for granted in families without explicit violence are based on similar assumptions about women's deference to men's needs: assumptions that women should work to provide service and that men are entitled to receive it. Though battering represents an extreme version of inequity between husbands and wives, it highlights the significance of the observations that will follow, and suggests a vicious circle: the idea that some version of womanly deference is "normal" may contribute to an ideology of male entitlement that supports violence against wives and mothers.

The households I studied were not, to my knowledge, ones in which violence was prevalent. Only a few of the people I interviewed spoke of any discord with their spouses. But their reports of daily routines suggested that implicit marital "bargains" were often based on taken-for-granted notions of men's entitlement to good food and domestic service. It was clear, for example, that in most households, wives are very sensitive to husbands' evaluations of their cooking. Teresa, a young Chicana woman, described the pressure of learning to cook when she was first married and her husband and brother-in-law, who ate with them regularly, were both "judging" her:

> It was really a lot of strain, to make two men happy, who
> were judging you. You know, "You don't make it half as good
> as my mother did." So that kind of pushed me a little to
> learn fast.

After seven years of marriage, her husband still has a great deal of influence over her routine. He buys most of the meat for their household, since they both agree that he knows more about butchering and can purchase better meat than she does. He has high standards and communicates them clearly. When he goes shopping with her, Teresa reported, "I go through the canned food aisle, and he'll say, 'Why are you taking so many cans?'" Teresa does not think of her husband as particularly demanding. She not only accepts her husband's preferences, but also thinks of her occasional failures to satisfy them as "cheating":

> I do cheat a little and I—like beans take about an hour to
> make—so if I forget that I've run out of beans and I don't
> make any, I'll just open a can of beans and just warm them
> up. But when he tastes them—I don't know, there must be
> something about the taste—he'll say, "These are canned
> beans, right?" No matter how hard I try to hide the can.

Teresa told me proudly that he likes the way she cooks and that he has gained so much weight that people tease him about what a good cook she must be. But she is still anxious about judgments of her cooking:

> Maybe that's why I still don't like cooking, because I know
> that every time I serve something on the table I'm going to
> be judged and criticized, and you know, "This tastes awful."
> [MD: Do you really get that?]
> No, no. But I'm afraid of it, right.

She describes a more relaxed kind of meal on the days when her husband works a second job and she eats casually with the children:

> Now Saturday, my husband works on Saturdays, and that's
> the day that my kids are home also. So Saturday would be
> hot dog day . . . To them it's a big treat to have hot dogs. And
> to me it's another treat, because I don't have to go to the
> whole trouble of doing or preparing a whole dinner . . . [She
> explains that her husband works until 10 or 11 at night.] So
> that means the whole day, we don't have a father to yell over
> us. That's what Felix says, he says, "Oh, we don't have a dad
> to yell over us." So we'll have some kind of Campbell's soup,
> some kind of vegetable or chicken or something, out of a
> can.

Some writers have suggested that men are especially authoritarian in Hispanic families, and the pattern that Teresa describes— with "a dad to yell over" the family—is consistent with such an idea. However, I found instances of a similar attitude among women in all of the class and ethnic groups included in this study. While none of these women—including Teresa—described their own attitudes in terms of service or deference to husbands (in fact, many took some trouble to explain to me that they were not mere servants in their own households), they spoke of accepting husbands' demands in a matter-of-fact tone that illustrates the force of male preference. For example, one affluent white woman explained:

> My husband doesn't like a prepared salad dressing. So I
> make my own. And he now is on a kick of having me make
> orange juice, rather than buying the frozen concentrate. So
> I'm going to have to go out and get an orange juice squeezer.

Her tone suggests that she takes for granted that his preferences should determine her work: that he is "on a kick" means that she will buy new equipment and adopt a new method for preparing juice. The same idea appears in one of Donna's comments, as she talked about the foods that she and her husband like:

> I used to have pork chops three or four times a week. And then he just said, "I don't want pork chops and that's it." And I haven't bought them since.

She tells a small story here that conveys the drama involved in such mundane matters. By casting her report in this way, she indicates how easily (and thus, we assume, how legitimately in her mind) he puts forward his claims: "he just said . . . And I haven't bought them since." Susan, remembering times when she had to scrimp and save, explains how things are different now: "If the man wants a steak, he gets it. Period. No questions asked." Again, the sense is of men's entitlement to make claims and have them met within the family.

A number of women referred to husbands as the sources for elaborated standards. For example, a recently divorced, white professional woman commented on how the change had affected her cooking; before the divorce, meals for her husband and children had been rather elaborate:

> The expectations of supper, you know, the big meal of the day. I knew that I had to have meat and potatoes, and you know, the usual fanfare. But you know, that really required me to be home, by five o'clock in the afternoon, to get all of this ready by six. But I knew that was expected of me.

After the divorce, food was "not a priority," and her routines became "very simple." She is concerned about nutrition, and carefully monitors her children's eating, but she no longer prepares elaborate meals:

> After my husband left, things got very simple with food. I found, you know, I didn't have to be in the kitchen, and shopping all of the time. I had always flirted with the idea. But you know, being married, you're just a slave to the kitchen. And once I got out of that, I just had more choices. I mean I had more flexibility in what I could do and couldn't do.

She does not explain exactly why her choices expanded; we do not know precisely how her husband influenced her decisions before the divorce. But she describes a shift from "the usual fanfare" to a "very simple" routine, and her language is clearly that of constraint and permission: her husband's presence—whether explicitly or through her own expectation—dictated what she "could do and couldn't do."

The fact that many women seem unaware of this tone of deference toward husbands, or at least are unable to articulate its basis, does not detract from its force. Indeed, for those who value some form of egalitarianism in their marriages, the requirement to serve a husband—which might be resisted if it were more explicit—is not necessarily diminished by its invisibility. One white woman, whose husband is an executive, provides an example. When she is home alone during the day, she eats very casually, and she talked about how difficult it is, when her husband occasionally works at home, to prepare a "really decent lunch." When I asked why he could not eat the same lunch that she does every day, she was unable to explain except on the basis of an inarticulate "feeling." She attempts to explain her concern as an issue of nutrition, but her talk about nonfattening food is peppered with references to meals that are "really decent" in some other way:

> It would be hard, if I had to feed him every day, to think up really decent lunches. I eat yogurt, and peanut butter and jelly, all kinds of fattening things that I shouldn't, and every day I say I shouldn't be doing this. But it's hard to think of a well-rounded, man-sized meal.

I asked what she might prepare for him, and she gave an example:

> All right. Yesterday, we thought our girls were coming out the night before and I had bought some artichokes for them, so I cooked them anyway. So I scooped out the center and made a tuna salad and put it in the center, on lettuce, tomatoes around. And then, I had made zucchini bread . . . So that was our lunch. If I had to do it every day I would find it difficult.
> [MD: When you make a distinction between the kind of lunch you would have and what you'd fix for him, what's involved in that? Is it because of what he likes, or what?]
> I just feel he should have a really decent meal. He would not like—well, I do terrible things and I know it's fattening. Like I'll sit down with yogurt and drop granola into it and it's great. Well, I can't give him that for lunch.
> [MD: Why not?]
> He doesn't, he wouldn't like it, wouldn't appreciate it. Or

peanut butter and jelly, for instance, it's not enough of a lunch to give him.

This woman's discussion is quite confusing: when she is alone, she does "terrible things" that her husband "wouldn't appreciate." Yet she went on to report that in fact, he likes peanut butter and jelly and would probably enjoy a peanut butter sandwich. Still, it is "not enough of a lunch to give him." In fact, her explanations—the references to nutrition concerns and what he "appreciates" or not—obscure what seems the real point, that "not enough of a lunch" means simply that she has not done enough to prepare it. Her example shows how much trouble she takes to prepare a "decent" meal and serve it attractively. A "man-sized meal" may not be so much larger in quantity, but should be a meal she has worked on for him.

What we see in all of these comments are specific versions of a socially produced sense of appropriate gender relations, a sense that certain activities are associated with the very fundamental cultural categories "man"/"husband"/"father" and "woman"/ "wife"/"mother." (Haavind [1984] discusses similar interpretive frames for marital exchanges among Norwegian couples.) These associations are learned early and enforced through everyday observation of prevailing patterns of gender relations; they are rarely justified or even articulated explicitly, but explicit statement is hardly necessary. For most people, these understandings have become part of a morally charged sense of how things should be, so that even those who strive for some version of equity are prey to their pervasive effects.

Men Who Cook

Perhaps the one who cooks tries, "naturally," to please the one he or she cooks for, regardless of gender. That is, in homes where men did as much cooking as women, perhaps the inequalities of service and deference found in typical family settings would be less pronounced. The possibility is one that is difficult to assess, precisely because gender is so strongly associated with activity. In the sample of households I studied, only three men cooked more than occasionally. Of these three, only one (Rick, a white transportation worker) has taken on almost all of the cooking, as women have typically done in traditional families; one (Ed, a black psychologist) prepares the dinners most evenings, but usually by finishing the preparation of foods his wife organizes during the previous weekend; and the third (a white professional worker) reported cooking about twice each week. Since even Rick reported that his wife is the one who organizes their routine, reminding him what needs to be done each day, none of these men has taken on the kind of sole responsibility for family work that has been the most common pattern for women, and none seems to do even half of the coordinative work of planning. In short, they cook, but they are only beginning to share the work of "feeding the family" in the broader sense I have been developing. These few men's reports cannot provide any definitive answers to questions about gender and household activity, but they are worth examining alongside their wives' accounts if only as suggestive pointers toward understanding how men's and women's understandings of family work might differ. Their comments indicate that they have begun to learn and practice household skills such as preparing specific foods, juggling schedules in order to bring the family together for a meal, and improvising with the materials at hand. However, their reports also suggest that they do not feel the force of the morally charged ideal of deferential service that appears in so many women's reports.

When women talked about what they cook, they frequently referred to husbands' and children's preferences as the fixed points around which they designed the meals. Such comments are mostly absent from the reports of these men, except for occasional references to particular foods that young children will not accept. Rick, for example, likes cooking partly because he can be inventive; his explanation emphasizes his own creativity more than the tastes of those he serves:

> I don't use any recipes. It's just by what I want to put in the thing. And if I like it . . . It's just whatever I have up here, what can I think of now?

He reported that his wife and child like his cooking, but only late in the interview, in the context of a longer exchange. When I asked him what kinds of cooking he did best, his answer again suggested freedom from external standards even as he mentioned his attention to his wife's tastes; he explained that he has not mastered baking, and then continued:

> Other than the meats and stuff, it's just my imagination, whatever I want to do with it. And whatever Robin, you know, I might ask her, like the taste of this, do you like it? And if she doesn't like it I won't put it in.

Picking up on this last comment, I attempted to probe for some elaboration of his feelings about the evaluations of others:

> [MD: So what about Robin and Kate? Do they think you're a
> pretty good cook?]
> Yeah. I surprise them. I surprise myself sometimes
> [laughing].
> [MD: Yeah. They don't have too many complaints, then?]
> No. If so, I don't know . . . [laughing and shaking his head as
> if the thought had never occurred to him].

Rick takes on more responsibility than the other men I talked with, and he does so even in the face of some pointed teasing from some of his working-class friends who disapprove. But even though he understands the urgent demands of children who need to be fed, he seems able to set limits for his efforts more comfortably than most of the women I talked with, and has more success saying no to the tasks he simply does not enjoy. Both he and Robin reported that she cooks when they entertain large groups; he explained that she cooks "if it's gonna be any effort out on cooking—you know, let's go, go for it—instead of just fixing one or two things like I do." And in contrast to the many women who spoke of their own "laziness" and "bad habits," his matter-of-fact reporting of his faults, while perhaps more reasonable, is striking in its lack of shame:

> I don't remember a lot of things, I'll let things run down and
> just let things go completely out. I do that quite frequently.
> Keeping things in your head—well, I know what I really
> need. But it's going out and getting it—and having the
> money. Or just going out and getting it, that you know, if I'm
> extra tired and I don't feel like going out, I'm just not going
> to go out. The heck with that. I'll think of something else, or
> do something else with it, or not use it, whatever.

Like the women I have discussed, Rick takes advantage of the flexibility built into housework to avoid work he dislikes; unlike many women, he seems to do so guiltlessly.

A somewhat different situation provides another version of this attitude. Ed took up cooking not because he enjoys it but because he had to, when his wife's new job and long commute meant that she returned home too late to prepare their meals. As he explained the routine, she plans meals for each day, but he decides when he begins the cooking whether or not to follow her plan, and she accepts whatever he decides. I saw the system in operation when I

observed a dinner at their house. Just as he started to serve, Ed
stopped and said, "Oh, I forgot—Gloria would have liked us to have
a salad." But then, shrugging, "Well, I didn't get to it." The ability
simply to dismiss the work that cannot be completed, without the
anxieties that plague so many women, springs at least in part from
differential cultural expectations: the notion that caring work is
optional or exceptional for men while it is obligatory for women.

These comments can only be taken as suggestive, since so few
men were interviewed, and since even these represent only a few of
the variety of household arrangements that are possible. Still, the
language of these few men points toward some rather different understandings of what in the work is "burdensome" or "convenient." Ed, for example, sees as a "burden" an aspect of planning
that the women I talked with took so much for granted that few
even mentioned it. He reported:

> We occasionally get some fresh vegetables, but we usually
> have frozen vegetables. Because the fresh stuff, somebody
> has to be there to consume it, you can't delay. Then it
> becomes my burden, you know, I have to be thinking, and
> orchestrating, how to use such a variety of food.

And another man explained to me that he and his wife never use
"convenience foods," but then defined as a "convenience" the extra work that she puts in on the weekends:

> One convenience that we will use sometimes is this. You
> know when you come home from work and you have to
> cook you don't really have much time. You don't have time
> to simmer sauces or anything like that. So sometimes on the
> weekend Katherine will make up something, or if she has
> time maybe two or three things, something that can be
> heated up later in the week and will actually taste better
> then.

Here, we see how thoroughly women's household work is obscured
from view and thus framed as not requiring discussion or negotiation. Even as they began to share this work, all three of these men
continued to attribute imbalances in the division of labor to their
wives' "personalities," defining much of the extra work that wives
did in terms of fortuitous propensities for organization or planning.

Men who care for children alone probably take the work of
feeding more seriously, simply because they are forced to take sole

responsibility for this work that most men are unaccustomed to doing. In addition to the men who served as informants in this study, I talked briefly with two single fathers who do all of the work to care for their families. Both emphasized the terrific worries produced by the necessity of feeding their children. One talked of an "overwhelming anxiety" that began each day as he finished work and realized that he had to get a meal on the table for his three demanding children; the other wrote me that I should emphasize "the STRUGGLE involved in this feeding work," and the fact that "behind closed doors, dinner is often a nightmare." These are the comments of men who cannot rely on partners even to help out or fill in (much less to plan menus and prepare meals during the weekend), who are forced to learn, as most women do, that "if I don't do it, no one else will." Such comments may also reflect the lack of guidance—and resulting panic—for men who must unlearn cultural expectation, disentangling work and gender, separating "care" from "woman"; they must learn to provide service instead of receiving it.

Struggle and Silence

Overt conflict about who will do housework is surprisingly rare.[1] Informants in only two of the thirty households I studied discussed any sustained, explicit conflict about who would do the work or how it should be done, and results from a large survey are similar: over half of the wives responding reported no difference of opinion over who should do what, and only seven percent reported "a lot" of difference of opinion (Berk 1985:188; see also Haavind 1984). Fairly quickly, most houseworkers develop adjustments that are satisfactory enough to mute potential complaints from household members. The boundaries that produce complaints become the givens of the work, and those who do it find ways to manage around these givens. The perception that routine is chosen provides an interpretive frame for redefining the adjustments that are made.

1. This is not to say that other kinds of family conflicts are not sometimes expressed through the provision of food or reactions to it. I was less interested in these emotional dynamics associated with food than with the practices of organizing, preparing, and serving it, and I did not ask interviewees to speculate about the significance of food in conflicts other than those focused on family work issues. Charles and Kerr (1988) provide somewhat more information about food practices as expressions of interpersonal struggles, especially between parents and young children.

Susan, who is quite happy with her household routine, told a story from the early days of her marriage, of her first definitions of her work, an episode of resentment, and its resolution:

> When we first got married, I played "Suzy Homemaker." I was young and stupid—what did I know? We lived in the suburbs and I worked in the city, and I had to get up at five every morning to get to work. And then on my days off, I'd get up to fix him breakfast, and you know, put on makeup, all that kind of thing. After a while my sister-in-law kind of pulled me aside, and told me I'd better cool it, or he'd get used to that kind of thing.
>
> I still remember, once I came home after a grueling day, and there was my old man, sitting in front of the TV with his potato chips. I said, "God, in my next life I hope I come back as a 26-inch Zenith, I'd get more attention!" That was probably our first fight. But it had been brewing for about four months. You know, we were just getting used to our differences.
>
> I like the way I do things, I'm used to it. I just get it all done on Monday and then I don't have to worry about it. If I don't do it, I'm a wreck by Wednesday. It's not that I like this kind of work, but you have to do it.

She thinks of this as something other than conflict over work: they were "getting used to [their] differences." She knows that she "has to do" housework, so she has found a way of doing it that she "likes," or at least, that she is "used to." Now, her husband goes to work before she is up; he has coffee and a doughnut, or buys something to eat on the job, and she sleeps until her daughter wakes up. She says, "If I'm in a pinch, my husband's not beyond doing the laundry, or washing a floor." But it is clear that she accepts responsibility for the housework: it is her domain, and though she would not say that she likes the work, she has accepted what seems to her a satisfactory compromise.

In many households, like this one, such compromises are negotiated with little overt struggle. Some men accept more responsibility, or are less demanding than others; some women are satisfied to take on the family work with little help. But accommodations cannot always be found. When conflict about housework does arise, it can be quite painful, at least partly because it carries so much emotional significance. Women who resist doing all of the work, or resist doing it as their husbands prefer, risk the charge—

not only from others, but in their own minds as well—that they do
not care about the family. When I talked with Jean, for example,
she was engaged in an ongoing struggle to get her husband to share
the housework. She spoke of her continuing frustration in two interviews, a year apart, and I felt her ambivalence when she told me:

> In spite of all this, I love him. [Laughing, but then serious]
> No, I do love him, and I'm willing to make some sacrifices,
> but there are times when I really just go off half-crazy.
> Because the pressure is just too much sometimes. I just feel
> it's not fair. It's not a judicious way to live, a fair and equal
> way to live.

She seems afraid that any complaint will be heard as her lack of
feeling for her husband. She insists, indeed, that she is willing to
make "sacrifices," as a loving wife should. His resistance to helping with family work is apparently not subject to such an interpretation.

Since feeding work is associated so strongly with women's love
and caring for their families, it is quite difficult for women to resist
doing all of the work. Bertie, for example, had been married for over
twenty years when I talked with her, and had experienced a long
period of difficult change. She told the following story:

> There was a time when I was organized, did things on time,
> on a schedule. I cooked because I felt a responsibility to
> cook. I felt guilty if I didn't give my husband a certain kind
> of meal every day . . . When I made the transition it was
> hard. For me and him. And he's still going through some
> problems with objecting to it. But I felt that I had put undue
> pressure on myself, by trying to do what people used to do,
> you know . . . when the husband could pay the bills, and the
> wife took care of the house . . .
> I told my family that there were certain things that I
> needed, which went neglected for many years. And when I
> recognized my own needs, there was a problem . . . I had
> given so much of my life to my husband and children, that
> he thought that I was wrong, not to give them that much
> time anymore. But I needed to go back to school, needed to
> improve myself, I needed time to myself . . . They've come
> to accept it now. Five, six years ago it was really rough. But
> now they accept, that you know, I'm a person. I am to be
> considered a person. I have rights, you know, to myself. It

was a rough ride for a while. And I suppose it could have gone in another direction. But it didn't.

Things had changed by the time I talked with Bertie: she was pursuing a degree and spent less time cooking elaborate meals. Her husband and children have not taken on much of the work burden, and typically do without meals when she is away from home in the evening—sometimes the girls will prepare sandwiches—so Bertie continues to be responsible for the bulk of the work, simply doing less than in the past. Yet when she talks about their struggles, she still worries about being "selfish":

> I do take that time now for myself. But I count my study time, and my class time, as my own, you know. You know, so that I don't—I try not to be selfish.

When I asked what "being selfish" meant, she replied:

> I make sure that I have time with them. If my stuff gets to be too much, whatever is necessary, whatever, whatever is important, I try to do. Because we still have the children to raise. So there must be some sharing. They're still there, I can't treat them as though they're not there. Even though they're pretty independent, on their own, they still require a lot of attention. So I have to be careful not to give too much to myself. Because you can fall into that. You know, studying too much. It's hard to describe.

It is, indeed, hard to describe. She claims that she has "rights," like any other person. Yet she will do "whatever is necessary" for her family, and must be "careful not to give too much" to herself. Her talk reveals quite different standards for evaluating her own needs and those of others. Raising such issues within the family requires this intense scrutiny of a woman's own desires.

Bertie's system for accounting her time was not unique. Jean, the other woman who was struggling with these issues, reported considering her situation in similar terms. She identified two blocks of time as "hers," but both were hers in a rather ambiguous sense:

> I feel the only real time I have to myself is usually my lunch hour [at her job]. I consider that my time for myself.

She has to be firm to maintain even this break officially sanctioned by her employer. Her husband, who works at night and wakes up around noon, would like her to come home so that they could spend time together. But, she reported:

I do kind of resist that, on any kind of a regular basis.
Although, in order to keep a marriage going I should maybe
not do that. It's hard for me. Because I know there's a need
there, I feel that too. But this gets into all kinds of other
issues, about him not helping. I feel that if he would help out
more around the house, I'd be more willing to come home
and spend more time with him. But you know, I feel like this
is my own time for me.

On Sundays they go to church, partly for the children, and partly
because she and her husband enjoy the "social aspect," and she
counts this activity as her own time as well:

So Sunday morning is never a time when I can do chores or
anything. And in a way, I mean, I count that as time for me,
in a different sort of way.

These women have asserted to their families that they are people
too, with rights (and it is surely striking that they feel a need to put
forward such a claim). However, they still must calculate which
time to claim as "theirs," and the logic of caring for others labels
any too-active exercise of their rights as "selfish."

These women's stories help to show why there were only two of
them in the group I studied, why conflict about housework is infrequent. They illustrate how, in the family context, a mother's
claims for time to pursue her own projects can so easily be framed
as a lack of care, and a mother's claim even to be "a person" may be
taken as "selfish." If the act of pressing a claim for time off or help
from others is so fraught with interpersonal danger, it is perhaps
not surprising that so many women choose to accommodate to inequitable arrangements instead of resisting them.

The Language of Choice

Many women spoke of doing work they did not enjoy in order to
please their husbands. However, very few of them expressed explicit discomfort about these efforts, and only those described
above reported any sustained, overt conflict with their husbands. I
was puzzled and a bit dismayed by their complacency about what I
saw as inequity. But as I analyzed their reports, I began to see how
the organization of family work contributes to their responsiveness to husbands' demands. As I showed in the last chapter, individuals have considerable flexibility in designing household
routines, and they choose routines shaped to the idiosyncrasies of

those in the family. They find ways to adjust to special demands, and then take their adjustments for granted, often describing them as no particular trouble. These choices, and the sense of autonomy that comes with making them, combine to hide the fact that they are so often choices made in order to please others.

Both deference and a sense that her deferential behavior has been freely chosen can be seen in Donna's comments, for example. Her husband, a mail carrier, is moody and unpredictable, difficult to please and quite openly critical when he does not like the meal she prepares. Although she told me several times that he is "not fussy," she also reported checking with him about every evening's menu before she begins to cook. I remarked that his preferences seemed quite important, and she responded:

> Yeah. I like to satisfy him, you know, because a lot of times I'll hear, 'Oh, you don't cook good,' or something like that.

The possibility of such criticism becomes part of the context within which she plans her work. She thinks ahead about what to prepare, but final decisions depend on his responses. When I asked what she would prepare the night of our interview, she could not answer:

> I haven't talked to him today, so I really don't know . . .
> [MD: Does he always know what he wants?]
> Well—I give him choices. Or he'll say "I don't care." So then it's up to me and I just take out something. Hopefully tonight—I would like to have the pot roast—so maybe he'll say yes. Because he actually bought it the other day, so he might want it.

Donna finds ways to build a routine that provides some shape for her work and still allows accommodation to his day-to-day tastes. She explained, for instance, how she plans her shopping:

> Like I'll ask him, what do you want me to pick up? you know, what kind of meat do you want me to pick up? And he'll go through the paper, and he'll tell me, do this, get this. But as far as really making it out [a menu], I just don't. Because sometimes he might not be in the mood for it, he might not want it, or something like that. So I just leave it up in the freezer.

Her scheme sometimes involves an extra trip to the store:

> Then if he wants something, then I'll just go to the store and get what he wants. It's really kind of day by day. I find it

easier that way. I couldn't sit there and write what I'm
having for dinner every day. I just can't do that.

When I asked why not:

I don't know, I figure maybe it's just me. I just can't sit there
and write, well, we're going to have this and this and this.
And then that day you might not have a taste for it. And
then you'll want something else. That's the way I look at it.

She "finds it easier" to plan meals day by day, and she presents this
as just her way, a personal inclination. It seemed clear to me that
her strategy was shaped by her husband's demands, in response to
his moodiness and in order to avoid his sharp words of criticism.
Within the constraints of their relationship, she does make choices
in order to avoid trouble. Interpreting her accommodations as
choices freely made, she translates his peculiarities into a general
observation: "you might not have a taste for it. And then you'll
want something else." And thus she presents the result of her
strategizing as her own belief: "the way I look at it."

Even when family members are not so demanding, the pattern of
choosing to adjust to others is common. Another woman explained
how she has chosen a breakfast routine that lets her sleep a bit later
instead of eating with the family:

During the week I usually get their food to the table and
then I make a lunch [for her husband]. It's more pragmatic. I
could get up earlier and do that, but I choose to stay in bed
and avoid sitting at the table.

Such comments stress autonomy and choice; however, it is clear
that these women's decisions are not so freely made as they suggest. When husbands decide to press their claims, these become
the fixed points around which adjustments and "choices" are
made. One white woman, married to a journalist, reported a more
conflictual negotiation over the breakfast routine, and explained
how she has adjusted her morning schedule to accommodate her
husband's ideas about breakfast:

Breakfast has turned into more of a social occasion than I
perhaps would care for. For my husband it's a real social
affair, and we got into huge fights years ago. He always from
the day we got married expected me to get up and fix his
breakfast, no matter what time he was going anywhere.
Then we lived overseas and we had two maids, and I couldn't

see any point in getting up just to sit with him—I didn't
even have to *make* the breakfast. Well, that was a "dreadful,
dreadful thing." Finally he got over that, and I don't mind
getting up, you see, all right, that's a personal thing . . . So I
usually fix breakfast for the two of us. Which is nice—but I
would like to be able to read the newspaper, myself.

On this issue, her husband is adamant—it is a "dreadful, dreadful
thing" not to have breakfast together—and she has adjusted to this
"personal" preference. But she also describes her adjustment in
somewhat contradictory terms: she "doesn't mind getting up," it's
"all right," even "nice," but still, she would rather read the newspaper.

The choices that women talk about are not entirely illusory: in
many ways, houseworkers can choose to do the work as they like.
They adopt different general strategies: some maintain that they
"couldn't live with" a regular routine, while others describe themselves as "disciplined" and "big on rules." To some extent, people
even choose not to do the kinds of work they dislike. One woman,
who would like to "just forget about" cooking, has simplified her
food routine so that her work is quite automatic: she prepares
meals that are "very easy to cook, and very quick also." And Sandra, who enjoys cooking and prepares elaborate meals for her husband (in addition to simpler, early meals for the children), thinks of
her efforts as "compensation" for the cleaning that she does not
enjoy, and often does not do. Still, these real choices—some of
which certainly do ease the burdens of housework—seem also to
provide a rationale for deference: women emphasize their free-
doms and minimize their adjustments to others.

As women make choices about housework, their decisions include calculations about when to press their own claims and when
to defer to others. The choice to do something in the way one prefers oneself is made to fit among the more compelling demands of
others, especially husbands. The houseworker comes to understand her work in terms of a compromise that seems fair: since she
is free to choose in some ways, it is only fair to defer in others. Most
women seem only partly conscious of this logic. They, and others,
notice the choices but not the deference. In their talk about decision making, they tend to conflate benefits for the household group
all told with their own more specific interests and preferences.

Such calculation can be seen in this affluent white woman's
comment about going out to dinner. She explained that she does

not really enjoy cooking and "always looks forward to" going out. But she often thinks that her husband is not so interested, and "being sensitive" to him can interfere with her enjoyment:

> If it's just family, and we wait a real long time, I keep thinking of all the things I could be doing instead of waiting, and then I wonder if it's really worth going out for dinner. And I think part of that is being sensitive to my husband's thinking. Because he has to eat out every noon anyway. And sometimes a couple of times a week he has to take people out for dinner. So it's not a great pleasure for him, to go out again just to get me out of the kitchen. So if it takes a real long time, I just feel, why did I do this, you know?

She does not feel this way—and can relax and enjoy herself—when she eats out with her son; knowing her husband's feeling changes her own, to the point that she wonders, "Why did I do this, you know?" Donna, managing a household with little extra money, worries about the expense of eating out, but talks about the decision to go out in much the same way:

> To me, I can go to the store and pay for two days' meals, or go to a restaurant and pay for one meal. And a lot of times the kids don't finish their meal . . . I was going to suggest for Easter, going out to eat. But maybe I'm better off just getting something and having it here.

Her own preferences disappear into those of the household group: though she might enjoy a holiday, the children might not eat and money spent would be wasted. In the end she concludes, "I'm better off" doing the work of cooking at home.

These are issues that are difficult for many women to discuss; their talk is often hesitant, sometimes contradictory. But my point is not that they are confused or disingenuous about their positions relative to others. Rather, I mean to show that they are in a situation not easily described in terms of either autonomy or control. These women do make choices about their work, though many of those choices are made within a structure of constraints produced by others. The work itself is defined in terms of service to others, and husbands' demands are given special force through cultural assumptions about appropriate relations between husbands and wives. What a husband insists on typically becomes a requirement of the work, and a woman who arranges the routine to satisfy her own preferences as well as his may simply be making her work more difficult. The fact that so many women frame these accommodations as "choices" means that they are less likely to make choices more obviously in their own behalf when the interests of family members conflict. In such situations, women seem to assume that they have made enough choices, and often come to define deference as equity.[2]

Dominance and Subordination in Everyday Life

I have argued throughout this book that the work of "feeding a family" is skilled practice, a craft in which many women feel pride and find much satisfaction. Such a view suggests that wives care for family members not because they are coerced or compelled by despotic husbands, but because they believe the work of care is valuable and important. The discussion in this chapter, however, suggests as well that the work of caring—however valuable or valued by those who do it—is implicated in subtle but pervasive ways in relations of inequality between men and women. Some husbands insist quite explicitly that their wives display subordination by providing domestic service. For most men, however, such coercion is as unnecessary as it would be unpleasant. In most households, wives display deference to husbands simply because catering to a man is built into a cultural definition of "woman" that includes caring activity and the work of feeding. For many women and men, patterns of "womanly" service for men simply "feel right." In some cases, the recognition of a husband's claim to service is quite direct ("Like I said, whatever he wants, I'll make it the way he likes, and everything he likes with it."); in other reports, references to "really decent," "man-sized" meals point toward a more diffuse sense that a husband, because he is a man, deserves special service. Both kinds of statements show how the everyday activities of cooking, serving, and eating become rituals of dominance and deference, communicating relations of power through nonverbal behavior (Henley 1977).

Many women take pleasure in preparing food that pleases, in serving family members, in rewarding a husband for his work at a

2. Haavind, in an analysis of "Love and Power in Marriage," based on studies of Norwegian couples, makes a similar observation about understandings of "choice" that accompany marriage based on romantic love: "If you have the right to marry whom you please, the responsibility for how it works out is also yours. Therefore, it is difficult to share our disappointment with anyone outside our own marriage" (1984:161).

difficult job. Many think of the craft of attentive service as work they choose. But few women· are themselves the recipients of a similarly attentive service in return. We might assume that men who cook like to please the ones they cook for. But they do not talk about preparing a meal that is "enough for a woman." Indeed, they cannot talk (or think) this way: the idea of a "woman-sized meal" is so dissonant with prevailing cultural meanings that it sounds quite wrong. Here, we see how categories of expression interact with people's everyday family activity. The gender inequalities inherent in language and in a multitude of nonverbal behaviors are woven into the fabric of social relations produced as people go about the mundane affairs of everyday life. Even when fathers cook, their activity—however similar to that of mothers who cook—is framed differently. There are no terms within which men think of cooking as service for a woman, no script suggesting that husbands should care for wives through domestic work. Some women are beginning to insist on more equal relations, and some husbands are beginning to struggle at taking equal responsibility for family work. But these attempts are made without a cultural imagery to support them, and in opposition to established understandings about appropriate activities for men and women.

Because of the expectation that women will be responsible for caring work, their own independent activities are likely to conflict with requirements for family service. When wives and mothers assert their rights to pursue individual projects, they often discover the limits of choice and the force of cultural expectation. When women resist—by demanding help with housework or a respite from serving others—they challenge a powerful consensual understanding of womanly character by suggesting that women's care for others is effort rather than love. Many have trouble speaking plainly about the limits of caring work, and many find that in the long run it is easier to do all the work required than to press claims for an equitable division of labor.

The invisibility of the work that produces "family," the flexibility underlying perceptions of "choice" about the work, and the association between caring work and the supposedly "natural" emotions of a loving wife and mother all tend to suppress conflict over housework. Since the work itself is largely unrecognized, and often misidentified as merely "love" rather than also effort, redefinition is required before questions of dividing the work can be discussed. Those who have benefited from the work often have trouble recognizing it as such, and indeed, have little incentive to do so. Further, many women find that they can make enough choices and adjustments in some areas that accommodation in others seems preferable to sustained conflict. Those who insist on negotiating new household patterns must confront their own and others' sense that they do so out of "selfishness" or insufficient concern for others. Even as they struggle for more equitable arrangements, these women carefully ration ("count") the time and attention they give to their own needs, while attempting to provide "whatever" their families require. Their demands for themselves are painfully visible within the family, while their accommodations to others remain largely unacknowledged.

The claim that caring is work, or that this work should be shared by all those who are able to do it, must be made against powerful beliefs about the naturalness and importance of family life, and about men's and women's dispositions and roles. For a woman to provoke and sustain conflict in this area is to risk the charge that she is unnatural or unloving. The costs of conflict are high. Conversely, when a husband complains, or even hints at complaint, his claims carry with them the weight of generations of traditional practice and a body of expert advice about housekeeping and family life based on the assumption that women will serve others. As women adjust and accommodate, choosing deference to others and fitting their own projects into frames established by others, their actions contribute to traditional assumptions about woman's "nature." Thus, we see that in addition to its constructive, affiliative aspect, the work of care—as presently organized—has a darker aspect, which traps many husbands and wives in relations of dominance and subordination rather than mutual service and assistance.

Part Three

Feeding Work and Social Class

7   Affluence and Poverty

In the preceding discussion, I have often alluded to material circumstance as context for the work of feeding, since the resource base for household life inevitably comes into view in discussions of the particularities of household life. Here and in the next chapter, I will focus more explicitly on the significance of class relations for the conduct of feeding work. Feeding, like most household work, is performed as direct service for family members, outside of cash-mediated relations, and is often experienced as freely given, out of "love." But the means for providing a household life are commodities that, for the most part, must be wrested from a cash-mediated market. In the United States, where there is some measure of income protection for most workers and a greatly expanded sphere of "consumption," basic necessities can be obtained more easily than in many societies. However, this observation obscures more disturbing facts: that income differences mean considerable variation in the amounts and kinds of food consumed; that many in the United States must spend a far higher percentage of their income merely to eat; and that a significant group of people continue to experience hunger and malnutrition.[1]

The establishment of an official "poverty threshold" recognizes the impossibility of providing for a family without at least a minimal cash income, and social welfare assistance provides minimal

---

1. According to USDA estimates, Americans spent about 12 percent of their disposable personal income on food in 1988. However, those in the 20 percent of households with the lowest incomes spent 42 percent of that income on food while those in the highest 20 percent spent only 9 percent on food (Blaylock, Elitzak, and Manchester 1989).

cash payments to at least some of those who cannot earn a living wage. The poverty threshold is based on a "household budget" that estimates necessary expenditures.[2] Such a budget, however, says nothing about the kind of work required to translate these minimal sums into household life for a group of people (in much the same way that time-budget studies of household work are mute on the invisible tasks of monitoring, planning, and coordinating family life). The differing material bases of household/family groups—connections to wealth and occupation, the resulting amount and stability of cash resources, and redistributions of resources by the state—all combine to construct quite different conditions for the conduct of household work. These different conditions mean that the work itself is experienced and understood differently, and that the "families" produced through housework are different as well.

In this chapter and the next, I consider how class relations shape and are shaped by distinctive patterns of feeding work and household life. My discussion is based on a conception of social class as dynamic social process, organizing the activities of individuals and families both in very direct ways—such as through the wages flowing into households, or the demands of particular occupations—and also in less direct ways, through locations in particular neighborhoods, schools, and other social groups. My aim is to show how the social structures of class construct contexts for household life and work, and also to show how different ways of conducting household life and work are implicated in the reproduction of class relations.[3] I discuss profound differences in the work of "feeding a family," but I also take notice of the ways that these differences are obscured. I will suggest later that cultural discourses about class-less "wives" and "mothers" are powerful ideological tools that hide the realities of many women and their families.

I assume that class position, though produced primarily through occupation, is more accurately assigned to households

2. The USDA's Human Nutrition Information Service computes the cost of providing the foods included in each of four menu plans, ranging from "thrifty" to "liberal," and uses the "thrifty" plan as the basis for setting food-stamp benefit levels. These cost estimates assume that food for all meals and snacks is prepared at home. See U.S. Department of Agriculture (1987a).

3. My approach conceives class as organized activity rather than simply in terms of social categories. For exemplary writing on class and family, see Rapp (1982), Smith (1985), Davidoff and Hall (1987), and Acker (1988).

than to individuals (at least for the purposes of this study; see chap. 1, note 9). The conditions and requirements for household work are contingent upon the total resources available to the household group. Most family/households gain income from wage work by one or more members. Some inherit family wealth, and virtually all benefit, though in very different ways, from government re-distributions, such as provisions for tax relief and social welfare benefits. Occupational position and income are related, but they rarely coincide neatly. Thus, neither occupational categories nor income levels alone are completely satisfactory ways of "sorting" households, especially for a discussion of issues related to con-sumption, which are more directly tied to income than to work-place experiences. In general, those in professional/managerial occupational positions have higher incomes than those in working-class/white-collar positions. But as the description of this sample shows (table 1—see above, p. 21), there is a large area of overlap between these two groups, produced partly but not en-tirely by the income contributions of wives who work for pay in the working-class/white-collar group. In fact, some of the class-related effects on the conduct of household work are closely related to income, while others arise from the patterns of sociability of groups linked to different types of paid work. Thus, I consider these matters separately, examining the significance of money in this chap-ter, and the organization of occupational class groups in the next.

In the first part of this chapter, I discuss in a general way the sig-nificance of money in people's accounts of household work, and some variations in their spending and saving practices. Then, I take a closer look behind the predominant image, of the affluent homemaker, at households sustained on the meagerest incomes.

Money and the Market

In the most general sense, all of these people face a similar prob-lem: the allocation of their total money resources to food and other expenses. For most people, a general level of spending on food is a settled question, a background assumption that underlies their more specific everyday strategizing about planning and purchas-ing. But attention to food expense is necessary for some and volun-tary for others. Slightly less than half of all these interviewees (43 percent) talked of having a "budget" for food expenditures, and those who did so were more heavily represented in the lower-income groups.[4] Whether they budget or not, those with very low incomes are most directly aware of economic constraints, and their awareness appears in their talk. In the poorest women's accounts, there are many spontaneous comments about money. When they reported on shopping routines, they often began by mentioning the amounts of money that structure their decisions: how much money they have each month, and how much they spend on food. These references appeared both earlier in the interviews and more often than in the accounts of more affluent informants. Margaret, a white single mother who works part-time at a low-wage job, offered as an introductory comment in the first few minutes of our interview:

> With cooking and stuff like that, we stick to chicken, hamburger meat, and hot dogs. Because we spend over $100 a week, on food alone.

Like others with limited incomes, she had developed an idiosyncratic but effective system for sticking to an informal "budget":

> Usually if I fill the basket up, it's about 130 . . . When the basket is full, that's a little over $100. Because I buy the same amount of stuff. But if it's getting a little over the basket, that's when I have to buy like, deodorant and toilet paper, which I don't buy every week. Or shampoo and toothpaste. And then that makes it 140, 130.

Another woman makes one large shopping trip each month, and insures that she will stay within her budget by taking with her only the amount she intends to spend:

> OK, when I go I have $200 even, and that's including the tax and everything. And with that $200, that's including soap, toilet paper and all the household things. That's $200 for everything.

The $200 limit she has established reflects her earlier practice, when she relied on food stamps and had less cash income available. At the time of our interview, she was working for pay and no longer

4. In making these calculations, I relied on interviewees' commonsense understandings of the term "budget," and did not always probe to learn exactly what they meant. In most cases, I asked whether they had a budget, and their answer to this direct question provided the basis for assigning them to one of these categories or the other; in a few cases, I relied on spontaneous remarks about being "on a budget" or making decisions because of "my budget."

received food stamps; however, her low-wage job had not significantly increased her overall resources. She explained her reasoning about a food budget, once again structuring the account around specific money amounts:

> When I got food stamps, I would spend—I'd come out spending $200. My 168 in food stamps, plus another $50 in money. That's the way it worked out. So that's the way I did it when I got a job. I just, you know, went on spending $200.

Those in households with more resources often reported a similar result—a generally stable level of expense. They talked of routinizing their purchasing decisions, and of avoiding particularly expensive foods in order to hold their expenditures at a constant level ("He doesn't get filet mignon at home," or somewhat more ambiguously, "I don't buy junk.") In addition, the shopping strategies of some of those in moderate-income households were also tied to specific amounts of money, which came into the household at particular times. But those who had more money to work with talked about these matters more abstractly, and infrequently mentioned how much they spent. For example, when Janice described her weekly shopping, she referred to the checks she and her husband received, but not to the amounts of their incomes:

> I get paid every other Friday, and my husband gets paid every Friday. And the payday that I have I use my money, and on the payday that he has, that I don't, I use his. Which is a lot less than what I have, so I try to do my bigger shopping on my payday, and get as many things as I can. On his, I'll fill in with a lot of vegetables and fruits.

In part, the differences in these accounts seem to arise from differences in attitude, the reticence of more affluent interviewees reflecting a characteristically middle-class "etiquette" of keeping such information within the family. In this study, for instance, the poorest interviewees talked most directly about money, while others were more likely to talk in general terms about whether things were "tight" or "comfortable" (though all except one informant—the wealthiest—were willing to tell me the amount of their household income when asked). This pattern is consistent with other studies of very poor and very wealthy households. Carol Stack's (1974) study of poor families shows how income pooling is an adaptive survival strategy in poor communities, and suggests that as a result, knowledge about the resources available is relatively wide-

ly distributed. Rosanna Hertz (1986), by contrast, shows how affluent dual-career couples can afford to use their discretionary money
to express individuality and autonomy, and how in some cases,
spouses withhold information about their salaries even from each
other. But these studies also suggest that such differences arise not
only from attitudes toward money, but from material conditions
that construct quite different relations to money in poor and affluent households. Those in very poor households must use very
small amounts of cash income to maintain their households, and
these minimal amounts set narrow limits for expenditure on survival needs. As a result, poor women discussing their food expenses often talked rather specifically about their rent or other
household expenses as well, something that others rarely did.
When I asked about her income, a black woman caring for six
children produced a succinct summary of her monthly budget:

> I do get food stamps—food stamps, I get, uh, $291. And the
> check [from AFDC] is about 500. OK. Now my rent's about
> $300. Then I have the light bill, and the gas bill, and the
> phone bill. And then I have to figure out ways to get washing
> done. And somebody's always going to be needing
> something.

Her account displays the calculus that is ever present in these
women's strategizing, the balancing of meager income against
fixed expenses, unpredictable needs, and the areas—like food
expense—where expenditures can sometimes be reduced through
careful purchasing or extra effort. In situations like these, when
there is virtually no margin beyond subsistence, even small
amounts of money loom large, and particular prices are significant.

Charles and Kerr (1988) also found that poor women are more
likely than others to report that cost is an important criterion for
shopping decisions, and they suggest that poor women are less able
to concern themselves with the "goodness" of food purchases.
However, Charles and Kerr relied on a structured interview technique that required ranking such factors, and therefore made cost
and "goodness" competing concerns. The accounts of informants
in this study did not suggest that poor women were less concerned
with the quality of food they purchased; rather, their task was to
strategize about obtaining "good" food with very little expenditure.

In addition to a heightened concern about expenditure in low-
income households, efforts to save money on food purchases in-

volve different practices and have different meanings. For all of these people, food is an essential, but variable rather than fixed expense. Thus, almost everyone, from the wealthiest to the poorest households, talked about food expenditure as a possible area for saving money in order to make more available for other purchases. This mode of thought produces a surface similarity in people's accounts. Most, though not all, talked of trying to limit their food expenses, comparing prices in the store while shopping, watching for bargains and stocking up on items on sale, and purchasing cheaper generic products rather than brand-name items.[5] The interviews revealed a general trend toward greater emphasis on economizing among poor and working-class families, but also considerable individual variation.

In all groups, those who engage in these economizing practices typically describe them as necessary ("Of course now everyone is very cost conscious"), or as self-evidently intelligent or admirable behavior ("It's like a game, that I say, oh, wow, I only spent you know, a certain amount—it's oh, you did good!"). Those who do little economizing treat such practices as matters of personal inclination, and tend to minimize their value. Virtually all of the accounts, however, display considerable ambivalence about the efficacy of economizing, reflecting the difficulty of calculating actual savings when there are so many decisions to be made simultaneously. Those who are most committed to economizing do not express their ambivalence directly, but rather in extensive discussion of alternative purchasing strategies, a kind of talk that suggests continuing anxiety about saving as much as possible. For others, ambivalence is expressed more directly ("You have to watch . . . and make sure you're not spending more with your coupons"), or in negotiation with other household members. In several of the professional households, for example, husbands were especially concerned about potential savings on food, and either shopped themselves in order to save as much as possible or pressured their wives to economize more. Typically, their wives acknowledged the rationality of attending to cost, but they often

5. Generic products were first introduced in some stores in 1977, and were widely available in urban supermarkets by the time I conducted interviews. During the early 1980s, they were widely discussed in mainstream media, in features that typically presented their appearance as an industry response to consumer interest in lower prices (Hawes 1982). This media attention helps to explain why almost all those I talked with made some reference to generic products, whether they used them or not.

expressed doubts about the value of specific practices these husbands suggested. One white woman described her partner's attention to relatively small savings with an amused tolerance:

> My husband likes to clip coupons. And I tease him about
> this. I say, "A lawyer? Clipping and cataloging coupons?" I
> said, "I don't bother with that, I don't think it's worth the
> money. But you're welcome to do it." So then I have to go
> and look for his coupons, to make him happy, see if he's got
> anything new.

Her report displays the uncertainty about savings that was characteristic of so many accounts, but it also shows the power of a husband's statement of economic logic. Even though she herself
considers this kind of activity inessential—not "worth the
money"—she finds it difficult to argue that clipping coupons is not
virtuous activity, and she feels obliged to "make him happy" by
using the coupons he has collected.

In spite of considerable individual variation in the extent to
which shoppers attempt to save money, and their particular means
for doing so, there are also fundamental differences produced by
having more or less money to work with, and these begin to come
into view when we look at the meanings of economizing in different sorts of households. Income levels themselves do not always
convey the objective situation of particular household groups, or
their subjective assessments of their situations. Families with relatively high incomes sometimes reported severe financial pressures, usually because of heavy obligations and debt. In the
following discussion, therefore, I have not sorted households by income levels or class groups alone; instead I characterize several relatively distinct approaches to reasoning about economizing,
which were loosely associated with both class group and income
level.

Most of the wealthiest interviewees, all from profession-
al/managerial households, made some reference to economizing,
though virtually all acknowledged that they did not need to "worry
about money." They took for granted a certain kind of attention to
money; the underlying assumption, that one should not spend
more than necessary on food, seemed not to require elaboration.
But these families' incomes—and the security of stable incomes—
allow rather generous definitions of what is "necessary." Like others, they sometimes talked about the boundaries to their purchasing decisions—which items they would not buy because of price.

But they were less likely than others to rule out particular kinds of food and more likely to report that they decided when to buy things because of price: "If grapes cost more than $1.19, I just don't get them."

Most informants in higher-income households reported that they compare prices, watch for sales, and use some coupons or generic items. But the calculus of cost, need, and preference is quite flexible for these families, and they discuss the cost of food as one factor to be considered among others. They are concerned with the variety and quality of their food, and there is little indication in these accounts that cost places significant limits on what they buy. The practice of "stocking up" on sale items—used by others to save money on standard purchases—is often used by wealthier shoppers as an opportunity to purchase especially favored foods, expanding the household repertoire of menus, rather than simply reducing cost. A white professional man, for example, who does the shopping for his household precisely because he believes he can save more money than his wife, reported proudly: "This winter I've invested heavily in shrimp and scallop futures."

These families with more resources can accommodate their preferences more easily; saving money is desirable, but optional. While these people usually refer to the importance of economizing, they also speak without worry about decisions to forego savings for other benefits in particular situations. The voluntary character of economizing is clearest in the account of a relatively affluent white single mother, who reported that she does not worry about saving money on food because time is an even scarcer resource in her life. She explained:

I used to go to the big supermarkets, and try to save a penny here, a penny there, you know. And occasionally I'll look at the, you know, the sale items. But I gave that up. That is the most ridiculous waste of time.

Since her divorce, as she begins a new career and cares for her two children, she chooses to go to a smaller store where she can do her shopping more quickly:

They get you in and out! Oh—it's wonderful. And all of a sudden that became more important to me than any money I was saving or anything.

A final feature that appeared in the talk of a few wealthy women was a concern with the negative implications of economizing, a sense that too much attention to price might be unseemly. For example, one affluent white woman, reporting that she had purchased orange juice on sale rather than squeezing it herself, worried that I would think her "a tightwad." And a white professional woman explained that she clips coupons occasionally because her husband will use them, but that she is uncomfortable with the image of "couponing": "there are always these horrible ladies on television who, you know, 'I only spent 39¢ on my— feeding my family of four because I saved all these coupons!' . . . there's a lot of affect associated with my not saving coupons."

In middle-income, mostly working-class, households, relatively secure but with considerably less income than the most affluent families, typical practices of economy are more limiting. As they describe their routine shopping, these people talk of firmer boundaries to their purchasing, mentioning more items they simply never buy in order to keep their expenditures within relatively predictable limits. Laurel explained:

> We don't buy the best cuts of meat, except to entertain, we
> don't, you know, we buy 39¢ chickens when they're on sale,
> by the tens, that sort of thing.

Even when the logic of shopping is similar here and for more affluent shoppers, with special items purchased on sale, the resulting stock of foods is rather different. While those with more money reported watching for bargains on shrimp and scallops, Jean told of making standard purchases of ground beef and chicken, and buying pork chops "if they're not too expensive."

Whatever their actual purchases, those in middle-income households seem more conscious of cost as a real limit to their enjoyment of eating, and for several, "steak" served as a convenient vehicle for discussing difficulties at the boundaries. Bertie, for example, talked of the conflict between her concern with cost and her husband's preferences:

> There are a lot of things that I don't buy because they're too
> expensive. We do without—since beef has gotten so high.
> My husband is not as conscious of food prices as I am, since
> he doesn't buy food as much as I do. He will go out and buy
> steaks. I won't.

The issue is one that arises in some form in most of these households. Donna, for example, makes the same decision as Bertie, and displays more of the reasoning behind her choice:

> Like my one brother-in-law, they have steaks every week.
> And they never have any money. And you know, I say, at
> least we have food—I'd rather spend $5 on two different
> kinds of meat than on one steak.

Others choose in favor of taste when they can—especially if their
husbands are more insistent. (Indeed, these two accounts suggest
again the force of husbands' wishes, and the dilemma produced for
wives who have too little money to satisfy them. Donna, whose
husband was quite demanding, concluded this discussion by ac-
knowledging that she doubted he "really likes steak that much.")
But even the accounts of those who choose to spend money on
more expensive items are full of an awareness that such choices are
not always possible. Susan, for example, explains that "it all re-
volves around how much money's coming in." She reported that
when her husband was unemployed they ate "a lot of macaroni and
cheese," but that now her husband gets steak. Even as she explains,
the choice is tied to the possibility of facing hard times again:

> I can't see depriving my husband, or myself, of the better
> quality if I can afford it. Because the day might come that
> we'll be back at square one again.

Susan's talk of "deprivation" recalls—in a somewhat different
register—the tone of the more affluent wives who were concerned
not to be "tight" with their families. But while there were occasional echoes of this attitude, most of the working-class wives I
spoke with talked positively about their efforts to use their resources carefully. They constructed economizing even more
clearly in terms of responsibility and virtue, and seemed more anxious than wealthier informants about choices in favor of preference
or convenience.

Income is less stable in these households than in profession-
al/managerial families, and several interviewees told about times
when they suffered losses. Reporting on these episodes, they described minimal meals that became standard fare and allowed
them to survive. Jean, for example, described some typical meals
when she and her husband were separated for a time, a few years
before our interview:

> Well, pancakes and eggs. A lot of times we'd have grilled
> cheese sandwiches. A lot of times we'd have spaghetti, like I
> just—the kids love this—when I just cook plain spaghetti
> and mix it with butter and parmesan cheese, not tomato

sauce, just that, with a salad. I liked it too. Had that a lot . . .
Sometimes for a treat, like a big treat would be a bacon,
lettuce, and tomato sandwich. I'd buy half a pound of bacon
and make it last all month, you know [laughing]. I'd fry, like
for four, for three sandwiches we'd have three pieces—no,
we'd have like two pieces of bacon, and they'd be cut, you
know, in all these little—everybody'd have like crumbled
bacon. And that's how we used to do it. But it was fine, you
know, we all survived.

Such difficulties inevitably reveal food as one of only a few variable categories of expense. For example, both Robin and Rick were
working at the time of the interview, but their expenses for a mort-
gage, utilities, day care, and transportation to work were so high
that food was "very low on a priority list . . . [though] it shouldn't
be." Rick explained, "we're hurting right now. So now it's just like,
three days—I'll go out and get enough food for three days." Both of
them stressed the various ways they save money on purchases:
driving to discount stores, comparing prices and saving coupons
for items they need. But when they reach the limit of this kind of
economizing, sometimes they simply cannot buy adequate food.
Robin explained how they make decisions at these times:

If we repeat a meal for three days, it's no big deal to us. To see
a nice piece of meat, like a steak or something, is really rare.
It's usually the hamburgers and hot dogs and cheese
sandwiches and stuff. We just can't afford anything else . . .
If it gets down to it, we buy to feed the kids . . . And then
we'll eat whatever we can scrounge together.

In several ways—including their limited diet and their dissatisfaction with it—this account was similar to those of much poorer
families. Ironically, in such cases financial achievements—home
ownership and the expenses associated with full-time jobs—have
the effect of requiring radically reduced expenditures on food.

In households with incomes near poverty levels, or where food
expenditures are especially reduced, another irony appears.
Though these families are most in need of any savings produced by
economizing, some of the prescribed techniques of "smart" shopping are not always appropriate or even possible. The poorest wom-
en I talked with were well aware that the stores in their
neighborhoods charged more for many food items than stores in
other areas. But few of them had transportation to other shopping
areas. One black woman, for example, knew of several stores where

she could find bargains, but had to rely on friends or her sister for transportation, or consider whether to spend extra money on a delivery service. In addition, these women often choose to buy more expensive brand-name products simply because they do not have enough cash to experiment with cheaper items and risk wasting money on unsatisfactory purchases. While more affluent shoppers could recite long lists of bargain items they had tried—some acceptable and some not—poor shoppers tended to report more conservative strategies for selecting foods, emphasizing the cost of a single mistake:

> I go for quality . . . I'd rather go and get Del Monte corn . . .
> I have bought some of these—like they had four cans for a
> dollar. And when you got it, all the husks and stuff was
> inside it and it was just money wasted, when I could have
> just took that dollar and bought that one can of Del Monte
> . . . To me, it really is a waste of money.

For these women, any waste seems very consequential. Wealthier shoppers seem comfortable thinking of themselves as consumers who freely choose from items on the market, simply rejecting items not up to standard; poor shoppers are more likely to think of the market antagonistically. Affluent shoppers were aware of price differences in different stores and neighborhoods; for them, these patterns were background information they referred to as they reported where they go to shop. Shoppers with little money were mostly unable to respond to these differences by shopping elsewhere, and were more likely to talk about higher prices in the areas they could reach as unavoidable features of the market environment. One woman complained that "in some areas, you can go and buy one item this week and it's at a reasonable rate, and you come back the next week, and it's 50¢ higher," and Margaret observed that, "Especially food and stuff, things that you really need, they take advantage of it."

These poor shoppers work at "making do," in as many ways as they can. They compare prices carefully, watch for special bargains, and to the extent possible, shop where prices are most reasonable. But they are severely constrained by circumstance, usually limited to shopping in depressed neighborhoods and with no discretionary cash to subsidize economies that could be produced by traveling to cheaper outlets or experimenting with cheaper products. Their frequent references to the dangers of wasting food reveal the differences produced by their quite limited budgets in comparison to others' more ample resources. While most shoppers would like to spend less on food, these women know that they can only spend so much, and their most urgent concern is to make sure that they can make their meager allowances last. The ways in which this concern permeates the everyday experience of poor women will be explored in the next section.

Poverty and the Work of Survival

In this section, I consider the work of five women caring for children in households sustained on minimal cash income. This group should not be taken as representative of all poor households, since that group includes more than just single-mother families. However, single-mother families make up a large and significant segment of the poor: in 1986, 60 percent of poor households were headed by single women (U.S. Bureau of the Census 1989). In the group of five I studied, three mothers lived in households of their own, and two thought of themselves and their children as independent "families," but at the time of my interviews resided with parents in what might be described as "subfamily" arrangements.[6] One woman was widowed, two separated or divorced, and two were never-married, though both of these had had relationships of some duration with their children's fathers. One reported that her children's father was often in the household, and usually shared their meals.

All these women were "on their own" in some sense. Though one described herself as engaged and planned to marry soon, the others, like many single mothers, were conscious of their difference from a more accepted form for family life. While the two women in their thirties seemed to take for granted that they would raise their children mostly on their own, the younger women— both in residence with their own parents—seemed to think of their single status as temporary, and expressed some worry about living in households that were not "proper" families. Margaret, for example, emphasized that her present living arrangement was a transitional one, and took care to explain how her routine would be different if she were living on her own: the children would set the table, for example, and she would "experiment" more and take more time with the cooking.

6. I have adopted the term used by the U.S. Census Bureau, which defines a "subfamily" as a married couple, or parent with one or more children, who live in a larger household and are related to the primary householder or spouse.

All but one of these women were unable, for one reason or another at the time of the interviews, to command a living wage. Two were in their early twenties, and had few marketable skills. One of these two, and one other of the five, reported she was temporarily unable to hold a paying job owing to a recent disturbance in her life (one was recently widowed and severely depressed; the other was recovering from a bout with drugs). One cared for six children, all younger than ten years old. And the only one who worked at a full-time job received such a low wage that she was able to manage only because she lived in a rent-subsidized apartment. Accounts of financial arrangements in these households reveal complex relations of adaptation, a process of piecing together enough resources to survive. All received some kind of government assistance, whether in the form of a direct payment, food stamps, or subsidized rent; several received material help from family members; and two held jobs, both of which paid minimum wage or below. These sources of income were interrelated, in ways mediated by the bureaucracy of state assistance. For example, the two women who lived with parents thereby forfeited their right to food stamps; a woman working full-time at minimum wage was ineligible for AFDC (Aid to Families with Dependent Children), while another woman worked only part-time in order to retain her benefit. These "patchwork" combinations of material resources are summarized in table 3. The information revealed is consistent with what we know of the welfare system: because increments resulting from wage work or family assistance usually mean a reduction in government aid, the total resources of each woman hover at roughly similar levels that barely provide for their subsistence.

Because they depend at least in part on direct government assistance, these women's lives must be understood in the context of the welfare state in the United States. (Government subsidies support wealthier families as well, but less directly, and thus less intrusively.) Mimi Abramovitz (1988) shows that, historically, social welfare policy has included some provision for the support of mothers and children, but has also regulated their lives through restrictive and often moralistic policy. She argues, with others (e.g. Gough 1980; Dickinson 1986; Corrigan 1977), that the state recognizes the need to reproduce and maintain a healthy labor force, and subsidizes women's household labor in order to do so. At the same time, however, welfare provisions are designed to insure that government assistance will not become a preferred alternative to paid employment or traditional family life. They do this chiefly by lim-

Table 3. Sources and Amounts of Income or Subsidy in Five Poor Families

Household composition	AFDC	Wages	Housing assistance	Food assistance	Estimated annual income (including FS)
Margaret + 2 children 3 in "sub-family," 9 in extended family/household (White)	$302/mo	$260/mo	Lives w/parents	Father buys food	$6,744
Ivy + 2 children 3 in "sub-family," 4 in extended family/household (Black)	$302/mo	—	Lives w/mother	Mother buys food	$3,624
DW + 2 children fiance sometimes in household (Black)	—	$500/mo	Rent subsidy	—	$6,000
Annie + 3 children 1 other child lives elsewhere with grandparent (White/ Hispanic)	$NA[a]	—	—	Food stamps $NA[a]	Unknown
LM + 6 children (Black)	$500/mo	—	—	Food stamps $291	$9,492

[a]Amounts of subsidies unrecorded.

iting eligibility for subsidies to those seen as "deserving," as well as keeping payments at levels below prevailing low-wage employment options. In spite of these regulatory effects, most social welfare programs have empowering effects as well, if only limited ones. They do contribute to the subsistence of those outside the labor market, and by doing so they provide a modicum of choice and make possible some resistance to the most severe forms of exploitation.

The program of Aid to Families with Dependent Children, on which several of the women I studied depend, was established in 1935, but developed in part from earlier Mothers' Pension programs established during the Progressive Era. Abramovitz argues that these programs, which provide direct subsidies for poor women raising children alone, have been built around a "family ethic" that assumes the naturalness of gender distinctions, and assigns child care and household responsibility exclusively to women. Concern for children has been expressed in terms of the importance of "proper mothering," which has been defined and enforced through education, supervision, and threats of ineligibility for assistance or the removal of children from poor women's homes. The biases in early Mothers' Pension programs had systematic effects: white widows received most aid, and never-married and black women were seldom on the rolls for assistance. The exclusion of large numbers of women from the programs meant that in spite of a rhetoric that supported women's household work, large groups of "undeserving" (especially black) women were channeled into low-paid wage work. Thus, the contradictions in the programs helped to mediate conflicting demands for women's household and market labor.

The operation of AFDC has reflected similar dynamics since its inception. Widespread ambivalence toward husbandless women has kept eligibility rules tight and benefit levels low. In the early years of the program, vaguely defined rules about "suitable homes" were used to justify continual scrutiny and harassment of recipients, and kept many women out of the program. During the 1960s, at least partly in response to the growth of a strong grassroots welfare rights movement (Piven and Cloward 1979; West 1981), the mechanisms of regulation shifted somewhat, opening up the program in response to pressure, and moving from a coercive to a more paternalistic kind of regulation. A rhetoric of social services to support "proper mothering" began to substitute for some of the harshest program rules, though in practice only limited service was actually provided. As AFDC expanded during the 1960s and 1970s, public and political antagonism toward its recipients grew. In spite of its regulatory agenda, the program did support and in some sense legitimate single mothers living alone with their children. Abramovitz (1988:352) summarizes:

> [I]nstead of supplying the market with low paid women workers and delegitimizing female-headed households [as program framers intended], AFDC enabled welfare mothers to avoid dangerous marriages and jobs, to prefer public assistance to either wedlock or work, and to accept public aid as a right.

Since it was increasingly seen during the 1970s and 1980s as a challenge to the "family ethic," AFDC has been subject to a series of new modifications and restrictions. Welfare "reforms" introduced in 1981 included stricter eligibility requirements, new requirements for work outside the home, and lower real benefit levels. Thus, my interviews with AFDC recipients took place during a period of limitation and cutback in the program; inflation during the period worsened their situations as well.

The food stamp program, which supplements AFDC for two of the women I interviewed, has a similar history (DeVault and Pitts 1984). This program—which provides vouchers to be used in purchasing food items—functions chiefly as income supplementation, since it means that recipients can spend their cash income on other needs. However, like AFDC, it incorporates regulatory provisions that control recipients' use of the program: benefits are provided "in kind" (to be used for food only) rather than directly, as additional cash. While this program feature was intended primarily as a subsidy for American agriculture, it also reflects an underlying distrust of recipients and a desire to control the purchases of those in the program.[7] As supplementation to AFDC, it suggests that spending money on food ("wisely," of course) can legitimately be enforced as part of "proper mothering." The more recent Special Supplemental Food Program for Women, Infants and Children (WIC)—which provides in-kind food aid and nutrition education—emphasizes the relation of food and mothering more

7. Congressional concern with the regulative aspects of food-stamp policy is evident in hearings on the program, as members of Congress debate issues such as whether recipients should be allowed to buy processed foods: in the early years of debate, some reasoned that "convenience foods" should be excluded because the government should not pay to substitute for poor people's labor.

explicitly, and is more restrictive than the food-stamp program. (One of the women I interviewed had participated briefly in a WIC program; her experience will be discussed below.)

These social welfare provisions can be seen as part of a transition from private to "public patriarchy" (Brown 1981), with reproduction increasingly subsidized and controlled by the state instead of by individual men as family heads. Johnnie Tillmon, a welfare rights activist (cited in Abramovitz 1988:313–14), compares welfare to a "supersexist marriage":

> You trade in "a" man for "the" man. But you can't divorce him if he treats you bad. He can divorce you of course, cut you off anytime he wants. But in that case "he" keeps the kids, not you. "The" Man runs everything. In ordinary marriage, sex is supposed to be for your husband. On AFDC you're not supposed to have any sex at all. You give up control over your body. It's a condition of aid . . . "The" man, the welfare system, controls your money. He tells you what to buy and what not to buy, where to buy it, and how much things cost. If things—rent, for instance—really costs more than he says they do, it's too bad for you.

Many welfare recipients are sharply aware of the punitive restrictions that condition the assistance available to them, especially since the emergence of a welfare rights consciousness during the 1960s. But recipients' perspectives on the system are also conditioned by prevailing cultural ideologies about work and individual achievement, as well as by the ideology built into welfare policy. Most seem to experience a complex mixture of feelings, and are subject to dissatisfaction and resentment about their situation, which can be directed both outward and inward. In the following discussion, as I examine the feeding work of the poorest women I interviewed, I will attend to the ways in which the contradictory purposes and consequences of welfare policy intersect with everyday struggles to feed and care for children.

These interviews, as a group, were the most difficult for me to conduct and analyze. I spoke, as a middle-class researcher, with women whose lives were very different from my own. Our conversations were mostly comfortable—the women generously accommodated my curiosity, and in at least some cases, seemed to welcome my listening, perhaps as company. But with some distance from the interview situation, I began to realize how unprepared I was to know their lives, and how frightened I could be by their situations. These realizations developed at different times, and in different ways: sometimes unsurprisingly, as when I drove nervously into unfamiliar parts of the city; sometimes much later, as I have studied the transcripts of our conversations, noticing gaps in my understanding and questions I might have asked. Such gaps in understanding present problems for any middle-class researcher talking with those whose lives are quite different from hers (see, for example, Riessman 1987). One approach to a solution involves prolonged immersion in the lives of those studied (e.g. Stack 1974); another involves a more collaborative research strategy (e.g. Mies 1983). In this study, however, I adopted neither of these strategies, but interviewed poor women in the same relatively conventional way as others. An awareness of this problem recommends reading my account here somewhat cautiously, as an attempt to begin to see what is missing from a more middle-class view of feeding work. What we find, I will suggest, is a hint at the dark underside of women's caring work, the most brutal expression of the pitfalls built into women's inexorable responsibility for the well-being of others.

One of the features of these interviews that made them different from others is that they were less neatly compartmentalized; my conversations with these poor women often ranged far beyond their feeding routines, including larger life stories, reflections on their hopes and ambitions, and, in some cases, discussions of relations among several generations of women and children. I did not seek such comments, though I did not discourage them either. They emerged in response to the same questions I asked others, perhaps because of different understandings of the conduct of a research interview, but perhaps also in recognition of my ignorance about the conditions of these lives, from a desire to show me the context for household routine. I sometimes became caught up in the dramas of these lives, and lost my focus on feeding as we talked—other kinds of stories seemed more important. But I wonder now if this phenomenon I experienced as a "loss of focus" should be taken as an indication of a significant feature of these women's lives: the fact that feeding is only one difficult task among many, part of a total life experience that needs broader explication precisely because it does not fit a middle-class norm.

To my knowledge, these households were not visited by hunger and malnutrition, in the clinical senses. However, several comments leave this statement open to some doubt: one woman reported giving her children two meals instead of three during the winter when they slept later and were less active; another's two-year-old daughter had grown so slowly that she had been hospitalized for a time; and a third described one child who "just gobbles . . . down (her food)" and is always "wanting more, wanting seconds." Still, the overall sense of these accounts is one of a skillful management of quite limited resources that makes possible the survival of these household groups. In many ways, these women engage in precisely the same kinds of work activities as mothers with more resources. They pay attention to the needs and preferences of their children, they shop for provisions with which to prepare "proper" meals, and spend time planning such meals, and they work at teaching their children about proper eating, through experience and example as well as direct instruction. But the insufficiency of their cash income adds an additional layer to the web of conditions within which they do this work, and gives the provision of food a different meaning for the household group.

These women talked straightforwardly about the difficulties of their situations. As one black woman explained:

> Being on public aid is a very—well, to me, it's, you know, a hassle. I don't like it. You know, first of all, because the amount of money you receive from public aid is not really enough to, you know, for a person to take care of their family. It's really not enough.

They see quite clearly that their decisions are structured by the restrictive, even punitive regulations that define public aid. The only woman working full-time, for example, explained that since she has started work, she is no longer eligible for enough food assistance to make it worthwhile to apply: "I know the changes I would have to go through downtown with them—it's not worth it, when they're not going to give me, maybe $30." But as they considered their lives within this context, all of these women expressed some pride in their abilities to manage, and especially to care for their children. Some saw themselves as protecting their children in a hostile environment. For example:

> They [the children] know that there's a single parent here, so they do try to be helpful . . . But I don't push it on them a whole lot . . . I want them to enjoy their childhood while they can, because once they start getting big, then they're going to be, "Oh, it's bill time," "Oh, it's food," "Oh, it's this and that." You know, so I feel that they should stay young.

And for Margaret, pride is tied to a sense that she manages in spite of the difficulties produced by the market:

> I enjoy doing it. Because I know, I can feed—I can get around all these people who think they're going to, you know, BS everybody else. You know, I'm smarter than they are.

With one exception (Ivy, who will be discussed below), these women were active and determined, working to fill in with extra effort for the money resources they lacked. One works at a low-wage telephone job she describes as "a bitch," but "better than sitting home all day"; another cares for six children and also works in a community group; and a third, Annie, reported how she keeps track of all the kids on the street in her area, serves as secretary for a neighborhood organization, and helps Spanish-speaking mothers deal with their children's problems at school.

The lives these women lead can be better understood by examining Annie's in some detail. Annie was a white woman in her late twenties, and lived in a predominantly Hispanic neighborhood with three of her four children when I interviewed her. She had been married briefly, to a Puerto Rican man, but her husband had left the family almost a decade earlier when he discovered he was too ill to provide for them. Annie had worked at a variety of low-wage jobs until she became ill herself, and then, as she recovered from surgery, began to use drugs. By the time I interviewed her, she had succeeded in quitting drugs and seemed to have reestablished a relatively stable household life. However, she reported that her health was poor and that she had had "a couple of nervous breakdowns." When I interviewed her, she was not working for pay; she explained, somewhat ruefully, that she was "supposed to be taking it easy." Much of Annie's life was structured by conditions in her neighborhood, an area with a lively and sometimes dangerous street life. Her oldest daughter, who "couldn't handle it," had been sent to live with a relative in a rural area, and Annie spent much of her time keeping an informal watch over the neighborhood's children as well as her own.

Annie acknowledges the help she receives from family and friends, but she also emphasizes her own work and her self-sufficiency: when she told about some workshops offered through her children's Head Start program, she explained, "I figured, 'Well, I'm going to play mother and father, and work, and I've got to learn something.'" She also reported that her sisters are sometimes jealous, and tell her she is "lucky," but she stresses her own effort as the source of whatever comfort she enjoys:

> They don't see how I can make it so good, and not have no money and live on welfare. But I told them, "If you budget yourself, and penny-pinch, you can do it." Because I do. I go to No-Frills, I go to Diamond's, I go to the fruit market. I mean, I don't care, if I have to walk all over the city to get it.

Accounts of "penny-pinching" were prominent in the reports of other poor women as well. Just as they were more likely than others to talk spontaneously about their overall budgets, poor women were more likely than others to include the prices of foods they selected as they talked about their shopping. Another woman, for example, told me in detail about several "good buys" she had located in various markets:

> They have these beef sausages—I think it's a good buy, you know, you get a whole—I guess it stands as long as me—for $10. Where going to the store and getting a little piece, you got to pay almost 2 or 3 dollars . . . And maybe I'll go down to Quik-Stop—they have these, 30 pounds of chicken for 14, 15 dollars. Which is not a bad buy.

And Margaret described her reasoning about which brands and sizes of products would be cheapest to buy, referring from memory to the prices for different brands of toilet paper and sizes of rice packages. What is striking in these accounts, and different from others, is the frequent reference to actual sums, the attention to exact prices, which marks these women's necessarily constant concern with the distribution of whatever cash is available.

By "penny-pinching," then, Annie manages to purchase supplies, and works to produce "family meals," as others do. She explained that they all sit down together for dinner:

> The meal is on the table, and I tell them if the steam leaves the bowl before they get to the table, the bowl goes right back in the stove and they don't get any supper. So they make sure they get to the table. And then that's our group discussion, this girlfriend played with that boyfriend at school, and—I hear everything.

As she describes their routines, it is clear that she is conscious, like more affluent mothers, of using food to construct social relations and mark special events in the week. When she describes a typical meal, we can see the sense of group sociability that arises from having a "house specialty," and also the attention to individual preference that marks the family as "personal":

> Oh, that's our house specialty, macaroni and cheese. And my daughter usually makes that. I guess she's got her way of making it, because when I make it she says I don't make it right . . . And then plus, the 11-year-old, she doesn't like ground beef in her macaroni and cheese. So hers is made separately. They make the macaroni and cheese, the ground beef, and then before they add the ground beef, my 12-year-old will take out a big bowl and put a separate [gesturing to indicate a separate portion]—for the 11-year-old—and then she'll keep on making the rest of it.

Because she works with such limited resources, Annie must be especially clever about making use of what is available. This requirement became especially evident when I considered her organization of household space. I interviewed Annie in her apartment's "living room" (perhaps twelve by twenty-four feet), which contained not only a couch and television but also a cooking area with refrigerator, stove and small work counter, a small kitchen table for eating, and a work table where we sat for our talk and where the children do their homework. As she described her routine, Annie referred to the sense of space she has created for the family by using different areas in the room for different purposes, and enforcing different rules in each one. She explained, for instance, that on weekends breakfast is different, because she allows the children to watch cartoons while they eat:

> I don't want them to eat cereal in here [the "living" rather than "kitchen" end of the room]. They could eat here [the table where we are sitting during the interview], but I won't put the TV here because they have to study here. So on Saturdays and Sundays they have to bring a tray [to the couch] . . . And usually I make a banana shake . . . They have to bring a tray, they have to have a napkin, their roll's in a bowl . . . They're real good about it.

In many ways, the logic of "constructing family" is the same here as in more affluent households, though the "products" may differ—these families enjoy macaroni and cheese rather than a steak dinner or stir-fry, and treat themselves with breakfast on the couch rather than the terrace. However, in spite of the similarities, a more thorough examination of the meaning of regular family meals will show that poverty constructs a distinctive relation to food and the work of care, both for those who do the work and those who are fed. Parents in households with more resources talk about using food, thoughtfully and creatively, to signify love, comfort, and pleasure. They seem rarely to be conscious of the possibility of scarcity, but this spectre is rarely absent from the consciousness of those who live in poverty. Thus, while poor mothers also use food to mean love, comfort, and pleasure, they teach a harsher lesson as well—that survival is never to be taken for granted.

A consciousness of scarcity appeared in the talk of some working-class informants who were not technically "poor," as well as in the accounts of the poor women who are the subjects of this section, and all of these people talked about the particular significance of scarcity for children's health and well-being. When I asked how she "felt" about cooking—whether she enjoyed the work or not—a black single mother living on her clerical-worker salary replied: "I'm just glad that I can provide for my family, because you know, there are so many people who don't, children who don't have no one there to cook for them, or nothing to eat." And Robin and Rick, the two-paycheck couple beset by expenses and debts who were quoted above, reported: "If it gets down to it, we buy to feed the kids." In these households, as in others, providing food sends messages of interdependence and caring. But in these households, "caring" is also understood in terms of urgent necessity, and it loses some of the romantic gloss it often has in more affluent families. Cooking and eating, like other household activities, are organized around the exigencies of survival.

In poor households, children learn early, through direct observation, that their parents are caught up in economic circumstances over which they have little control. In spite of parents' attempts to protect children from the worst consequences of their poverty, children see their parents' frustrating labors, and they typically understand that they must often do without (Stack 1974). Parents face a dilemma: while they would like to let children "enjoy their childhood," they are also concerned to prepare them for independence. Thus, Annie's caring for her children is expressed in part through tough, energetic discipline, and determination and self-sufficiency are part of an attitude toward life that she teaches them quite directly:

> I told them, "You stand up and say 'I am somebody,' because
> if not, you're just going to be with the rest of them" . . . So
> my kids, they know, they stand up for themselves. If not,
> they get stepped on. I tell them, "That's the way it goes."

Her message to the children should be understood in the context of
the family's difficulties. Like the black mothers described by their
daughters in a study by Gloria Joseph, she is both "tough and tender" (1981:101). Joseph found that, while daughters recognized their
mothers' shortcomings, they had tremendous respect for mothers'
work, both outside and inside the home:

> [A]ggressive and harsh behaviors were acknowledged and
> appreciated in light of their being carried out in the context
> of caring for the daughters (and other family members) and
> trying to instill the need to be prepared and to be able to
> cope within a society where choices for Black women are
> frequently between the dregs of the keg or the chaff from the
> wheat. (1981:102)

Poor families like Annie's, and many black families whether poor
or not, are in situations requiring that they adapt to hostile en-
vironments, and a protective "toughness" emerges as part of the
caring work that maintains family members in the present and prepares them for challenges ahead.

Annie relies on her children to help with household work and to
begin caring for themselves at an early age. When she worked in the
afternoon, they took care of themselves after school and she would
leave them a list of chores: "Sometimes I'd forget . . . So they'd call
and say, 'What's there to do today, and what time can we go out?'
Very well organized." When she is not working, Annie does most of
the housework herself, but she still strategizes about how much
help the children should provide, balancing their need to spend
time on schoolwork against the importance of learning responsibility and household skills. This general feature of their relationship appears in a specific form in her talk about feeding them:

> Everybody has to do something in order to eat . . . I don't
> never let them go without a meal, but I just tell them,
> "You're not going to eat if the sink is dirty. If I have to start
> supper with dirty dishes I won't do supper that day."

Children in more affluent households help with chores too, usually also because their parents want them to learn responsibility

and household skills.[8] But in poor families like Annie's, the necessity behind children's independence gives them a distinctive sense of the struggles their parents face. As a result, these children learn that to struggle for physical maintenance is "natural" (as Annie explained, "That's the way it goes."), while more affluent children take survival for granted, and learn to feel a sense of entitlement to the pleasures that food can provide.

The gender organization of feeding work is also expressed in a distinctive form in these poor households. Since all of these poor families were headed by single mothers, questions about a division of labor between spouses do not arise. But these mothers' sole responsibility for children can be seen as part of a larger community-level division of labor. The predominance of single-mother families among the poor in the 1980s can be attributed to a variety of factors, including high rates of male unemployment and incarceration among the poor, the relative unavailability of income assistance for two-parent families, and increasing rates of divorce and single childbearing among the population as a whole (Wilson 1987). These trends, together, tend to produce a particular pattern of gender segregation, with poor women more likely than men to be attached to household and children. Thus, poor women cook at least in part simply because they are more likely than men to live in relatively stable households with children who must be fed. Often, they cook for men who do not live with them, but join their households for meals through kin or "fictive kin" relationships (Stack 1974). Annie, for example, often cooks for a boyfriend, and sometimes for his brother as well. The men usually bring something in exchange—some soda, perhaps—but these exchange relations are delicate ones, and Annie reports that her boyfriend is sometimes embarrassed at how much his brother eats. His worry hints at expectations that surround such relations of service and exchange: they all accept that Annie should provide food for the one man she is attached to, however informally, but her responsibilities toward others are more ambiguous. Thus, even in the ab-

---

8. I did not question informants in great detail about children's labor, and in any case, this study does not permit a definitive finding as to whether children in poor and working-class households help more than those in professional/managerial ones. However, my sense was that few of the wealthier parents relied on children for much actual assistance. Several reported that they believed in encouraging children's work, but found organizing and supervising it effectively more burdensome than doing the work themselves. Many informants' children were still too young to provide real help with household chores.

sence of a legal marriage relationship or even cohabitation, the relations of service and entitlement that organize feeding and eating are organized around the heterosexual couple.[9]

As we talked, Annie revealed an awareness of a gendered division of labor, and also some ambivalence about it. Her construction of her situation as a single mother—"I'm going to play mother and father"—relies both on a dichotomy between men's and women's activity and on a confidence that she can transcend the dichotomy. She reported that many of her men friends cook, and that her son has learned cooking skills in his Head Start program. But she emphasizes cooking skills for her daughters rather than her son, and she worries about his development as an acceptable man, encouraging him to spend time alone with her boyfriend. She is uncertain about changing expectations for men's and women's activity: "I was brought up with the same beliefs that my mother taught me—boys are boys and girls are girls. And boys don't do girls' things. But nowadays it's different." Her daughters, drawing on more traditional cultural expectations, insist that their brother should not work in the kitchen:

> I've got a lot of friends that are bachelors, and I've took my daughters over and seen them, and said, "See, he cooks." So they're kinda letting him participate. But they also used to say that if he does it, he gonna be funny, you know, gay.

Annie tries to negotiate a reasonable compromise that takes account of several conflicting demands and beliefs here: her son's desire to be with the girls in the kitchen, her daughters' more traditional demands for gender segregation, her own appraisal of concrete evidence of changing patterns, and the ideology of gender equality that is taught at preschool, but not in the girls' elementary school. She encourages her daughters to be more open to male participation in housework, but she also advises her son that he is old enough to begin to "separate himself" from the girls. In their struggles over this issue, they encounter and respond to a cultural ideology that emphasizes the distinction between male and female, and

9. The habit of cooking for others outside the family may be characteristic of black working-class communities as well. Bertie reported that she always included someone from the church in her family's Sunday dinner. And her comment suggests a special concern for men unattached to household groups: "We always have somebody in to eat. From church, some member who wants to stay for church in the evening . . . or some student who lives on campus. Or some young man who doesn't cook."

in the girls' worry about homosexuality we see how the enforcement of traditionally gendered activity supports heterosexuality
as well. Annie, a single woman who "plays mother and father,"
takes responsibility for feeding, and even as she questions a gendered division of labor, reinforces it with her children.

Most of the poor women I talked with, like Annie, thought of
themselves as managing relatively well, even with their limited resources; indeed, they are probably a more successful group than
would be found through random sampling, since those who are
managing well are most likely to agree to be interviewed. The kind
of maintenance work they do has often been understood as an essential contribution to communities under siege by the wider society; Patricia Hill Collins suggests that black women, for
example, "see their unpaid domestic work more as a form of resistance to oppression than as a form of exploitation by men"
(1990:44). The household and feeding work performed by slave
women for their families (Davis 1981), by working-class mothers
(Caulfield 1974), by Southern black "Mamas" for civil rights workers (Evans 1979; Jones 1985), and by poor women for networks of
kin (Stack 1974) has been essential labor that contributes directly
to group survival. In groups such as these, women's responsibility
for feeding is significantly different from that in more privileged
families: rather than a work burden that excludes middle-class
white women from the more remunerative activity and status enjoyed by their male counterparts, feeding others is a work task that
also provides an opportunity to promote the survival and well-
being of the less privileged community, including men, children,
and women themselves. But we will see below that this opportunity, which can bring honor to those women able to fulfill such
roles, can also be cruelly demanding for those who are not so gifted
or fortunate. One of my informants, Ivy, was in a period of considerable stress and depression, and her story highlights some of the special difficulties of being a poor mother who cannot cope so well
with the difficulties of her situation.

Ivy, a black woman in her early twenties, had come to the
United States from the Caribbean about ten years before I interviewed her. When we talked, she was recovering from the death of
her children's father and a subsequent period of grief and disrup-
tion. In spite of public assistance and financial help from her mother, she acknowledged that feeding her children was "very hard"; it
was a matter of great concern because her young daughter had been
hospitalized briefly the year before for failure-to-thrive. Her daugh-

ter's hospitalization marked her as a mother in need of help, and since then she had been especially vulnerable to the scrutiny of medical and social welfare professionals. Ivy's situation illustrates the complex reality of troubles with caring work. She had real difficulties managing the care of her children, and she needed and, for the most part, welcomed expert advice. However, her reports about the help she has received reveal significant gaps between what is offered and what she can use. And to some extent, the counseling intended to help Ivy seems to have contributed to her depression and sense of inadequacy.

Though she lives with her mother, who pays for much of their food and often does the shopping, Ivy is responsible for the work at home; her mother, she explains, is tired when she returns home from her very demanding service job. Ivy takes her children to nursery school in the morning, and spends most of each day at home alone. Her account hints at the curious contradictions of a state of anxious depression. Though she does not enjoy cooking, she reports that she cleans energetically: "I'm a workaholic. As a matter of fact, I love cleaning up . . . I'm not used to the type of life of sitting and relaxing, it's not me." Yet a few minutes later, when I ask if she usually cleans the dishes after supper:

> No, sometimes I skip that, you know, I watch TV, or try to play with them. I don't do that very often. Or I just sit and watch TV. And you know, you get depressed now and then. You know, I try to play with them. And then after, do the dishes. Sometimes I leave them overnight, because you know, I have to conserve my energy, I'm using up so much trying to get everything done.

This excerpt illustrates a tone that characterized all of Ivy's talk in the interview: an emphasis on things she "tries" or "needs" to do, alongside apologetic accounts of how her actual practice usually falls short.

This characteristic mix of anxiety and discouragement was even more prominent in Ivy's accounts of food routines. For example, when I asked what they would eat for dinner the night of the interview:

> Have to look in the freezer and decide. Because I gave them spaghetti yesterday night. Have to find something. [After a pause] I can cook, but—you know, I need to learn how to fix different varieties of stuff. It's not easy.

The same tone appears in her account of the afternoon routine:

> Around 3:00 I start, just to get it out of the way. I hate to
> cook late, especially when I have to go pick the kids up . . . I
> try to cook as early as I can.

And although they usually eat in front of the television, she reports that they sit at the table "now and then," and adds, "We should get into the habit."

Ivy, like anyone in a contemporary industrial society, lives surrounded by a discourse that emphasizes the importance of food in family life and women's responsibility for preparing food. She wants desperately to do better, and attends to media discussions of nutrition and food preparation, but her depression limits her ability to use what she learns. Still, this discourse appears frequently in her talk, and seems to contribute to her perception of herself as an inadequate mother. Explaining the breakfast routine, for example, she referred to something she had heard on the radio:

> There too I still have to try to get some variety. Instead of
> fixing them eggs, eggs, every other day. Like I heard on the
> radio they had this nutrition program and they said that you
> could—instead of fixing the same thing you could even fix
> spaghetti for breakfast. You know, it's nourishing. Things
> like that.

It is clear from other comments that these media features are not limited to nutrition information, but also reinforce the idea that food is central to the quality of family life: Ivy hopes to learn more so that the food she prepares will be like the food in books that looks so "eatable" and "delightful." And it is also clear that the media create standards for food work with which women like Ivy are obliged to compare themselves. When I asked about shopping, for example:

> Like I say, I need to get organized. Like when I shop I'll just
> pick up anything, that's not very good shopping. I don't
> really look, and read the label and you know, find out what
> different kinds of food, you know—You know, some people
> when they do their shopping they're always organized, they
> know exactly what they're going for.

These public sources of information create standards for all women, but those who are better able to follow these discursive prescriptions refer to them less directly, incorporating them more smoothly as "background information" into their accounts of their own routines. Ivy's difficulties living up to an image of the ideal homemaker bring the coercive character of this discursive construction more clearly into view.

Because she had been identified as a mother with problems, Ivy had received several kinds of expert advice. She was seeing a psychologist, with whom she talked about her problems with the children; she had talked with doctors (not much help, she reported) and other hospital personnel about nutrition (they had mainly provided "booklets"); and she had discussed her children's eating habits with teachers at their nursery school. She had also participated briefly in a WIC program, and mentioned that the extra food provided was "very helpful," even though she was sometimes unable to make the trip downtown to pick up her coupons at the required time. But when she talked about these relationships, she seemed curiously detached, stuck in everyday realities that seldom fit with the information provided. When I asked if the WIC program helped her learn about nutrition, for example, she acknowledged that such teaching was built into the program, but could only talk about it in a vague and general way. Her comment suggests that somehow the instruction offered through the program was only something to "listen to," and that she was never able to tell them "her part" or get answers to her own questions:

> Yeah, that was part of it, they had someone to tell you, you know, what you should feed. But I never really did get to tell them, you know, my part. You know, I was just listening to what they had to say. I didn't, like, ask them questions. I didn't take much interest in that.

I do not mean to diminish the importance of information about food and nutrition. But Ivy's problem is not primarily a lack of knowledge. She is severely depressed, with no marketable skills, isolated at home, and responsible for two small children. Given her material and psychological difficulties, the social services emphasis on instruction for homemaking seems primarily to have heightened her anxiety about the work of care.

The depression and discouragement that was so marked in Ivy's case showed up in subtler ways in all of the poor women's accounts, suggesting that however well they manage from day to day, they experience common psychological costs. All of them seemed relatively isolated: they lived in small, crowded apartments, and referred to their difficulties traveling outside their neighborhoods for appointments or to shop. All of them referred to their need sometimes to "just sit," conveying a sense of alternating periods of effort and listlessness. Perhaps most significantly, several of these women referred to their own lack of appetite and indicated that they often simply did not eat. Ivy, for example, complained, "Sometimes the food gets very boring. [Laughing a bit] You know, boring, boring, boring food." When I asked what she liked to eat, she could hardly think of anything:

I don't know, I'm a picky person, I hardly know what I like. But I don't know—sometimes I get hungry and I look— there's food, but sometimes it's just not what I like. So you know. I look in the freezer, I look in there and there's nothing that you like to eat.

Another woman explained that she usually does not eat until mid-afternoon when the children are off to school or taking naps. Then she has "a sandwich, or maybe some junk food" [pointing to a soda and some doughnuts on the coffee table nearby]. "I like salads," she went on. "But I don't do that very often . . . I'm on a budget, so I can't just go out and get whatever I've got a taste for, you know, like just go out and get a steak or something." And Margaret reported: "I usually don't eat, because I can't—if I'm on the go all day, I can't eat. Because I just—my stomach gets goofed up. I have to be relaxed to eat."

These disruptions of appetite probably have multiple sources. It is not uncommon for women of any class to feel ambivalent about eating, for a variety of reasons (Kaplan 1980; Charles and Kerr 1988: chap. 7). In addition, these women seem to be expressing a heightened sense of the more widespread notion that women's own food is less important than that prepared for others. But the fact that these poor women were the only ones among these interviewees who spontaneously talked about simply not eating suggests that their loss of appetite is directly related to their poverty. Their comments suggest an alienation from their family work, a distaste for food that arises from the fact that it is always a problem, and unavailable as simple pleasure. Further, social welfare policy seems to invade even this intimate physiological aspect of these women's lives. The one woman who was working full-time was the only one of the poor women I interviewed who did not appear to have difficulty with her own eating, or feel guilty about it. This single exception suggests that those receiving assistance are undermined by the public dictum that they are to be valued and assisted only in their roles as "proper mothers." They actually play out this ideology in their everyday lives, working to feed their children as well as possible, but not themselves.

The Illusion of Similarity

In this chapter, I have looked beyond surface similarity to examine the ways that feeding work is organized through access to cash income from different sources. The ideology of a capitalist economy emphasizes similarity in the situations of household/family groups, constructing households as "consumption units" and individuals as consumers who choose freely from what is offered on the market. In this model, each household must garner cash resources, usually by sending some members out to work for a wage. Then, household members decide how to use their resources, allocating them to the necessary expenses of sustenance and other purchases, as desired. Every consumer seems to be doing the same thing: deciding to exchange cash for some desired product. Careful budgeting—shrewd decision making about how much to exchange for what products—seems to determine how well families live.

This simple, ideological model of consumer behavior omits the structural economic factors that determine what kinds of access families have to cash resources, what kinds of products are available on the market, how their cost is determined, and how they are distributed and marketed.[10] But this simple model is the one that underlies discussions of housekeeping in advertising, expert advice for women, and much public policy discussion. The "smart shopper" is the central image in this discourse: she is the woman who carefully tends the family resources, purchasing wisely in order to "make ends meet." This "smart shopper" is class-less: whether she has plenty of money or only a little, she virtuously balances cost and need, spending only what is necessary to provide for her family.

There is, of course, a material base for this image: women (and some men) do budget and calculate as they purchase goods for their families, and many husbands and children would live considerably less comfortable lives but for women's efforts at making ends meet (Luxton 1980). However, the class-neutral character of the image

10. Professional economists, of course, develop more sophisticated theories that take account of such factors. Their theories also have an ideological cast, but a discussion of this issue goes beyond the scope of this book.

obscures crucial differences in the work of provisioning and in the different kinds of "family" people are able to produce.

Economizing is activity that some people engage in voluntarily; they can make choices about when and how to economize. Others "make do" from necessity, and are rarely able to purchase what they want. Thus, concepts like consumer "choice" and "power" apply to only some consumers. The work of feeding is very different for women of different classes: the woman with plenty of money is able to operate more like a manager, considering the market and making "executive" decisions about purchasing for the family (perhaps this is why more middle-class than working-class men seem interested in shopping for food; see Charles and Kerr 1988:176), while the woman who does not have enough is more like an unprotected daily laborer, dependent on the local availability of products and unpredictable fluctuations in prices.

Also missing from this picture are those workers in the burgeoning service industries whose labor provides time-saving "conveniences" for those houseworkers who can afford them. For example, Margaret's paid work in a laundry provides essential maintenance work for others, but also limits the time she can spend with her children and renders her too exhausted to eat herself when she returns home late in the evening. Many such workers are members of disadvantaged racial and ethnic groups, and Evelyn Nakano Glenn (1990) suggests that the increasing marketization of household maintenance work reshapes a longstanding racial/ethnic division of labor. Rather than purchasing the labor of women of color directly, as domestic servants, affluent white women increasingly benefit from the labors of others less directly, and perhaps more comfortably because relations of oppression and privilege are less visible.

These differences mean that feeding and eating are experienced quite differently as well. In families with more resources, food becomes an arena for self-expression, providing a chance to experience family as a reward for achievement; in poor families, feeding and eating are themselves the achievement. Since the ability to maintain family members cannot be taken for granted, all family members are recruited into interdependence through necessity. In working-class and poor households, the person who does the work experiences its two sides quite sharply: though she often understands her activity in terms of enabling the pleasures of eating, she also works with more urgency to provide sustenance, and often has the unpleasant task of deciding which desired items must be eliminated from the family's diet.

Finally, it must be clear that, given the market distribution of food, some families enjoy plenty of healthful food, while others do not. The poor have access to such minimal cash resources that they can only obtain an adequate diet through extraordinary effort. They are often blamed for their own deprivation. Social programs are based on calculations that assume that households are managed by "smart shoppers" who will be able to stretch meager resources. Social policy simply assumes that women will do this work, and Ivy's story illustrates how thoroughly mothers are held responsible, whatever their circumstances or individual difficulties. Discourses about such programs emphasize knowledge and skill as a condition for survival, and largely ignore the energy, will, and luck that are also necessary. Thus, they help to maintain an illusion—that families share a similar experience of purchasing and preparing foods, and that differences in their diets must indicate that some are at fault, that some "deserve" healthful and satisfying meals, while others do not.

8   The Significance of Style

A household's class location has important and quite direct effects on the cash resources with which family members can work to produce family life, and some of these effects were discussed in the preceding chapter. But class relations also influence patterns of sociability and styles of eating. In households with sufficient money, those who have enough to eat relatively well without constant worry make many decisions about what to eat and how. Some of these decisions are relatively idiosyncratic, dependent on particular tastes and preferences. But many of them emerge from the organized social relations of class groups, and reflect bonds forged not only among family members but between family and others as well. In this chapter, I discuss two contrasting ways of organizing meals, one based on custom and habit, characteristic of working-class families, and another based on textual standards for stylish eating, characteristic of families in a professional/managerial class group. While such differences are often identified as arising from simple cultural preferences, I will argue that these different practices are based in the organization of class groups and have significance for the maintenance of social class divisions.

Learning to Cook: Tradition and Text

I began to notice these class-related differences in food patterns as I talked with women about learning to cook. Some women described the process as a relatively simple one. They relied heavily on their mothers or other female relatives, and they tried to learn to reproduce the kinds of meals they had grown up with. Teresa, for example, claimed that she learned to cook "on the phone":

> I would always be on the phone when it was right around
> supper time. "Ma, I have this and this. What do I do?" You
> know, and then she'd tell me. I'd be in the kitchen, with the
> phone at my ear, and she'd be telling me, "Now put oil in the
> pan." [Laughing] It was that bad. "Let the pan heat up a
> little." It was funny, now that I remember it.

She laughed as she told me the story, but she also reported quite
proudly that she still cooks just as her mother does.

Some of these women reported that their cooking was less elaborate than their mothers', or differed in ways that reflect changes in
widely disseminated nutritional recommendations—that they
make more of an effort to avoid cholesterol, for instance—but the
overall sense was of similarity. These women reported learning
cooking skills through "trial and error": often asking their mothers or female relatives for help, and occasionally consulting books
or magazines. However they acquired cooking skills, for these
women, mothers' practices provide the model.

Another group reported that they cook very differently from
their mothers, and eventually I came to understand the difference
as one based in class. These women usually felt they had learned
general principles from their mothers—a sense of how to organize
their cooking, or of the importance of balanced meals—but they
were often sharply critical of their mothers as cooks. They frequently discussed the defects in their mothers' practices ("She was
a very plain cook, a very unimaginative cook") and were proud of
cooking differently, better than their mothers ("Often I think that
she served the same thing twice in one week. That didn't bother
me when I was a child, but I don't do that"). They repudiated their
mothers' reliance on custom or tradition, and instead emphasized
their own attention to general skills that could be applied to cooking as an abstract task. When they talked about learning to cook,
they described an intellectual endeavor. They emphasized their reliance on books and recipes, often naming the particular cookbooks they used or discussing their study of specific cuisines. For
example:

> Most of it was French-based, at first, because the James
> Beard cookbook had that basic French touch to it.

For these women—who were more likely to live in profession-
al/managerial households—cooking was not a practice to be
learned imitatively, but a new terrain for study.

The story of one woman, upwardly mobile through marriage, illustrates the changes in her attitudes toward cooking in more detail and foreshadows the themes of this chapter. Phyllis, a single mother with a professional job at the time of our interview, remembered her mother's cooking with some ambivalence:

You know, Jewish cooking—they always prided themselves on their cooking, so food was an important part of our lives. But my mother didn't ever read cookbooks, or try to learn fancy new recipes. It was whatever you knew, it was the tradition of the cooking rather than the creativity of the cooking. It never occurred to her to look in a cookbook to figure out something new to make. You made whatever it was that you knew about.

She remembers the importance of food, and that there was a rich ethnic tradition. But looking back, she seems puzzled that her mother never thought of learning new skills. Her mother, she said, had taught her about "plain cooking":

What you would cook for your family. Like you take a chicken, and you put it in a pan, and you throw paprika on the top, and stick it in the oven for an hour. That's plain cooking. With two baked potatoes.

Such cooking was not only sufficient but pleasing for the family. But now that Phyllis has left that family, she thinks differently about her mother's abilities:

I used to think that my mother's cooking was the best. But it turns out that she wasn't a particularly gifted cook . . . She never got into any of this stuff as an end in itself, it was always a means to an end.

When she married into a different social circle, Phyllis began to learn new attitudes toward food and its significance. When she met her in-laws, she encountered new kinds of food as well:

Eggs benedict. It was a big treat, Sunday morning brunch . . . Things like beef stroganoff, I mean, what did I know from beef stroganoff, I didn't know anything.

From her husband's family she began to learn a new kind of "attention to food." Looking back, she says that as a newly married woman she "didn't know anything." However, she continued to learn about new kinds of food because of the kind of entertaining that she and her husband participated in as a couple:

We used to—that's how we entertained each other, people had dinner parties. So I had the *New York Times Cookbook,* and I used to read it, and try to decide what to make, and follow the recipe. And then, I don't know, I watched Julia Child, that kind of thing.

In her account of this process, we see the kind of textual reference that was characteristic of professional women's accounts of their learning about food. And we see how the process is connected to a particular location in the society. For Phyllis and no doubt for others, participation in the social circles of a professional/managerial group both provided and also required a particular kind of learning about food. Learning to cook as her mother did was no longer sufficient. Instead, with marriage, she entered a period of new class relations and new learning which meant that she had to look beyond her parents' ways to a more generalized set of styles and codes. Phyllis, like most wives in professional households, tells of using cookbooks to learn a specific type of cooking—cooking not tied to household or family tradition but to the more general standards of an established cuisine. Her story points to the importance of textual sources for instruction in the use of food, and also to the relevance of entertaining for professional and managerial couples. It suggests that different ways of using textual sources for cooking practice are related to class differences in the organization of social meals.

Food and Sociability

Studies of family and community have documented contrasting patterns of kin and social connections in working-class and middle-class households. Both American (Rainwater, Coleman, and Handel 1959; Komarovsky 1962; Rubin 1976) and British (Bott 1957; Allan 1979) studies indicate that working-class families live relatively close to their relatives and spend a large part of their social time with kin. Husbands and wives often have separate social groups, and their friends tend to be local people they have known for many years. Middle-class couples tend to draw friends from a wider geographic area and a greater variety of settings. They are geographically mobile, and less likely than working-class families to be near their relatives; they tend to spend most of their social time with the immediate nuclear family or in joint social activities with other couples (Benjamin 1988).

Such differences have often been labeled "cultural," or attributed to varying attitudes about sociability. However, Rayna Rapp (1982) argues that they are best understood as features of social life that emerge from the differing material bases of working-class and middle-class families. Working-class families survive by "sending out" household members to work for wages. Domestic labor is devoted to protecting and supporting wage-earners, and the needs of wage-earners are accorded high priority. Larger networks of kin spend time together and often pool material resources in times of trouble. Thus, working-class families can supply mutual aid (Humphries 1977) and "a sense of continuity and permanence" (Seifer 1973:47).

Middle-class nuclear families tend to have more stable resource bases; in addition to salaries, they can rely on such nonfamilial resources as expense accounts, pensions, and the availability of credit, so that they have less need for resource pooling through extended families. Kinship ties are more lineal, with resources passed to sons and daughters instead of through larger extended kin groups. Relationships with extended family members are not unimportant, but joint activities and support are relatively infrequent. The distinctive middle-class pattern of social life emphasizes joint friendships outside the family and entertainment with other couples.

Middle-class entertaining seems to be based solely on "enjoyment of interaction with one another for its own sake" (Allan 1979:52), but in fact it also has significance in the mobilization of these individuals as actors in their class: it brings together "insiders" to a dominant class, and marks their common interests. This form of sociability has taken on a new significance because of changes in the form and dynamics of capitalism. Accumulation increasingly occurs through corporations and trusts rather than individual ownership, and economic activity and class groupings have come to be organized on a national and international level rather than locally or regionally. People become agents of a ruling apparatus through their positions in organizations (and the series of positions we know as a career) instead of through kinship ties. The ordering of these positions is expressed through the development of various codes (of dress, behavior, and social activity), which identify insiders and outsiders to the system. Styles become the "visible signs" (Smith 1985:21) that constitute class as an everyday phenomenon.

These differences in the organization of working-class and

middle-class households can be seen for the families in this study in the characteristics of "social meals," those with people beyond the immediate family. In working-class and white-collar households, social meals occur when extended families assemble. In most of these households, relatives routinely meet to eat together once a week, or every few weeks. Such meals are important events. Barbara, for example, explained that such gatherings are traditional for her extended family, with significance for everyone:

> That was the time we talked over things, at meals . . . And we always have all the little kids—kids have always been in the same party, right in the same room.

The importance of these meals comes from the fact that they bring people together; the food and conduct of the meal are secondary. These gatherings are comfortable precisely because they are familiar, and they often have a taken-for-granted, almost ritualistic character. Susan, for example, reported:

> I plan 4:00 dinners. We don't usually eat till six, for some reason. Like last week, I started cooking at 11:30, it should have been done at 3:30. But it wasn't—we ate at six. And it's always screwing up *60 Minutes*. No matter how early I try.

The food served at such meals is special, not everyday food, but it is traditionally based. Janice described a typical meal: "Maybe I'll make a roast, and with it, everything that one would have with a roast—potatoes and salad and all that kind of thing." The pattern is one that she learned from her mother; the changes she reports represent a modern version of her mother's practice, which eliminates some of the time-consuming preparation while retaining the overall form and significance:

> I tend then to cook as my mother cooked, except half of what she does. She might have four appetizers for dinner. Egg rolls, and meat balls, and chopped liver, and one other thing. When I make dinner, we're lucky if we get an appetizer.

Thus, "special" meals are routinized and customary; they are special because everyone is together.

Professional couples have more difficulty maintaining such relations, because their kin are less likely to live nearby. Only one of the ten professional families I studied had relatives living in the metropolitan area, compared to eighteen of the twenty nonprofessional families.[1] Thus, social meals for professionals are usually meals with other couples outside the family group. In these situations, people cannot rely on family traditions; instead they must search for common interests, often topics of conversation associated with shared experiences of travel, cultural pursuits, training for professional positions, and so on. In this context, food itself can be used as a tool to promote sociability with those who may be relatively new acquaintances. For example, several professional couples had lived overseas, and they knew about and enjoyed exotic cuisines. They reported that their special knowledge is often useful in social situations. One woman, for example, draws on her Asian heritage and "performs" when she entertains by preparing an elaborate Chinese meal; and Sandra reported that she and her husband and their friends often talk about food when they get together, and added, "Because our friends have lived in various parts of the world, we can get into these interesting kinds of discussions."

There are generalized standards for social meals with other couples, which are understood as "unspoken laws." A white woman who frequently cooks for her husband's business clients reported, "I would not give company a turkey here, very often. Not if it's company that you are obligated to, you know, to pay back a dinner." Asked to explain, she replied:

> Part of it is how it's served. And another part of it is what
> you serve . . . If I was to do chicken at all, I would do it rather
> fancy, with some kind of a special recipe. Otherwise, beef,
> such as tenderloin, and then have, you know, maybe molds,
> and fancy salads, or a cold vegetable marinated or some-
> thing. It's almost an unspoken law, you know. You have to
> think up a really acceptable menu, with a fancy dessert. It
> has to be beautiful, and it has to be on platters, and it has to
> be served a certain way.

Some women, of course, report that they enjoy this kind of "fancy cooking," but the standards for professional/managerial entertaining have a coercive aspect as well. The comment of a divorced woman who looks back on her married life with some dismay illus-

---

1. Distance from kin seems greater for this group in my sample than in the wider population, perhaps because the group is composed primarily of professionals rather than managers and entrepreneurs, who would more likely have ties to local areas. However, class differences in contact with kin are consistent even when there is less geographic dispersion for the middle class.

trates the influence of a social circle, as well as the emphasis on performance for others:

> I used to subscribe to *Gourmet* magazine when I was married, and I used to—if I had people over for dinner—really try to go all out. My friends were into it too, so—but I hated it. I mean, I really hated it, and I used to have escargots, and you know, all that stuff. I don't know why I did it. I guess I felt like people wouldn't like me, you know, there was part of that too, that I had to show how good, how talented I was.

This kind of cooking is not traditionally based; in fact, unusualness is an important element. Sandra reported proudly, "If my friends want roast beef they can roast it themselves." An implicit assumption is that all of these couples can afford food that is merely good; the requirement for their social gatherings is that the meal should be interesting enough to serve as a focus for conversation and sociability.

Both working-class and professional couples use food as a vehicle for sociability, but professional and managerial families—in spite of the advantage of more financial resources—are limited by living apart from their kin. Their sociability beyond the household group has a problematic, extra-local character: it must be constructed outside the immediate family, on more tenuous bases than traditional kinship ties. In this context, food becomes a tool to be deployed with a different sort of skill. It constitutes a common code that can mediate relations among professional and managerial couples, and that these couples bring back into their everyday family lives.

Family Eating: The Meal as Entertainment

Although they recognized the importance of food for nutrition and sustenance, people in professional households also talked about their meals as important sources of entertainment and pleasure. This woman, not working for pay herself but married to a professional man, explained:

> Bob and I gain great pleasure from food. I mean, it's pleasurable. Eating is fun, you know. And I enjoy going out, and having people over, and having a pleasant dinner talking and being sociable.

It is not far from such an observation to the establishment of pleasure as a measure by which meals are judged. Phyllis, for example, explained that she tries to cook healthy foods, but wants her daughter to "eat affirmatively" as well:

> Of course I have to get things that Marilyn will enjoy. And eat affirmatively—it isn't just that it should be this terrible burden on us, to eat healthy food, it should be a pleasure, right?

In their efforts to make meals entertaining and pleasurable, these couples design elaborated routines that involve special attention to experimentation and the presentation of their food. The standards learned from entertaining influence their expectations about everyday eating as well. One professional woman, for instance, reported that she liked to make food look "as beautiful as a picture." Her husband shares this goal; he explained the difference between his mother's meals and theirs in simple but revealing terms: "They weren't bad meals, they were just poorly prepared and poorly presented. We like to make the meal more of an attractive thing."

Since eating is thought of as entertainment, the setting for the meal is important, and special places to eat can add an element of "fun":

> The summer, breakfasts are really fun, since we moved in this house. We have furniture out on the porch and I fix a plate of fresh fruit, and usually cheese and some kind of meat and toast or something. And we sit out there and read the newspaper. It's really pleasant.

Informants from working-class and white-collar households did not emphasize the pleasure they created for themselves with such arrangements. Many spoke of enjoying their meals, and some talked about variations on the everyday routine—barbequeing and eating outdoors, for example—but their talk did not share with these examples the self-conscious emphasis on designing (and rather pointedly enjoying) an "entertainment" as part of a meal.

When they talk about what they cook, women in professional households refer frequently to the kinds of textual sources that were prominent in their accounts of learning to cook. In these households, the concern with variation that is a part of everyone's meal planning is expanded to include an emphasis on creativity and experimentation. One consequence of the value placed on novelty is that women in professional households use cookbooks and recipes more often than others. None of the women I interviewed felt that they needed to rely on recipes for everyday cooking, but most women in professional households reported that they cook from recipes at least some of the time. A typical comment:

> I have an enormous collection of cookbooks. And I'll pull something out and say, "I haven't made this in ages," or I have to refresh my memory, or I'll look for something new.

By contrast, women in working-class and white-collar households said they rarely used recipes. When I asked, one laughed and pointed to her cookbooks, saying, "They look real nice on the shelf." And Robin explained:

> If we have any questions we'll go to my mom's old cookbooks. A lot of the stuff is pretty dated in there, but it usually gets us through whatever's wrong. Things like how many minutes a pound to cook a roast, that kind of stuff.

People in professional households stressed the importance of "trying new things," and often talked about experimenting in terms that revealed their conscious efforts to do so: "We try to try something out once every two weeks or so." Many described their cooking in terms of various "cuisines," and described routines that emphasized varieties of ethnic food. One woman, for example, listed the soups she makes regularly, carefully labeling each: "Dutch split pea soup, and an Algerian soup. And a cream soup with fennel in it, that's definitely a North African thing." Another reported that, unlike most of her friends, she is not very interested in ethnic cooking. Then, needing a label for her own practice, she suggested, "I think maybe it's more of the country style." Her sense of needing to identify her cooking reveals the influence of the very categories she claims are unimportant. In many working-class households, ethnic food is important as an expression of heritage (indeed, for immigrant groups, movement toward a more standard "American" diet is associated with assimilation and social mobility, though ethnic foods are often the last element of cultural identification to be dropped). The professional/managerial interest in ethnic food is different; it involves borrowing from various cultures and deploying new cuisines to add the novelty that makes a meal "entertaining."

Children in professional households learn that food should be different and interesting, and that eating should be an adventure. One woman explained:

I get a lot of positive feedback for experimenting. Even my little one will say, "Mom, this is fantastic." And he's very diplomatic, you know, he came up to me and he said, "I know you tried your hardest, but this doesn't have any zing to it."

By contrast, a working-class woman explained that her children like "pure, basic foods," and commented:

I guess it makes them feel more like home. Because they're used to it. And if you have something else, they'll say, "Oh, who's coming over?" and they'll feel a little bit uncomfortable.

"Trying new things" requires a good deal of study and a constant vigilance to learn new things and develop new ideas. Thus, informants from professional households talked at length about watching out for new recipes. The comment below shows how this Asian-American woman gathers information from a variety of sources, "always interested." And her language ("you know" and "of course" you do this or that) shows how thoroughly she takes such activity for granted:

We're both great recipe collectors. We'll clip anything out that we think sounds interesting. And I'm always interested—you know, if you go to someone's house for dinner, or whatever, trading recipes. I also have a lot of friends in a parents' group, and that seems to be another source of finding food recipes in regard to your child . . . And of course, you know, you watch Julia Child, and *The Frugal Gourmet*.

Even those who are not particularly interested in food spend time studying cuisines and searching for new information. A white woman who claimed that cooking was "not a priority" still reported:

I remember we went to a Thai restaurant, and we had lived in Thailand and we loved Thai curry. And then I found a Thai grocery store. So I thought, "Oh good, I'll try that."

The comment provides a particular reason for her family's interest in Thai food—their time in that country—but her final expression of satisfaction shows how this particular interest is immediately reframed as an opportunity to meet the more general goal of trying something new.

Women in working-class and white-collar households did not express this kind of concern with gathering new information. Some reported reading about food and cooking, or trading ideas with friends, but they do not particularly value experimentation for its own sake. When I asked about their current sources of information, about half of them simply said they were "not really interested" and left it at that. Others reported that they like to read about food in the newspaper or magazines (*Family Circle, Woman's Day,* and *Good Housekeeping* were most frequently mentioned); however, when they talked about this kind of reading they were more likely to describe it in terms of curiosity than as immediately practical knowledge they would use. A black woman working in a large word-processing group explained that the women she works with spend a great deal of time trading recipes and diets, but that she rarely uses recipes at home. She also reported enjoying women's magazines, but described her interest as "just looking at pictures." Similarly, Teresa explained:

> I usually do look for recipes. But it's more like the same way
> I read labels. It's not so much because I'm going to stick
> right to the recipe but because I'm curious. How do the
> Americans do this and that? It's more or less just to
> compare. How do they make it? Or what's their idea?

These women had developed standard repertoires that satisfied the members of their households; they seemed to feel little need for the experimentation that was so important in professional households. Donna explained why she does not need to collect new information:

> I cook all my meats the same, you know. And as long as he
> doesn't complain, why should I change it? He likes it, so
> there's no reason for me to change it.

The contrast is between a taken-for-granted expectation that food will be good because familiar, and an elaborated standard based on an expanded (and constantly expanding) field of knowledge about food that links pleasure with novelty and entertainment. In the next section, we will see how these differences are structured through differing relations to a discourse about food.

Discourse and Practice

Textual representations of everyday life—in advertising and the media—have proliferated in the twentieth century, and texts have become increasingly important in organizing contemporary life. Representations of household practice provide public, ideal images of family life—images that are influential even if they are not accurate reflections of actual household life or achievable by any more than a small fraction of the population. These representations provide "instructions" for people located throughout the society, who constitute part of a coordinated social system but are not in direct communication with one another. The more direct kinds of instruction and control characteristic of a locally organized society are replaced by a more diffuse coordination of many specific sites that are tied to extra-local institutions like large bureaucracies, professions, and national (or increasingly, multinational) corporations. This textual coordination has become an important constituent of the organization and maintenance of class, and produces the different styles of household work I displayed above.

Texts related to food work include cookbooks and books of instruction for domestic work, newspaper and television advertising and features about food and cooking, and the nutritional advice given by physicians, dietitians, home economists, and the mass media. Virtually all members of the society are well aware of the existence of these texts, and have some knowledge of their content. But in order to understand their effects, we must consider how these texts become part of everyday practice. I use the term "cooking discourse," following Smith (1984; see also Griffith and Smith 1987), to refer not only to texts, but to the activities involved in their production and use as well. The images and codes of discourse, expressed in particular texts, are public, and transcend local settings, but local expressions of the code are specific to particular individuals and material settings, and are products of individual effort. Smith's analysis of femininity as discourse (1990), for example, displays the relation between textual images of female beauty and the activities of shopping and makeup through which women work on their own bodies as expressions of these images. This extended concept of discourse—including both texts and their uses—provides a way of understanding how such media representations are linked to actual practice.

The body of textual material that I refer to here as part of a cooking discourse has developed in the context of broad social and economic changes. During the late nineteenth century, the expansion of women's education and the growth of bureaucratic forms of work organization brought a weakening of the barriers to women's participation in economic activities outside the home. Formal qualifications and skills, increasingly the basis for access to positions within organizations, did not clearly differentiate women from men. At the same time, productive activities within the household were shifting to the market, so that women's work at home was becoming less arduous and time-consuming, creating a "domestic void" (Ehrenreich and English 1978). At least partly in response to these changes, reformers and scientists began to develop ideologies of domesticity that reinforced women's household roles. The founders of home economics—largely women trained in the sciences but unable to find work in their fields—carved out a new discipline, arguing that housework should be a full-time profession based on scientific principles and knowledge. More and more middle-class women were educated, but their education was increasingly seen as preparation for domestic roles. Gradually, an older form of the organization of family work—based on the interdependence of men's and women's productive activities—was superseded by a more ideological kind of organization based on quasi-scientific and managerial theories of household life (Smith 1985). The development of nutritional science and its promotion through domestic science meant that technical knowledge came to seem essential to good housekeeping. Corporations began to use domestic science to sell their products, and women's magazines began to provide a combination of professional advice and advertising both supported by and supporting these new kinds of knowledge.

The texts of more modern food discourse—advertising and food journalism, cookbooks, and the instructions of health and food professionals—have continued to be legitimated through scientific authority and closely linked to commercial projects (Levenstein 1988). During the 1960s and 1970s, for instance, nutrition researchers began to highlight problems of excessive consumption, and the "health food movement" contributed to a growing public concern with nutrition and diet. Food industry managers fought this critique of the American diet, but they have also incorporated these new nutritional concerns into production and marketing strategies (Belasco 1989). Food journalists, combining these nutritional concerns with an emphasis on food as entertainment, have promoted elaborated styles of eating that activate new kinds of consumer interests. Their discourse emphasizes emotionalism and a "spirit of adventure," as they refer to foods that are "light and lively," "comforting," or "titillating."[2]

Virtually everyone in a contemporary industrial society is exposed to some sort of food and nutrition discourse, and many of the principles of nutritional science have become embedded in the ordinary practices of the food industry, marketing, and household work. Nearly everyone I talked with, for example, mentioned the importance of "balanced meals," and many spoke of "the four food groups." They talked of avoiding "junk foods," reducing cholesterol intake, and eating a variety of fresh foods, all significant themes in contemporary discourse. These comments indicate how the ideas of a food and nutrition discourse are disseminated through multiple routes. When asked about nutrition knowledge, most people remembered learning something about "food groups" in school. In addition, some learned more about nutrition through special training (for work in health care or with community groups, for example), or through participation in neighborhood workshops, clinics, or public-aid food programs. Black and Hispanic women seemed particularly conscious of special nutrition concerns associated with culturally specific food patterns: most of the Hispanic women I talked with mentioned that they were trying to cook with less fat, for example, and one black woman reported that her concern with hypertension came partly from her readings in black history, which suggested that health problems characteristic of black Americans may be related to dietary patterns that developed around the only foods available to slave populations.

While some people are able to cite this kind of direct learning, even those who do not have such experiences have been influenced by nutrition principles that have been so widely disseminated as to be built into everyday practice over time. Many of the people I talked with reported changes in food practices that correspond to changes in the content of nutrition teaching over the last two or three decades. They were usually unable to identify particular reasons for these changes, and attributed them to a general "aware-

2. The particular phrases come from field notes on my observations of a "Food Trends" panel at the Annual Meeting of the International Association of Cooking Schools (Chicago, March 20, 1982). Most readers will be able to supplement these examples by glancing at the food sections of any major American newspaper (now often named "Living," and typically appearing on Thursdays to support advertisers' enticements for weekend shoppers).

ness," or "just knowing" that some foods are more nutritious than others.

If this food and nutrition discourse is so pervasive, it may seem counterintuitive to suggest that it is the source for class differences in eating patterns. But ideas about food are disseminated through multiple sources, and are used differently by those with different interests. Women who become members of professional and managerial households use cooking discourse in different ways—more explicitly and with more studied attention—from those in working-class and white-collar households. Through education and participation in class-related activities, professional/ managerial wives learn to take expert instructions about everyday life quite seriously and to attend to the details of elaborated ideals for household practice.

Differences in people's relations to the food discourse showed up most clearly in their talk about nutrition knowledge and concerns. Women (and some men) in professional households reported following media accounts of nutrition research quite closely, and seemed more concerned than others about modifying their practices in accord with the most recent recommendations. Many described rather marked shifts in behavior that were associated with changes in nutrition recommendations. For example, several professional wives explained that they had "gone through a stage" of interest in healthier, alternative foods during the early 1970s ("Of course, that was in the seventies, and everyone was into health food . . . I believed a lot of it and I wanted to do a lot more reading about it"). Even when they were not concerned enough to change their food habits, these people were aware of the current issues, and saw them as important, so that they sometimes explained why they had not modified their practice. One woman, for example, reported, "Salt isn't such a concern to me because I probably don't add much salt at the table anyway."

People in working-class and white-collar households were also aware of this kind of news account, but they tended not to highlight nutrition concerns or follow the details of these research reports. One white woman reported that nutrition was an important factor in her decisions about cooking, but that her concerns were general ones:

> I'm just not very attuned to it. I guess I know that vegetables are better than candy. And I govern them [the children] on treats.

Scientific advice about nutrition seems less salient than for those in professional households.

One source for these different attitudes toward textual instructions for cooking is the education that goes along with entrance into a professional/managerial class: people learn not only that science should order their lives, but also how to read and interpret media accounts of expert advice. Smith, in an account of the development of women's education for domesticity, points out that the cultivation of such an orientation toward expert discourse was central to the educational project:

> Women of the dominant classes learned to treat the
> academic and professional sources of guidance with
> deference and to look to the expert for guidance in child
> rearing and in the management of interpersonal relations
> in the home. (1985:25)

Several informants from professional households had training in health-related fields, and brought specialized knowledge to their use of cooking texts. But even without formal training specific to food or health, women in professional households had learned general skills related to using a discourse. They knew about a wide variety of textual materials related to cooking, and were quite selective in their use of media food sources. Phyllis explained that she reads food articles in the newspaper, but added:

> I feel that I read them critically. I know better what I know,
> than what they can tell me. If they tell me stuff that seems
> to make sense given what I think is correct, then I'll listen,
> but I have a critical eye for that.

By contrast, most informants in working-class/white-collar households spoke of the discourse with a less schooled attitude, and often with considerable ambivalence. They did not exercise the selectivity with regard to textual sources that was characteristic of professional women: when they mentioned trying new recipes, they often referred to those that are easily available, printed on product packages or "stuck up by the fish counter" at the supermarket. Some spoke about the ambiguities of media reports, suggesting a sense of distance and a lack of ease with accounts of expert advice. Teresa, though concerned about nutrition issues, complained:

> You don't know what to think. You hear that everything
> causes cancer nowadays, you're afraid to breathe. You don't

know if they're overdoing it, or if you should even pay
attention to it. Maybe it's just out of publicity. You don't
know what it is.

The sense is that these individuals experience the discourse from
its margins. Textual ideals seem unreal, even absurd. Rick, for example, commented on the foods featured in television cooking programs:

You watch these cooking things. I mean, yeah, it's a master
at knowing how to make a cheese souffle or whatever it is.
But hell, I don't know anyone who eats that stuff.

His remarks are especially revealing because they indicate both his
unavoidable awareness of a ubiquitous food discourse and the way
this material can be discounted when it does not fit with everyday
knowledge and practice.

People in professional households—"insiders" who have
learned to use the discourse comfortably—talk quite differently.
Sandra, for example, explained in some detail how she uses her sub-
scription to *Gourmet* magazine:

Let's put it this way. Shallots are all very well and good, but
they're so subtle, that I can't see buying shallots. And if a
recipe calls for shallots, I think that's very nice, and I put in a
little onion.

Her comment shows that using the discourse does not mean following guidelines automatically or even completely, but rather
working with the text as a specialized tool. She feels the kind
of legitimacy as a discourse user—based on knowledge and
familiarity—that allows her to pick and choose from cooking
texts, modifying recommendations as she chooses. She does not
cook for her children from *Gourmet* magazine, but she explained,
"sometimes I'll find something in it that just sounds marvelous,
and Ward and I will enjoy ourselves immensely." She adapts discursive ideals, and incorporates them into food events like these "special" late dinners with her husband that she has made central to
their household life.

Although I have used terms like "learning" and interpretive
"skill" to refer to comfort with this discourse—terms generally
laden with positive value—my aim is not to celebrate profession-
al/managerial attachment to scientific and textual guidelines for
cooking and eating. I do not mean to argue that those who attend
closely to a food discourse have more concern for their families'

welfare or more capacity for understanding and interpretation. Rather, I intend to point to two quite different ways of thinking about standards and procedures for household work. In working-class and white-collar households, family life tends to be aimed at familiar comforts and practices patterned on the customs of previous generations. Knowledge comes from experience, and the "new ideas" of science and discourse are slowly incorporated into practice as they are shared among close friends and relatives, and, more importantly, built into advertising and marketing strategy. In professional/managerial households, science and style are prized over experience: a healthful and interesting family life is thought of as an achievement integral to professional being—a project to be worked on—and necessary for transmitting the advantages of class to children. Textual sources provide images of a desirable kind of personal life, as well as instructions for working to achieve it. The formal education associated with position in a professional/managerial class contributes to a receptiveness toward expert advice, and gives those in professional households familiarity with discursive categories and concepts. But anyone in the society *could* learn such skills. We will see in the next section that interests associated with occupational position (especially men's jobs) reinforce the orientation that comes with education, and maintain professional wives' greater use of textual guidelines for family life.

Men's Interests

I have argued above that women (and some men) in professional and managerial households use a cooking discourse—recipe books, gourmet magazines, and newspaper features—to support the production of distinctive styles of family eating. In general, this cooking discourse is a women's discourse: though more and more materials are designed for a mixed audience, much expert advice in this area is still disseminated through clinics and workshops aimed at wives and mothers, in books and magazines written mostly for women and in the traditional (though now usually renamed) "women's sections" of newspapers. The discourse is differentiated, so that women of different class groups tend to use it differently (attending to different sources of information, for instance), but much of it appears in the mass media; it is not only accessible, but to some degree unavoidable. Thus, almost all women know about the kind of class work underlying professional/managerial styles of eating, whether they do this work or not.

But the discourse about food and eating has a special significance in professional/managerial households: for these couples, food serves as a basis for meeting with others, socializing within their class, and through such activity, marking and organizing the boundaries of class. Therefore, cooking discourse is important for professional and managerial men as well as women.

In most of the professional households I studied, husbands were quite interested in cooking and eating patterns, whether or not they shared the work of cooking. In several of these households, husbands were the ones who urged more elaborated patterns on their wives, who would otherwise have opted for simpler routines. One of these men, an executive who does a great deal of business entertaining, has quite definite ideas about what his wife should serve to visitors, even for casual meals at their summer home:

> There are a few things, when people are visiting, that he
> feels embarrassed to serve them, and I don't. Such as
> spaghetti . . . he feels that I am giving them some kind of
> home economy meal or something.

Another woman explained that although she "used to be happy popping a TV dinner into the oven," her cooking has become more "elaborate" because of her husband's interest in food.

By contrast, several women in working-class or white-collar households were interested in food styles and experimentation, but were constrained by their husbands' lack of interest. These women explained that their husbands were "hamburger and hot dog type" or "meat and potatoes" people. Susan explained that she likes to "experiment" (and her comment echoed the professional women's references to ethnic cuisines), but she also indicated that her husband's attitudes set boundaries for her culinary explorations:

> There's only a certain amount of things he can tolerate. You
> know, Mexican maybe once in a short while. But I get
> international sometimes, I'll whip up some Chinese or
> Mexican. And he'll eat it. But he influences it a lot.

And Jean complained that she is an "adventuresome eater" who "would love to experiment a lot more with food at home," but is "bound in by a picky husband and two picky little kids."

Deference to a husband's tastes is consistent with a longstanding working-class pattern of preferential feeding of the male breadwinner. Late nineteenth-century poverty studies show that men in working-class families were served extra meat and fish, better quality meats, and sometimes extra vegetables, cheese, and eggs, while their wives and children ate less. Both Laura Oren (1974) and Christine Delphy (1979), reporting on these studies, argue that these patterns of inequality within the family have persisted with rising incomes, even though they seem less materially necessary, and Charles and Kerr provide supporting evidence from a contemporary study (1988: chap. 4). In fact, professional and managerial husbands make demands too, but their preferences have a different basis. These men are aware of food as a class code: they accept the importance of textual guidelines for eating and they are often willing to put aside idiosyncratic tastes in favor of more generalized standards and styles.

From contacts outside the home, professional/managerial men become aware of the existence of a science of food and nutrition that is presented as crucial to maintaining health and efficacy. Though wives are often the source of food and nutrition knowledge for these men, women have authority only as conduits for official pronouncements; they serve as translators who are expected to implement discursive recommendations in everyday practice. The tension produced by this mediational role can be seen in this woman's complaint about her husband's attitude toward the information she gives him:

> I can't convince him on these things, it has to be what he hears from someone else . . . Well, finally a man told him— somebody else told him—so all of a sudden that helped.

Since authority comes from outside the home, additional standards are imposed: food must be entertaining as well as sustaining, and healthy not only in a general way, but in accord with the most recent expert advice. Family members can themselves call on discursive recommendations in support of their own demands. Thus, this same woman reported catering to several different interpretations of guidelines for healthy eating:

> My son and I use diet margarine . . . And then one of my daughters who's a vegetarian and is *so* concerned about what she eats—she's very concerned about fiber and roughage— she uses straight butter, and she wants to have it in the house when she comes, but she doesn't use a lot of it. And my husband wants everything to be polyunsaturated. So I have to read all the labels. But then he wants to have cream

in his coffee, so what's the use? What's the use, if you're
going to keep having beef?

Her rather plaintive question reveals peculiar contradictions of her
position. Though she is "in charge" of the family's nutrition, she is
not the expert herself, but rather the one who implements textual
ideals and (at most) advises family members; in spite of her own
reading of nutritional guidelines—including, apparently, the ideas
that one should avoid cream and beef—she must find ways of reconciling practice with her husband's and children's own readings
as well as their personal tastes and preferences.

Because they see the significance of food and food styles outside
the family, men in professional and managerial positions reinforce
(or sometimes enforce) their wives' attention to food. Working-
class and white-collar husbands, uninvolved in the kinds of social
activities outside the home that produce this kind of awareness, do
not attach great importance to an elaborated attention to nutrition
or food styles. The discourse is "out there," and these wives may
compare their own practice with textual representations of varied
and stylish meals. But Donna's comment displays the irrelevance
of these images: "As long as he doesn't complain, why should I
change it?" The reasons for eating stylishly are rooted in the social
activity that organizes and maintains a professional/managerial
class.

Organizing a Ruling Class

Cooking is often cited as the most enjoyable kind of housework
(e.g. Oakley 1974), and we might expect that elaborate cooking
would be most common among women who enjoy the work. However, personal preferences seemed to have little influence on actual
practice. Working-class wives who enjoyed cooking traded recipes
and read food magazines, but they reported cooking a standard set
of meals for their families, experimenting only rarely (and usually
without much success). Professional wives who would have preferred not to cook at all still talked of searching for "new ideas" and
making elaborate efforts to produce "interesting," "entertaining"
meals. Husbands influence the work of feeding in different ways.
The preferences of working-class and white-collar husbands tend
to be personal and idiosyncratic. Professional and managerial husbands are more familiar with cooking discourse, and their demands are more likely to be based on textual standards: they want

to eat in particular ways they have learned are healthy or stylish. They may be somewhat more likely than others to share the work of feeding with their wives—or at least to think of feeding as a joint concern[3]—but they also pressure their wives toward more elaborate routines.

Women in professional and managerial households are in a paradoxical situation. They have more financial resources, but they also tend to be more isolated from kin than women in working-class and white-collar households. Thus, they take on the burden of producing "special meals" for their families without much help. These women often subordinate their own preferences in order to produce a version of "family" that imitates images from the "best" textual sources (Davidoff 1973), images they share with others of their class, and that come to serve as markers of success. Many describe the exotic cooking they do as completely voluntary—as a hobby or pleasure—and it would be difficult to argue that these people do not truly enjoy experimenting with new spices and tastes. But a recognition of this aspect of the experience in no way negates the class significance of such feelings. Women (and some men) in professional/managerial households learn such attitudes toward food because they are shared in their social circles, and they teach spouses and children to think of food as interesting and entertaining so that family members are prepared to participate in social encounters organized around food.

This analysis suggests that in spite of changes in family life, a version of elaborated "domesticity" is alive and still significant in the organization of a class hierarchy among families. The nineteenth-century "cult of domesticity" emphasized the construction of "home" life in opposition to the larger society, and depended on the association of women with home and men with public activity outside the family (Welter 1966; Cott 1977). Now, the woman at home, producing an orderly haven for men and children, is no longer a central symbol of middle-class status. Middle-class husbands have begun to participate in family activities in new ways. But these changes have been accompanied by

3. Charles and Kerr (1988) suggest that this is so, and some studies of men's participation in household labor find greater involvement among professional/managerial men, though the evidence is ambiguous (Coverman 1985). I found that, regardless of the actual participation of professional/managerial men in feeding work, their wives were more likely than others to speak of food practices as joint concerns, as in "We usually . . . " rather than "I usually . . . "

a renewed emphasis on the pleasures of eating, which seems to be one strand in a reconstruction of domesticity.[4] This emerging, new version of domesticity, like the older version, emphasizes the significance of home life, and draws the attention of both men and women of the middle classes to family and home, in part through the interest and excitement of food. But its effects on middle-class women seem quite different. While the nineteenth-century version of domesticity elevated these women's status, and even provided a rationale for increased activity outside the home, this newer version pulls women in the opposite direction, encouraging limits to public ambition or activism and greater investments in home life.

These emerging ideas about family life, like the older ones, are typically presented as class-neutral ideals, but in fact develop from the situations and interests of those in dominant groups. Cultural "ideals" for home life are integral to the organization and maintenance of the professional/managerial part of a ruling apparatus. Housework done in particular ways supports the involvement of professional and managerial couples in class-related social activities, and provides for their children the knowledge and orientation toward eating that will facilitate their later access to these same circles. As in the previous chapter, the analysis here shows how the cultural discourse obscures differences and their significance. The maintenance of different classes is built upon the distinctive activities of working-class and middle-class mothers and fathers. But part of the organization of class is its production as invisible. Since gender categories—"wife" and "husband," "mother" and "father"—appear to refer to class-less positions, they easily become constituents of ideologies that obscure class differences even as they produce them.

4. I refer here both to media and advertising celebration of "traditional" values, and to feminist writers such as Matthews (1987), who hope to revalue domestic activity without reinforcing gender inequality.

Conclusion

Representing Women's Work

Distinctive challenges arise in the investigation of women's experiences. Ordinary language often proves inadequate: women's activities are often obscured or distorted by the forms of thought and speech available, especially in public discourse. Examination of these linguistic inadequacies shows that they are not random absences, but part of an ideological web that defines "woman" as one who fits into a complex system of social relations. Discursive constructions of "woman" render invisible or mystify many central activities of women's lives, as well as many differences in the lives and experiences of actual women. These absences and mystifications in everyday language extend as well into ostensibly "objective" discourses, such as the vocabularies and frameworks of the social sciences. To represent women's lives more fully and adequately, then, is an act of resistance to partial, taken-for-granted, ideological understandings of social life. But we can only speak and write from within the systems of thought that we now see as partial, shaped by the interests and concerns of those men who wield power.

Feminist discussion of this vexed question of representation has a paradoxical character. We document, with increasing subtlety and detail, obstacles to the full expression of women's experiences. But precisely as we do so, we construct new meanings in spite of systemic barriers to that project. By noticing silences and absences, we begin to talk and write beyond them. Economist Marilyn Waring, writing about how international accounting systems obscure the bulk of women's work around the world, ends by emphasizing the power residing in women's knowledge of our own lives, and the urgency of asserting our own understandings: "We women are visible and valuable to each other, and must, now in our billions, proclaim that visibility and that worth" (1988:326).

This book builds from a strong line of feminist scholarship focused on the character and significance of women's household activity. Others have also noted—but too briefly, I believe—that housework involves interpersonal relations along with physical tasks, and that the work is often unnoticed and unacknowledged. This observation directs attention to the general problems of representation discussed above. It suggests examining the activities of housework alongside talk and public discourses about those activities, attending to the shape of consciousness about everyday household work. In this study, then, I have analyzed both activity and expressions about it, both work and accounts of work. My aim has been to move toward a view of women's household activity that more fully represents its "invisible," incompletely acknowledged aspects, and also shows how and why these are made invisible. I have shown readers a kind of activity and skill familiar to many women, but quite difficult to describe—activity that produces the sociability and connection of group life. It is activity essential to producing central cultural rituals of everyday life, but also activity whose invisibility makes it appear "only natural" for women.

I have argued that we lack an adequate language for the work of everyday caring and sociability. Thus, we too often fail to see the skill that produces group life, the effort of being constantly responsible and attentive, or the subtle pressures that pull women into the relations of subordination and deference produced by this work. Public discourse mystifies the activity: it locates "home" as a critical nexus for care and sociability, idealizes "womanly" care, and often blames women when problems arise. But public discourse only rarely hints at the complex character of caring work, and the effort and skill it requires. The "workful" character of this activity is often unrecognized even by those who do it. Many women feel that they "don't really do much housework," that the work is easy, and just "goes by pretty good." Since there is no ready language for sociability work, it rarely reaches conscious articulation. But women are often ambivalent, anxious about "making everything right," frustrated when their efforts fall short of their plans, and worried that they may not be doing enough.

My strategy in this research has been to focus on difficulties of expression as women talk about household work. I have wanted to explore gaps and contradictions in prevailing forms of thought, noticing and bringing to speech that which is not easily said. My analysis displays and interprets the accounts of informants, reading their words closely so as to reveal meanings of which each is only partly aware. The kind of talk I have analyzed, like what it describes, is ubiquitous; it is about activities we have all either performed or observed, the stuff of everyday life. The data presented here do not reveal unknown or exotic activity; although I helped informants to go further than is usual in articulating their experience, our interview conversations consist of rather familiar, everyday talk. I have used informants' words to capture fleeting realities and hold them still for close attention. I have included a good deal of talk from the interviews, and edited it lightly, in order to call attention to what people are (and are not) saying, and to illustrate a mode of analysis based on a particularly attentive kind of "listening" (M. DeVault 1990). This strategy relies on informants' human capacity for creativity of expression, as well as their willingness to engage with me in a "search" for adequate description of their experience (Paget 1983). It also relies on the fundamentally organized character of social life, the fact that when people talk about their activity, they refer, in various ways, to the recurring features of social context that organize that activity.

As a sociologist of work, I have wanted to understand the character of household food work, how its tasks are "bundled" together (Hughes 1984), how the work is organized and controlled. But I have also emphasized the sorts of interpersonal and emotional work that have only rarely been considered in traditional studies of work activity.[1] I have argued that "material" and "emotional" aspects of feeding work have been falsely separated. Feeding, like other caring work, is always embedded in a relation between people (Waerness 1984). When family members care for each other, they often overlook the fact that their activities are a kind of work. Many resist a view of feeding as work, for example, objecting that we degrade the experiences of family life by calling up the unpleasantness and coercive control so often associated with "work" (Daniels 1988). But this complaint assumes a dichotomy I have

1. Conventional workplace studies have sometimes recognized that emotions enter into the conduct of paid work; however, Hochschild (1983) has recently opened important new territory for investigation by calling attention to "emotion work" as the fundamental task in a variety of occupations.

tried to work beyond: a dichotomy that falsely opposes "work" and the pressures of necessity to "family" and autonomous choice. Fully representing feeding work means seeing its dual character, the fact that "feeding a family" involves not just the physical care and maintenance of household members but also the day-to-day production of connection and sociability. The physical tasks of food preparation—essential as they are—combine with equally important coordinative work that produces group life within a complex market society.[2]

My discussion has moved from an account of feeding as a general work process, with its own "logic," toward a more differentiated view. This movement involves more than simply describing variation; it also requires attention to how the discursive organization of "women's experience" hides the diversity of actual material settings. The work of maintaining a household group, and producing its daily life, is conditioned by features of the material setting for the work, as well as by the differing social relations and understandings of class and cultural groups. The category "woman" obscures these differences, however, by calling for a particular kind of activity, by modeling a dominant orientation toward family work that assumes particular features of material settings—not just money, but also time, space, equipment, the security of an adequate home and safe neighborhood, and so on. Discourses of "family life"—instructions for being a "wife" and especially for "mothering"—suggest that those for whom the models are often inappropriate should be held to the same standards as others, and if they do not measure up, should be blamed, as inadequate women, for their families' difficulties. By locating blame with individuals rather than structures, these discourses legitimate the hierarchies of access to resources that produce inequities.

Fully representing the work of "feeding the family," then, requires a kind of double vision: it means seeing the activity itself, and also the way the activity is constructed in public discourse. I opened this book with an idealized, public image of feeding work: the "spectacle" so appealing to Thomas Wolfe of the "beautiful

2. Although feeding work seems especially amenable to the kind of analysis presented here, I believe that other household work activities are similarly embedded in the "meaningful patterns" (Davidoff 1976) of everyday family life. For the beginning of such an approach to laundry, see the film "Clotheslines" (Buffalo Rose Productions, 136 W. 87th Street, New York, NY 10024), which combines images of laundry hung out to dry with women's statements about the work of washing, drying, and folding.

woman in the act of cooking dinner for someone she loves." Virginia Woolf's view from "inside" that image pointed to the complex, continuing effort and skill required to produce it. In the pages that followed, I introduced the reader to a group of actual women and men whose accounts, together, produce a much more complex view. Some of these women embrace the work of feeding as central to their identity and relations with family, while others simply get the work done as well as they can. Some do the work relatively easily, with many supporting resources, while others struggle under cruelly inadequate conditions. Some negotiate to share the work with partners and children. Most feel the strains of being responsible for their families' eating. Perhaps most disturbing is Ivy's story, which illustrates the special difficulties of feeding for poor women. Her account dramatically reveals social forces pressing on all women in families. Her story—precisely because it is the anomalous one, because she alone among these women has so much trouble with the work of feeding her family—displays the strength of this socially constructed responsibility. Though she speaks often of her inadequacy, she has not yet "failed"; if she had failed in an "official" sense, her children would likely have been removed from her care. But in spite of her effort and a good deal of formal and informal assistance, she barely manages to feed her children and herself. Even though she lives with extended family, she feels isolated, burdened with sole responsibility for the complex and demanding task of guarding the well-being of two young children. She seems quite different from the other mothers I have discussed, who are mostly pleased with the results of their efforts, and who typically dismiss their feeding work as not particularly difficult, "just part of being a parent." Such talk is possible for those who have found a way to manage some version of the socially required work. In their cases, the coercive force of social organization lies beneath their explicit talk, largely unacknowledged, only occasionally piercing the plane of everyday life to reveal a line of fault. The "iron cage" of women's responsibility becomes more visible when circumstances combine to exceed the "normal" demands and difficulties of caring—when there are few resources, or family members have unusually pressing needs—when "women's work" is nearly impossible, and still required.[3]

3. Traustadottir (1989), for example, discusses the astounding amount of work undertaken by many mothers of children with disabilities. These women talk of struggling, along with other family members, to produce a "normal family life," and their talk about this goal is quite revealing. Many report achieving a "normal

Conclusion

This study has focused on the work of women (and some men) in households with children. But many other women do similar kinds of caring work—for friends, intimate partners, children outside their own families, older or disabled people, co-workers, neighbors, and so on. Of course, not all women engage in feeding or caring work, and some consciously resist the heavy burden of responsibility I have discussed, whether through individual life choices, communal strategies, or attempts to share the work with other household members. But all women live their lives in the shadow of social demands for "womanly" care. Whether women embrace or resist responsibility for the work I have discussed, they are subject to cultural expectations surrounding women's personality and what we owe to others. As women act in the social world, discourses of caring are part of a context that powerfully shapes their actions.

Women and "Family"

This study explores women's tangled experiences of work and love, power and deference, intimacy and self-deprivation, as these emerge and are expressed on the terrain of food work and family life. It shares in a central tension in much feminist writing, which results from potentially contradictory insights about family work: family work is burdensome and oppressive, but also meaningful because it serves as a means for connecting with others. This tension appears with special prominence in writing about food, so basic not only to survival but to human pleasure as well. Women in all societies share long traditions of feeding others, and in many settings the work of producing, processing, distributing, and serving food provides a valued identity or a kind of power for women. Recognizing this aspect of food work, some writers emphasize women's active use of food in constructing meaningful lives for themselves, and point to food traditions as sources of power distinctively associated with women (e.g. Brown 1975; Counihan 1988; Sered 1988). Others, studying settings where food practices more clearly reinforce women's subordination, warn that such powers are not guaranteed by women's responsibility for feeding,

family life" when they are able to manage without major interference in a husband's career, even when the "career" of caring for the child has completely filled a wife's time.

which can also mediate gender asymmetry (e.g. Guyer 1981; O'Laughlin 1974).[4]

I have argued that feeding work in the American family setting is organized, at least in part, through relations of gender inequality. Although most of the women I interviewed do not think of themselves as subservient, their talk is shot through with a language of deference and subordination. They speak, for example, about the importance of pleasing others and the self-imposed discipline they adopt as protection against "selfishness." The reasons for this emphasis on deferential service are complex. Certainly, such patterns are upheld by women's lack of power in the wider society, as well as family ideology that identifies "woman" as the subordinate partner in intimate relationships. But in addition, women often choose to provide service because they recognize that their work contributes to sociability in groups, and sometimes, to a group's very survival. The principles and skills of attention to others are built into the work of feeding, and more generally, of care. The work is directed toward pleasing others as well as serving their more material needs for sustenance and comfort. And although I have sometimes looked beyond women's own claims about "love" as the basis for their work, it is clear that food does provide an important symbolic terrain, used expressively by family members in a variety of ways, and not easily dismissed as trivial.[5]

To insist that feeding work supports inequality runs counter to

4. Brown (1975), for example, discusses Iroquois women, who had high social status, great independence from men, and considerable control over food. There was little sociability in their society, or even joint activity between genders. Men and women did not eat together. O'Laughlin (1974) describes gender relations among the Mbum Kpau of Tchad: although women's productive activities are equal to men's, there is considerable gender inequality, especially with respect to the control of sexuality and reproduction. O'Laughlin argues that the contradiction between economic power and sexual powerlessness is rendered sensible to members of the society largely through food taboos. They believe that women must not eat chicken or goat because of danger to their reproductive capacities, and this cultural proscription supports a belief that women are naturally and essentially different from men, and more subject to the control of arbitrary natural forces.

5. While sociologists are just beginning to explore the significance of food in social relations, anthropologists have a stronger tradition of attention to food patterns. They most often discuss food habits as symbol systems revealing cultural structure, and they often ignore the work behind the practices observed. Charles and Kerr (1988), drawing heavily on anthropological theory, document in British families many of the same patterns I discuss, examining food practices mainly in terms of how they reflect social hierarchies, and, in my view, sometimes losing sight of feeding as work activity.

many people's beliefs about their lives. Most of these informants talked of very "practical" reasons for decisions about the household division of labor, minimizing the influence of gender. Women often explained that they cook simply because they are at home, because they are more skilled than their partners, or because they prefer cooking to other tasks. Such talk seems to assume that husbands and wives need not worry too much about who does what, that they should be "sensible" about such matters and just get the work done (cf. Haavind 1984:154). But a continuing identification of women as family cooks has consequences for equality at home that reach beyond the practical. It means that women continue to be the ones who take account of others in the household and who strategize about pleasing others, attending carefully to tastes so as to present a pleasing meal. Women bring the fruits of their work to table, offering them up for the approval of a (usually male) other. And they deal with the messiness of material life, quite literally transforming "raw" into "cooked."[6] It is true that men too sometimes use food to express their intimate connections to women, but typically their acts are quite different: they take women out to dinner and bring them gifts of food or drink (Charles and Kerr 1988). It still seems relatively rare for men to cook for women in the same way that women cook for men—with assiduous attention to their needs and preferences, carefully working to please, day after day. This kind of asymmetry reinforces a gender distinction: it contributes to the culturally produced idea that women and men are different, and that different behaviors are central to "being" men and women. Specifically, the gender relations of feeding and eating seem to convey the message that giving service is part of being a woman, and receiving it fundamentally part of being a man.[7]

6. The phrase, of course, is from Levi-Strauss (1969). See also Ortner (1974).

7. My claim intersects here with the arguments of Chodorow (1978) and Dinnerstein (1976), though my perspective is rather different. Our analyses share a focus on the significance of men's nonparticipation in caring work. And I would note, with them, how revealing it is that caring work is simultaneously revered and devalued—promoted as central to womanhood, yet in some fundamental sense considered so demeaning that men have been unwilling to take it on. However, these theorists, drawing on psychoanalysis, locate the importance of male participation in care primarily in early psychic development, suggesting that the predispositions toward connection or individuation formed there are the primary impediment to change. My perspective suggests that there are continuing effects of social organization that may be equally or even more powerful, and that the effects of male participation or nonparticipation in caring work on adult consciousness must be considered as well.

These perspectives on women and food work belong within a larger debate about reconstructing "family" life. Though feminists have carefully documented inequities in the distribution of family work, and have called for change, we have been less clear about the kinds of change that will preserve some version of "care" without recreating inequity. "Cutting back" on family work is apparently the most widely adopted solution to family work pressures, and is often discussed as a practical strategy for women (Oakley 1974; Hartmann 1981a; Hochschild 1988). But consideration of this strategy is limited by a lack of attention to the work itself, and consequent uncertainties about how much "cutting back" is possible or desirable. Several early feminist writers subscribed to the popular notion that housework has been so de-skilled that giving it up should be relatively simple. Lee Comer (1974:92), for example, expressed the hope that housework could be "dismissed, as it surely should be, as a necessary but boring chore, to be effected in the absolute minimum amount of time." But the persistence of the double day suggests that it is no simple matter to determine the "necessary minimum of housework" (Oakley 1974:241). Arlie Hochschild, in a more recent study (1989), discusses the importance of cutting back as a strategy for women involved in many activities, but writes with an awareness of the complexity of effort required by the "second shift." Hochschild worries about the consequences of cutting back on family work, but she can discuss only in general terms what is lost when women stop doing the family work they have done in the past. Meanwhile, recent feminist writers with similar concerns (e.g. Matthews 1987) have called for a reevaluation of domesticity and more sympathetic attention to domestic matters.

Sharing work among household members and forging new family roles for men are widely discussed as desirable changes with consequences reaching beyond the family (e.g. Chodorow 1978; Hochschild 1988; and many others).[8] Much research has been devoted to documenting small increases in male contributions to housework, and attempting to explain why most men do so little (Goode 1982) or why some men are willing to share with spouses (Coltrane 1989). These discussions are usually limited, however, by the fact that they conceive both problem and solution in terms of couple relationships. The research on work-sharing does not ad-

8. Hochschild argues that work-sharing will enrich marriage; Chodorow and Dinnerstein make the larger claim that men's participation in nurturing activity will alter societal concerns and projects.

dress the situation of single parents, and it is often unclear how it might be relevant for gay and lesbian couples (the study by Blumstein and Schwartz [1983] is quite unusual simply because it includes such couples).

Most studies of work-sharing indicate that change has been slight and slow, and that there is considerable resistance from men (and some women) to gender symmetry in household work. In one particularly interesting attempt at explaining the persistence of a gendered division of labor that parallels my analysis in this study, Berk (1985) argues that couples not only perform gendered work tasks in their homes, but actively "produce" gender as well. I have argued that the feeding work traditionally undertaken by women is both produced by and produces "family" as we have known it—the work itself "feeds" not only household members but also "the family," as ideological construct. Thus, taken-for-granted, largely unarticulated understandings of family stand in the way of equity.

Many analyses of household work assume that "families" are important, but without sufficient attention to the specifics that constitute family life, or to alternatives to family organization. Michelle Barrett and Mary McIntosh (1982) suggest that much resistance to careful analysis of family life stems from the undeniable appeal of the comfort and intimacy promised by prevailing understandings. They argue that feminists must analyze family as a "mythologized" package, looking critically at "the belief that kinship, love and having nice things to eat are naturally and inevitably bound up together" (p. 159). My discussion of feeding work is an attempt to show what is involved in the production of "family meals." I mean to suggest that the concept of a "family meal" is itself a mythologized package. Clearly, occasions of eating together produce sociability and connection in household groups. The satisfactions of participating in everyday ritual and indulging personal tastes can produce companionship, comfort, and security for both children and adults. But family meals as presently organized bundle these satisfactions together with the subordination of wives and mothers: too often, they depend on women's shouldering the burden of their production, and often on women's sacrificing their own satisfaction for that of others.

"The family" often becomes a politically charged idea, especially in times of considerable change. Recently, increases in women's labor-force participation and a growing number of single-parent households have put families on the public agenda. Public discourse highlights these changes, often pointing anxiously to the central symbol of the family dinner as a locus of particular concern. What is usually missing in the public account is a recognition of the work that produces this familiar ritual, and the woman who does that work. Like the family members who needed to learn that Bertie was "a person" with her own concerns (chap. 6), these partial representations need the expansion that would include women and their work. Those who produce familiar comforts might then be understood not as magically unselfish, but as people themselves, worthy of consideration, who should not be expected to produce sociability almost single-handedly with so little social support.

Caring as Work

I have drawn on a vocabulary of care and caring in the analysis of household work, but I have used these words with some trepidation, with an awareness of their power to reinforce traditional associations of women with nurturance and emotion. I have meant to locate this study within a line of thought aimed at transforming understandings of care and household life. Attention to care has become a strong theme in feminist scholarship, largely through the work of Carol Gilligan (1982), whose writing asserts the value of ethical perspectives associated with caring. While Gilligan herself assumes that activity is the source for an ethic of care, she abstracts from activity in actual settings to produce a general model for women's development, and thus loses the embeddedness of caring activity in particular, local settings. In much of the work built on Gilligan's framework, care becomes an aspect of identity, attached to individuals as a "trait," rather than a course of action to be chosen, resisted, or negotiated in some new form (see Tronto 1987 for a discussion of this problem). Thus, while the concept of "caring" has provided an opening for much provocative research, it has also begun to construct a psychology and morality for women that seems falsely normative and, sometimes, dangerously prescriptive. Further, the general concept of "care" has often served to conflate and distort the multiple realities of women's activities in specific settings. Yet the word persists in feminist discourse because it captures the significance of women's traditional activities, pointing to characteristic skills and strengths that arise from caring activity and its embeddedness in social relations.

238

"Caring," as a sensitizing concept (Blumer 1969),[9] has opened a wide field for investigation of work traditionally carried out by women, directing sociologists to a wide range of activities that have been ignored or undervalued.[10] Studies of caring focus on activities that are often unaccounted as work, and point toward the need for broader understandings of work itself. In social research—and to a large extent in folk understandings of work—the most prevalent assumption incorporates the economists' view that work is what a person is paid to do (Wadel 1979; Waring 1988). Such a definition serves as a clear and simple way of defining work. But it is increasingly clear that a full acknowledgment of women's contributions to social life will require moving beyond this wage-based mode of thought and rethinking definitions of work. The term "work" is a label, part of the language we use for defining reality. It often appears to be a technical concept, and functions as such in some contexts (in the calculation of economic statistics, and in theories of political economy, for example). As a "folk concept," it is sometimes used to refer to necessary but unpleasant activity—what people "have to do." But "work" is also, in all of these cases and more generally, an honorific label; it refers to activities that those with public, politically powerful voices take seriously as socially necessary.

As women's perspectives become more fully part of the social "we," previously neglected activities come into view, raising questions about standard definitions of work. Some feminist theorists (and a few others) have called for redefinition of the term, and their analyses provide important new perspectives on prevailing understandings.[11] But simply drawing boundaries in new places pro-

9. "Whereas definitive concepts provide prescriptions of what to see, sensitizing concepts merely suggest directions along which to look." (Blumer 1969:148)

10. On caring as paid work and in the "informal economy," see Abel and Nelson (1990); as an aspect of other paid jobs, Hochschild (1983); by volunteers and neighbors, Daniels (1988) and Wadel (1979); in conversation, Fishman (1982).

11. Illich (1981) coined the term "shadow work" to refer to unpaid activities tied to the economy and often organized through the labor market; in addition to housework, he includes preparing for work, commuting to a job, and being a client for paid workers (or being an advocate and helper for someone else as client). Novarra (1980) suggests a reversal, arguing that "women's work" has always included activities necessary for the survival of society—bearing and raising children, feeding and housing people, educating the young and caring for the sick—while the kinds of work that we think of as distinctively male—the elaborated activities that have developed into modern occupations and professions—developed around surplus production, and might be thought of more accurately as leisure than as work. Hooks (1984) suggests that middle-class feminists should "re-think" the nature of "work,"

vides an uneasy resolution of these new questions. What is most important, in my view, is to see that the concept of work itself is a powerful political tool in the construction of knowledge, both everyday and scientific. With this insight, we can begin to ask questions with relevance for public policy. Instead of "What is work?", we might ask: What are the consequences of calling this activity work and not that one? Who benefits from such a definition? What kinds of questions and issues does it obscure? Such questions look beyond access to existing "slots" in the social division of labor, toward a concern with the "shape" of the division of labor itself—a concern with what work needs to be done and how tasks are combined.

Recent feminist studies of caring work have begun to explore these issues, attending to problems with prevailing modes of expression and developing new vocabulary and meanings. For example, many writers agree that caring work, in most cases, includes both "caring for," or "tending" (Parker, cited in Ungerson 1983)— doing the maintenance work—and "caring about"—an emotional, personal dimension of the activity (e.g. Finch and Groves 1983; Waerness 1984; Abel and Nelson 1990). The English language, at least, provides only one word for these two ideas. This feature of language suggests asking why there has seemed no need for a differentiation, whose interests are served by the conflation of these two ideas, and what kinds of moral demands are produced by talk about care that includes both of these ideas at once. The association of caring with women's personality suggests that caring comes naturally for women, and the idea that women's "caring for" should be taken as evidence of "love" produces compelling social pressure to do the work, especially within families. Both of these ideas serve prevailing arrangements that depend on women's caring work without explicitly recognizing needs for care. If women seem to

too often understood in terms of a hierarchy of status associated with the labor market, and should take as a model working-class women's diverse and creative strategies for supporting themselves and others. Wadel (1979) calls for a radically inclusive approach, suggesting that any activity that contributes to the creation, maintenance, or change of socially valued institutions should be understood as work. Fisher and Tronto (1990:40) follow this line of thought as well, asserting that caring work includes "everything that we do to maintain, continue, and repair our 'world' so that we can live in it as well as possible." But broadening the concept of work is a strategy with diminishing returns, since any concept loses meaning as it expands. Thorne (1987:100) provides a cautionary comment on extensions of the work concept, arguing that we need more complex analyses of human activities, whether we call them work or something else.

"care" naturally, there is little need to strategize, as a policy matter, about how to organize care. These associations are built into recent advocacy of "family" and "community" care in preference to institutional arrangements; the implicit assumption is that women will be available and willing to provide care in families and communities (Land 1978; Graham 1983; Abel 1990).

This linguistic conflation also encourages a distortion of caring work done for pay. The relational aspects of service jobs are often obscured and the work trivialized by definition as simply menial activity. The work is often controlled (and perverted) through managerial techniques designed with the work of production in mind. Karen Sacks (1988) shows, for example, how the coordinative aspects of the work of hospital service and clerical workers—vital to the delivery of care—are unacknowledged and uncompensated. And Timothy Diamond's (1988 and forthcoming) study of nursing home life reveals that nurses' aides are kept so busy producing vital statistics and records that they have to "steal" time to sit and talk with their patients. These workers frequently act on a logic of "caring for," as well as "tending" their patients, but they operate within an organizational scheme that recognizes only physical care.

Most recent feminist analysis of caring work has focused on "caregiving" for children, elderly, disabled or chronically ill individuals, work that corresponds at least in part to the specialized activity of paid workers in education or health care. Many writers follow Kari Waerness (1984), who distinguishes such "caregiving" from "personal service," which she defines as work done by a subordinate for someone in a superior position. Personal service is nonreciprocal, as opposed to a third type of symmetrical caring among adults which might, in principle at least, be based on balanced give and take. This study has considered everyday aspects of caring work in family/households, which combine "caregiving," "personal service," and also something in between. Much (though not all) of the work of feeding a family involves serving family members who are capable of feeding themselves, or sharing in the work. Thus, it is, at least in part, the kind of work that Waerness calls "personal service."

In the family, the intermingling of the (potentially mutual) care fundamental to group life with personal service work produces much of women's characteristic ambivalence toward household work. Caring as skilled and significant work can be a source of pride and identity; caring as personal service can draw women into self-sacrifice and resentment. Between these two poles—between the work of sustenance and service—"feeding a family" is also a project of bringing people together, of constructing sociability and companionable comfort, of attending to particular tastes and desires. It is part of what produces a household group with a shared history, attention to the worth of unique individuals, the humor and celebration of sociability.

More complete and nuanced descriptions of caring tasks and relationships provide a basis for considering "needs" for care. Berenice Fisher and Joan Tronto (1990:40) point out that power relations always enter into processes of defining needs, so that "the caring process is not a gracefully unfolding one," but one that will often be conflictual and contradictory, however suppressed these elements may be. While needs seem relatively obvious in discussions of caring for children or disabled adults, they are more hidden in discussions of sociability—less available for straightforward articulation. This study provides an example of caring activity that raises questions about needs for a particular form of family caring and about mutuality in that work. The persistence of traditional family patterns—people's attachment to forms of relation that are often painful as well as rewarding—suggests that "family" produces social goods that are widely valued. The continuing commitment that many women make to work that contributes to their subordination suggests that they hold strong views about the importance of that work; they believe it is "necessary." But neither of these observations should be taken to mean that the form and organization of the work cannot change. Sociability work—in some form—may be necessary for group life. But this necessary work might be shared more widely, and better supported in our institutional lives, so that women are not expected to produce sociability at the expense of equity.

Representation and Change

Knowledge about women's activities circulates among women, but does not often, or easily, enter the circles in which men exercise power. These circles—together forming a loosely coordinated "ruling apparatus" (Smith 1987:54)—are the sites where managers and professionals produce the network of discursive "instructions" that coordinate women's unpaid work from outside the home. These coordinating discourses are designed to manage work activities in households so as to enable the functioning of organizations and institutions outside the family. They "see" women's lives only in pieces, as those lives intersect organizations. Schools, for example, require particular forms of mothering; health care institutions recruit women as "assistants" in the care of family members; advertisers and retailers depend on women's activity as consumers; and so on. Women find themselves at the intersection of a multiplicity of demands, faced with the work of interpreting, accommodating, complying with or resisting discursive models, and often "repairing" social relations—dealing with the problems that arise routinely, every day—when individuals do not fit neatly with institutional forms. Women's own perspectives on these institutional demands are rarely articulated, and conditions that make their work more difficult are rarely called into question.

To bring the work of daily maintenance and sociability into view is, in one sense, only to remind ourselves of that which we might see all around us if we would only look: the active, artful competence of women building social ties, constructing groups and maintaining and connecting them, in households, workplaces, and communities. Merely looking, however, does not change collective understandings, much less the organization of caring work. Mystifying and romanticizing the work of care and sociability will no longer do. But the practical, policy problems of adequately recognizing and supporting this work remain to be solved.

This study does not address the public policy issues that surround new understandings of women's work. But the insights that come from more complex representations of household activity can perhaps help to produce and enlarge a space from which to speak about what is needed. In the U.S., feminists and others working on these policy issues advocate a variety of workplace accommodations for parents and family caregivers.[12] A family leave policy, for example, would require that employers provide for times of special need or crisis in families, when a child is born or a family member is ill. Such provisions begin to provide for necessary caring work. However, this study helps to show why family work takes time every day, and that needs for family time arise from the routines of household life as well as the exceptional "problem." Current proposals for accommodating women in the labor force—such as the idea that some workers might follow career "tracks" that allow time off for family care—indicate that

12. For general discussions of family policy, see Kamerman (1979), Kahn and Kamerman (1987), and Gerstel and Gross (1987). Charles and Kerr (1988) discuss food-industry policy as context for women's responsibility for families.

policy makers have begun to recognize the need for some change. Feminists, in order to respond to such proposals, will need a vocabulary and discourse that permits full expression of the pitfalls built into any too-simple association of "woman" with "care." And we will need representations that explore how the experiences and consequences of caring are structured through race and class as well as gender relations.

To talk and write more publicly about the work of maintenance and care—*from the perspectives of those doing it*—is a move toward fuller representation of women's multiple interests. It focuses attention on the activity, and acknowledges the practical expertise and distinctive "rationality" (Waerness 1984) that arise from actually doing the work. With the emergent discourses forged through such talk, we are better prepared to insist that the work of producing connection and sociability, and especially those women who do the work every day in their diverse communities, figure much more centrally in public debate about families and caring.

Appendix Profiles of Named Informants

I experimented, while writing this book, with various ways of identifying and describing informants. On the one hand, I wanted to provide readers with quite specific information about the individuals interviewed, and to flag characteristics that might aid in interpreting interview excerpts. At the same time, my intent was to tell a "collective story" (Richardson 1988) about the work of feeding a family rather than to focus on individual situations. I did not want to produce a text overly burdened with identifying information, and I was reluctant to choose one or even several kinds of information to highlight for each excerpt, since each such decision seemed to imply that other kinds of variation were insignificant. My compromise involved two decisions. I have flagged many, though not all, excerpts with some kind of identifying information, primarily in order to remind readers of the variation within the group. I have also assigned fictitious names to about half of the informants—those whose situations I discuss in detail at some point—and I have identified those informants by name throughout the text. I imagine that most readers will follow at least some of these individuals through the book, and will come to "know" them in at least a general way. The following profiles provide, for reference while reading, brief demographic and family situation information for these named informants.

Professional/Managerial Households

Gloria and Ed: Married, both were interviewed; two children in elementary school. She works in social service administration; he is a psychologist; they share housework. Both are black.
Phyllis: Divorced; male friend lives in household but does not contribute to household maintenance; one child, in high school. She is a guidance counselor. She is white, Jewish.

Sandra: Married; two children, preschool and elementary. She is trained as an economist, does part-time free-lance consulting; he is a city planner. Both are white.

Working-class/White-collar Households

Barbara: Married; two children, preschool twins. Husband works in sales, helps occasionally with housework. Both are white.

Bertie: Married; two children, in high school. She does clerical work; husband is a barber. Both are black.

Donna: Married; two children, preschool and elementary. Husband is a mail carrier, helps occasionally with cooking. Both are white.

Janice: Married; two children, both high school graduates, live at home and contribute to household income; they share some housework. She is a nurse; husband is a plumber. Both are white.

Jean: Married; two children in elementary school. She is a legal secretary; husband works at night as a security officer. Both are white.

Laurel: Married; three preschool children. She runs a small business from home; he is an insurance adjuster, does most shopping and shares some housework. Both are white.

Robin and Rick: Married; two children, preschool and elementary. She is a records clerk; he is a local delivery truck driver; he does most cooking and they share other housework. Both are white.

Susan: Married; one preschool child. He is a construction worker. Both are white.

Teresa: Married; two children, preschool and elementary. He is a medical technician. Both are Mexican-American.

Poor Households

Annie: Single; three children present in the household, in elementary school; a fourth child lives with grandmother in another state. She receives AFDC. She is white; the children's father (no longer with the family) is Puerto Rican.

Ivy: Widowed; two preschool children; they live with her mother, who works in a service job. She receives AFDC. She is a Caribbean black.

Margaret: Divorced; two preschool children; they live in her parents' household, which has nine members altogether. She receives AFDC and works part-time in a laundry. She is white.

References

Abel, Emily K. 1990. Family Care of the Frail Elderly. In Emily K. Abel and Margaret K. Nelson, eds., *Circles of Care*, 65–91. Albany: State University of New York Press.

Abel, Emily K., and Margaret K. Nelson, eds. 1990. *Circles of Care*. Albany: State University of New York Press.

Abramovitz, Mimi. 1988. *Regulating the Lives of Women: Social Welfare Policy from Colonial Times to the Present*. Boston: South End Press.

Acker, Joan. 1973. Women and Stratification: A Case of Intellectual Sexism. *American Journal of Sociology* 78:936–45.

———. 1988. Class, Gender and the Relations of Distribution. *Signs* 13:473–97.

Allan, Graham A. 1979. *A Sociology of Friendship and Kinship*. London: George Allen and Unwin.

Barrett, Michele, and Mary McIntosh. 1982. *The Anti-Social Family*. London: Verso.

Becker, Howard S. 1982. *Art Worlds*. Berkeley: University of California Press.

Belasco, Warren. 1990. *Appetite for Change: How the Counterculture Took on the Food Industry and What Happened When It Did, 1966–1986*. New York: Pantheon Books.

Benjamin, Esther R. 1988. Social Relations of Separated and Divorced Men and Women: A Class Comparison of the Effects of Marriage on the Middle- and Working-Class Divorce Experience. Ph.D. diss., Northwestern University, Evanston, IL.

Berger, Peter, and Thomas Luckmann. 1967. *The Social Construction of Reality*. New York: Doubleday.

Berheide, Catherine White, Sarah Fenstermaker Berk, and Richard A. Berk. 1976. Household Work in the Suburbs: The Job and its Participants. *Pacific Sociological Review* 19:491–517.

Berk, Richard A., and Sarah Fenstermaker Berk. 1979. *Labor and Leisure at Home: Content and Organization of the Household Day.* Beverly Hills, CA: Sage Publications.

248

Berk, Sarah Fenstermaker. 1985. *The Gender Factory: The Apportionment of Work in American Households.* New York: Plenum Press.

Bernardes, Jon. 1985. "Family Ideology": Identification and Exploration. *Sociological Review* 33:275–97.

————. 1987. "Doing Things with Words": Sociology and "Family Policy" Debates. *Sociological Review* 35:679–702.

Blaylock, James, Howard Elitzak, and Alden Manchester. 1989. Food Expenditures. *National Food Review* (U.S. Department of Agriculture) 12(2):16–24.

Blood, Robert O., and Donald M. Wolfe. 1960. *Husbands and Wives.* New York: Free Press.

Blumer, Herbert. 1969. *Symbolic Interactionism: Perspective and Method.* Englewood Cliffs, NJ: Prentice-Hall.

Blumstein, Philip, and Pepper Schwartz. 1983. *American Couples: Money, Work, Sex.* New York: William Morrow.

Bossard, James H. S., and Eleanor S. Boll. 1950. *Ritual in Family Living.* Philadelphia: University of Pennsylvania Press.

Bott, Elizabeth. 1957. *Family and Social Network: Roles, Norms, and External Relationships in Ordinary Urban Families.* New York: Free Press.

Braverman, Harry. 1974. *Labor and Monopoly Capital.* New York: Monthly Review Press.

Brown, Judith K. 1975. Iroquois Women: An Ethnohistoric Note. In Rayna R. Reiter, ed., *Toward an Anthropology of Women,* 235–51. New York: Monthly Review Press.

Brown, Carol. 1981. Mothers, Fathers, and Children: From Private to Public Patriarchy. In Lydia Sargent, ed., *Women and Revolution,* 239–67. Boston: South End Press.

Cancian, Francesca. 1987. *Love in America: Gender and Self Development.* New York: Cambridge University Press.

Caplovitz, David. 1967. *The Poor Pay More: Consumer Practices of Low-Income Families.* New York: Free Press.

Caulfield, Mina Davis. 1974. Imperialism, the Family, and Cultures of Resistance. *Socialist Review* 4(2):67–85.

Charles, Nickie, and Marion Kerr. 1988. *Women, Food and Families.* Manchester: Manchester University Press.

Chodorow, Nancy. 1978. *The Reproduction of Mothering.* Berkeley: University of California Press.

Collier, Jane, Michelle Z. Rosaldo, and Sylvia Yanagisako. 1982. Is There a Family? New Anthropological Views. In Barrie Thorne with Marilyn Yalom, eds., *Rethinking the Family,* 25–39. New York: Longman.

Collins, Patricia Hill. 1990. *Black Feminist Thought: Knowledge, Consciousness, and the Politics of Empowerment.* Boston: Unwin Hyman.

Coltrane, Scott. 1989. Household Labor and the Routine Production of Gender. *Social Problems* 5:473–90.

Comer, Lee. 1974. *Wedlocked Women*. Leeds: Feminist Books Ltd. **249**

Connell, R. W. 1987. *Gender and Power: Society, the Person and Sexual Politics*. Stanford, CA: Stanford University Press.

Corrigan, Paul. 1977. The Welfare State as an Arena of Class Struggle. *Marxism Today*, March: 87–93.

Cott, Nancy F. 1977. *The Bonds of Womanhood: "Woman's Sphere" in New England, 1780–1835*. New Haven: Yale University Press.

Counihan, Carole M. 1988. Female Identity, Food and Power in Contemporary Florence. *Anthropological Quarterly* 61:51–62.

Coverman, Shelley. 1985. Explaining Husbands' Participation in Domestic Labor. *Sociological Quarterly* 26:81–97.

Cowan, Ruth Schwartz. 1983. *More Work for Mother: The Ironies of Household Technology from the Open Hearth to the Microwave*. New York: Basic Books.

Daniels, Arlene Kaplan. 1987. Invisible Work. *Social Problems* 34:403–15.

———. 1988. *Invisible Careers: Women Civic Leaders from the Volunteer World*. Chicago: University of Chicago Press.

Davidoff, Leonore. 1973. *The Best Circles: Society, Etiquette and the Season*. London: Croom Helm.

———. 1976. The Rationalization of Housework. In Diana L. Barker and Sheila Allen, eds., *Dependence and Exploitation in Work and Marriage*, 121–51. London: Longman Group.

Davidoff, Leonore, and Catherine Hall. 1987. *Family Fortunes: Men and Women of the English Middle Class, 1780–1850*. Chicago: University of Chicago Press.

Davis, Angela Y. 1981. *Women, Race, and Class*. New York: Random House.

Delphy, Christine. 1976. Continuities and Discontinuities in Marriage and Divorce. In Diana L. Barker and Sheila Allen, eds., *Sexual Divisions and Society: Process and Change*, 76–89. London: Tavistock.

———. 1979. Sharing the Same Table: Consumption and the Family. In Chris Harris, ed., *The Sociology of the Family: New Directions for Britain*, 214–31. Keele: University of Keele.

DeVault, Ileen A. 1990. *Sons and Daughters of Labor: Class and Clerical Work in Turn-of-the-Century Pittsburgh*. Ithaca, NY: Cornell University Press.

DeVault, Marjorie L. 1990. Talking and Listening from Women's Standpoint: Feminist Strategies for Interviewing and Analysis. *Social Problems* 37:96–116.

DeVault, Marjorie L., and James P. Pitts. 1984. Surplus and Scarcity: Hunger and the Origins of the Food Stamp Program. *Social Problems* 31:545–57.

Diamond, Timothy. 1988. Social Policy and Everyday Life in Nursing Homes: A Critical Ethnography. In Anne Statham, Eleanor M. Miller, and Hans O. Mauksch, eds., *The Worth of Women's Work: A Qualitative Synthesis*, 39–55. Albany: State University of New York Press.

————. N.d. *Making Gray Gold*. Chicago: University of Chicago Press. Forthcoming.

Dickinson, James. 1986. From Poor Law to Social Insurance: The Periodization of State Intervention in the Reproduction Process. In James Dickinson and Bob Russell, eds., *Family, Economy, and State*, 113–49. New York: St. Martin's Press.

Di Leonardo, Micaela. 1987. The Female World of Cards and Holidays: Women, Families, and the Work of Kinship. *Signs* 12:440–53.

Dill, Bonnie Thornton. 1986. Our Mothers' Grief: Racial Ethnic Women and the Maintenance of Families. Research Paper #4, Center for Research on Women. Memphis, TN: Memphis State University.

Dinnerstein, Dorothy. 1976. *The Mermaid and the Minotaur*. New York: Harper and Row.

Douglas, Mary. 1972. Deciphering a Meal. *Daedalus* 101:61–81.

————, ed. 1984. *Food in the Social Order: Studies of Food and Festivities in Three American Communities*. New York: Russell Sage.

Dudden, Faye E. 1983. *Serving Women: Household Service in Nineteenth-Century America*. Middletown, CT: Wesleyan University Press.

Edmond, Wendy, and Suzie Fleming, eds. 1975. *All Work and No Pay: Women, Housework and the Wages Due*. Montpelier, Bristol, U.K.: Falling Wall Press.

Ehrenreich, Barbara, and John Ehrenreich. 1979. The Professional-Managerial Class. In Pat Walker, ed., *Between Labor and Capital*, 5–45. Boston: South End Press.

Ehrenreich, Barbara, and Deirdre English. 1978. *For Her Own Good: 150 Years of the Experts' Advice to Women*. New York: Anchor.

Ellis, Rhian. 1983. The Way to a Man's Heart: Food in the Violent Home. In Anne Murcott, ed., *The Sociology of Food and Eating*, 164–71. Aldershot: Gower Publishing.

Evans, Sara. 1979. *Personal Politics: The Roots of Women's Liberation in the Civil Rights Movement and the New Left*. New York: Alfred A. Knopf.

Feldberg, Roslyn L. 1984. Comparable Worth: Toward Theory and Practice in the United States. *Signs* 10:311–28.

Finch, Janet, and Dulcie Groves, eds. 1983. *A Labour of Love: Women, Work and Caring*. London: Routledge and Kegan Paul.

Fisher, Berenice, and Joan Tronto. 1990. Toward a Feminist Theory of Caring. In Emily K. Abel and Margaret K. Nelson, eds., *Circles of Care*, 35–62. Albany: State University of New York Press.

Fishman, Pamela M. 1982. Interaction: The Work Women Do. In Rachel Kahn-Hut, Arlene K. Daniels and Richard Colvard, eds., *Women and Work: Problems and Perspectives*, 170–80. New York: Oxford University Press.

Freeman, Jo. 1975. *The Politics of Women's Liberation: A Case Study of an Emerging Social Movement and its Relation to the Policy Process.* New York: McKay.

Frye, Marilyn. 1983. *The Politics of Reality: Essays in Feminist Theory.* Trumansburg, NY: The Crossing Press.

Garfinkel, Harold. 1967. *Studies in Ethnomethodology.* Englewood Cliffs, NJ: Prentice-Hall.

Garmarnikow, Eva, David H. J. Morgan, Jane Purvis, and Daphne Taylor-son, eds. 1983. *The Public and the Private.* London: Heinemann.

Gerstel, Naomi, and Harriet Engel Gross. 1987. *Families and Work.* Philadelphia: Temple University Press.

Gilligan, Carol. 1982. *In a Different Voice: Psychological Theory and Women's Development.* Cambridge: Harvard University Press.

Glazer, Nona Y. 1980. Overworking the Working Woman: The Double Day in a Mass Magazine. *Women's Studies International Quarterly* 3:79–83.

———. 1987. Servants to Capital: Unpaid Domestic Labor and Paid Work. In Naomi Gerstel and Harriet Engel Gross, eds., *Families and Work*, 236–55. Philadelphia: Temple University Press.

Glenn, Evelyn Nakano. 1985. Racial Ethnic Women's Labor: The Intersection of Race, Gender and Class Oppression. *Review of Radical Political Economics* 17:86–108.

———. 1990. White Women/Women of Color: The Racial Division of Social Reproduction. Paper presented at the Henry A. Murray Research Center, Radcliffe College, April, Cambridge.

Goode, William J. 1982. Why Men Resist. In Barrie Thorne with Marilyn Yalom, eds., *Rethinking the Family*, 131–50. New York: Longman.

Gough, Ian. 1980. *The Political Economy of the Welfare State.* London: Macmillan.

Graham, Hilary. 1983. Caring: A Labour of Love. In Janet Finch and Dulcie Groves, eds., *A Labour of Love: Women, Work and Caring*, 13–30. London: Routledge and Kegan Paul.

Griffith, Alison I. 1984. Ideology, Education and Single Parent Families: The Normative Ordering of Families Through Schooling. Ph.D. diss., University of Toronto.

Griffith, Alison I., and Dorothy E. Smith. 1987. Constructing Cultural Knowledge: Mothering as Discourse. In Jane Gaskell and Arlene McLaren, eds., *Women and Education: A Canadian Perspective*, 87–103. Calgary: Detselig Enterprises.

References

Gubrium, Jaber F., and James A. Holstein. 1990. *What is Family?* Mountain View, CA: Mayfield.

Gussow, Joan. 1987. The Fragmentation of Need: Women, Food and Marketing. *Heresies*, no. 21:39–43.

Guyer, Jane I. 1981. The Raw, the Cooked, and the Half-Baked: A Note on the Division of Labor by Sex. African Studies Center, 125 Bay State Road, Boston, MA 02215.

Haavind, Hanne. 1984. Love and Power in Marriage. In Harriet Holter, ed., *Patriarchy in a Welfare Society*, 136–67. Oslo: Universitetsforlaget.

Hartmann, Heidi I. 1981a. The Family as the Locus of Gender, Class and Political Struggle: The Example of Housework. *Signs* 6:366–94.

———. 1981b. The Unhappy Marriage of Marxism and Feminism: Towards a More Progressive Union. In Lydia Sargent, ed., *Women and Revolution*, 1–41. Boston: South End Press.

Hawes, Jon M. 1982. *Retailing Strategies for Generic Brand Grocery Products*. Ann Arbor: UMI Research Press.

Hayden, Dolores. 1981. *The Grand Domestic Revolution: A History of Feminist Designs for American Homes, Neighborhoods, and Cities.* Cambridge: MIT Press.

Henley, Nancy M. 1977. *Body Politics: Power, Sex and Nonverbal Communication.* New York: Simon and Schuster.

Hertz, Rosanna. 1986. *More Equal Than Others: Women and Men in Dual-Career Marriages.* Berkeley: University of California Press.

Hertz, Rosanna, and Joy Charlton. 1989. Making Family Under a Shiftwork Schedule: Air Force Security Guards and Their Wives. *Social Problems* 36:491–507.

Hochschild, Arlie Russell. 1983. *The Managed Heart: Commercialization of Human Feeling.* Berkeley: University of California Press.

Hochschild, Arlie, with Anne Machung. 1989. *The Second Shift: Working Parents and the Revolution at Home.* New York: Viking.

Hooks, Bell. 1984. *Feminist Theory From Margin to Center.* Boston: South End Press.

Hood, Jane C. 1983. *Becoming a Two-Job Family.* New York: Praeger.

Hughes, Everett C. 1984. *The Sociological Eye.* New Brunswick, NJ: Transaction Books.

Humphries, Jane. 1977. The Working Class Family, Women's Liberation, and Class Struggle: The Case of Nineteenth-Century British History. *Review of Radical Political Economics* 9:25–41.

Illich, Ivan. 1981. *Shadow Work.* Boston: Marion Boyars.

International Association of Cooking Schools. 1982. Food Trends Panel. Discussion presented at Annual Meeting, Chicago, March 20.

Jones, Jacqueline. 1985. *Labor of Love, Labor of Sorrow: Black Women, Work, and the Family from Slavery to the Present.* New York: Basic.

Joseph, Gloria I. 1981. Black Mothers and Daughters: Their Roles and

Functions in American Society. In Gloria I. Joseph and Jill Lewis, *Common Differences: Conflicts in Black and White Feminist Perspectives*, 75–126. Boston: South End Press.

Kahn, Alfred J., and Sheila B. Kamerman. 1987. *Child Care: Facing the Hard Choices*. Dover, MA: Auburn House.

Kahn-Hut, Rachel, Arlene Kaplan Daniels, and Richard Colvard. 1982. *Women and Work: Problems and Perspectives*. New York: Oxford University Press.

Kamerman, Sheila B. 1979. Work and Family in Industrialized Societies. *Signs* 4:632–50.

Kaplan, Jane Rachel, ed. 1980. *A Woman's Conflict: The Special Relationship Between Women and Food*. Englewood Cliffs, NJ: Prentice-Hall.

Komarovsky, Mirra. 1962. *Blue-Collar Marriage*. New York: Random House.

Ladd-Taylor, Molly. 1986. *Raising a Baby the Government Way: Mothers' Letters to the Children's Bureau 1915–1932*. New Brunswick, NJ: Rutgers University Press.

Land, Hilary. 1978. Who Cares for the Family? *Journal of Social Policy* 7:257–84.

Lave, Jean, Michael Murtaugh, and Olivia de la Rocha. 1984. The Dialectic of Arithmetic in Grocery Shopping. In Barbara Rogoff and Jean Lave, eds., *Everyday Cognition: Its Development in Social Context*, 67–94. Cambridge: Harvard University Press.

Leibowitz, Lila. 1983. Origins of the Sexual Division of Labor. In Marian Lowe and Ruth Hubbard, eds., *Woman's Nature: Rationalizations of Inequality*, 123–47. New York: Pergamon.

Levenstein, Harvey A. 1988. *Revolution at the Table: The Transformation of the American Diet*. New York: Oxford University Press.

Lévi-Strauss, Claude. 1969. *The Raw and the Cooked*. Translated by John and Doreen Weightman. New York: Harper and Row.

Lopata, Helena Z. 1971. *Occupation: Housewife*. New York: Oxford University Press.

Luxton, Meg. 1980. *More Than a Labour of Love: Three Generations of Women's Work in the Home*. Toronto: The Women's Press.

MacKinnon, Catharine A. 1987. *Feminism Unmodified: Discourses on Life and Law*. Cambridge: Harvard University Press.

Matthews, Glenna. 1987. *"Just a Housewife": The Rise and Fall of Domesticity in America*. New York: Oxford University Press.

Mies, Maria. 1983. Towards a Methodology for Feminist Research. In Gloria Bowles and Renate Duelli Klein, eds., *Theories of Women's Studies*, 117–39. London: Routledge and Kegan Paul.

Mishler, Elliot G. 1986. *Research Interviewing: Context and Narrative*. Cambridge: Harvard University Press.

Murcott, Anne. 1983. "It's a Pleasure to Cook for Him": Food, Mealtimes and Gender in some South Wales Households. In Eva Garmarnikow, David H. J. Morgan, Jane Purvis, and Daphne Taylorson, eds., *The Public and the Private*, 78–90. London: Heinemann.

Noddings, Nel. 1984. *Caring: A Feminine Approach to Ethics and Moral Education*. Berkeley: University of California Press.

Novarra, Virginia. 1980. *Women's Work, Men's Work*. London: Marion Boyars.

Oakley, Ann. 1974. *The Sociology of Housework*. New York: Pantheon Books.

———. 1981. Interviewing Women: A Contradiction in Terms. In Helen Roberts, ed., *Doing Feminist Research*, 30–61. London: Routledge and Kegan Paul.

O'Kelly, Charlotte G. 1980. *Women and Men in Society*. New York: D. Van Nostrand.

O'Laughlin, Bridget. 1974. Mediation of Contradiction: Why Mbum Women Do Not Eat Chicken. In Michelle Zimbalist Rosaldo and Louise Lamphere, eds., *Woman, Culture and Society*, 301–18. Stanford, CA: Stanford University Press.

Oren, Laura. 1974. The Welfare of Women in Laboring Families: England, 1860–1950. In Mary S. Hartman and Lois Banner, eds., *Clio's Consciousness Raised*, 226–44. New York: Harper and Row.

Ortner, Sherry B. 1974. Is Female to Male as Nature is to Culture? In Michelle Zimbalist Rosaldo and Louise Lamphere, eds., *Woman, Culture and Society*, 67–87. Stanford, CA: Stanford University Press.

Paget, Marianne A. 1983. Experience and Knowledge. *Human Studies* 6:67–90.

Piven, Frances Fox, and Richard A. Cloward. 1979. *Poor People's Movements*. New York: Vintage.

Pleck, Joseph H. 1985. *Working Wives/ Working Husbands*. Beverly Hills, CA: Sage Publications.

Rainwater, Lee, Richard P. Coleman, and Gerald Handel. 1959. *Workingman's Wife*. New York: Oceana Publications.

Rapp, Rayna. 1982. Family and Class in Contemporary America: Notes Toward an Understanding of Ideology. In Barrie Thorne with Marilyn Yalom, eds., *Rethinking the Family*, 168–87. New York: Longman.

Rich, Adrienne. 1976. *Of Woman Born: Motherhood as Experience and Institution*. New York: W. W. Norton.

Richardson, Laurel. 1988. The Collective Story: Postmodernism and the Writing of Sociology. *Sociological Focus* 21:199–208.

Riessman, Catherine Kohler. 1987. When Gender is Not Enough: Women Interviewing Women. *Gender and Society* 1:172–207.

Robertson, Claire. 1987. Never Underestimate the Power of Women: The Transforming Vision of African Women's History. Paper presented at the Annual Meeting of the Organization of American Historians, April, Philadelphia.

Rollins, Judith. 1985. *Between Women: Domestics and Their Employers.* Philadelphia: Temple University Press.

Ross, Becki L. 1985. The Lodging of the Time Budget Method in Sexist Bedrock: A Feminist Excavation. Paper presented at The Motherwork Conference, October, Simone de Beauvoir Institute, Montreal.

Rothman, Sheila M. 1978. *Woman's Proper Place: A History of Changing Ideals and Practices, 1870 to the Present.* New York: Basic.

Rubin, Lillian Breslow. 1976. *Worlds of Pain.* New York: Basic.

Ruddick, Sara. 1980. Maternal Thinking. *Feminist Studies* 6:342–67.

———. 1989. *Maternal Thinking: Toward a Politics of Peace.* Boston: Beacon Press.

Sacks, Karen Brodkin. 1988. *Caring by the Hour: Women, Work, and Organizing at Duke Medical Center.* Urbana: University of Illinois Press.

Seifer, Nancy. 1973. *Absent from the Majority: Working Class Women in America.* New York: National Project on Ethnic America, American Jewish Committee.

Sered, Susan Starr. 1988. Food and Holiness: Cooking as a Sacred Act Among Middle-Eastern Jewish Women. *Anthropological Quarterly* 61:129–39.

Smith, Dorothy E. 1984. Textually-Mediated Social Organization. *The International Social Science Journal* 36:59–75.

———. 1985. Women, Class and Family. In Varda Burstyn and Dorothy E. Smith, *Women, Class, Family and the State,* 1–44. Toronto: Garamond Press.

———. 1987. *The Everyday World as Problematic: A Feminist Sociology.* Boston: Northeastern University Press.

———. 1990. Femininity as Discourse. In *Texts, Facts, and Femininity: Exploring the Relations of Ruling,* 159–208. New York: Routledge.

Sokoloff, Natalie J. 1980. *Between Money and Love: The Dialectics of Home and Market Work.* New York: Praeger.

Stack, Carol. 1974. *All Our Kin: Strategies for Survival in a Black Community.* New York: Harper and Row.

Strasser, Susan. 1982. *Never Done: A History of American Housework.* New York: Pantheon Books.

Thorne, Barrie. 1982. Feminist Rethinking of the Family: An Overview. In Barrie Thorne with Marilyn Yalom, eds., *Rethinking the Family,* 1–24. New York: Longman.

———. 1987. Re-visioning Women and Social Change: Where are the Children? *Gender and Society* 1:85–109.

Thorne, Barrie, with Marilyn Yalom, eds. 1982. *Rethinking the Family.* New York: Longman.

Tilly, Louise A., and Joan W. Scott. 1978. *Women, Work and Family.* New York: Holt, Rinehart and Winston.

Todd, Alexandra Dundas, and Sue Fisher, eds. 1988. *Gender and Discourse: The Power of Talk.* Norwood, NJ: Ablex.

256

Traustadottir, Rannveig. 1989. Constructing a Normal Family: Disability and Family Life. Unpublished paper. Center on Human Policy, Syracuse University, Syracuse, NY.

Tronto, Joan C. 1987. Beyond Gender Difference to a Theory of Care. *Signs* 12:644–63.

Ungerson, Clare. 1983a. Why Do Women Care? In Janet Finch and Dulcie Groves, eds., *A Labour of Love: Women, Work and Caring*, 31–49. London: Routledge and Kegan Paul.

————. 1983b. Women and Caring: Skills, Tasks and Taboos. In Eva Garmarnikow, David H. J. Morgan, Jane Purvis, and Daphne Taylorson, eds., *The Public and the Private*, 62–77. London: Heinemann.

U.S. Bureau of the Census. 1989. *Statistical Abstract of the United States*, 109th ed. Washington, D.C.: U.S. Government Printing Office.

U.S. Department of Agriculture, Economic Research Service. 1987a. Food Spending and Income. *National Food Review*, 1987 Yearbook, 24–33.

U.S. Department of Agriculture, Economic Research Service. 1987b. Foodservice Trends. *National Food Review*, 1987 Yearbook, 10–15.

Vanek, Joann. 1974. Time Spent in Housework. *Scientific American* 231:116–20.

Wadel, Cato. 1979. The Hidden Work of Everyday Life. In Sandra Wallman, ed., *Social Anthropology of Work*, 365–84. London: Academic Press.

Waerness, Kari. 1984. The Rationality of Caring. *Economic and Industrial Democracy* 5:185–211.

Walker, Kathryn E., and Margaret E. Woods. 1976. *Time Use: A Measure of Household Production of Family Goods and Services*. Washington, D.C.: Center for the Family, American Home Economics Association.

Waring, Marilyn. 1988. *If Women Counted: A New Feminist Economics*. New York: Harper and Row.

Weinbaum, Batya, and Amy Bridges. 1976. The Other Side of the Paycheck: Monopoly Capital and the Structure of Consumption. *Monthly Review* 28:88–103.

Welter, Barbara. 1966. The Cult of True Womanhood: 1820–1860. *American Quarterly* 18:151–74.

West, Guida. 1981. *The National Welfare Rights Movement: The Social Protest of Poor Women*. New York: Praeger.

West, Candace, and Don H. Zimmerman. 1987. Doing Gender. *Gender and Society* 1:125–51.

Willis, Ellen. 1972. "Consumerism" and Women. In Vivian Gornick and Barbara K. Moran, eds., *Woman in Sexist Society*, 658–65. New York: New American Library.

Wilson, William Julius. 1987. *The Truly Disadvantaged: The Inner City, the Underclass, and Public Policy*. Chicago: University of Chicago Press.

Woolf, Virginia. 1927. *To the Lighthouse*. New York: Harcourt, Brace.

Wright, Erik Olin. 1979. *Class, Crisis and the State*. London: Verso.

Wynn, Ruth L., and Jean Bowering. 1987. Homemaking Practices and Evening Meals in Married and Separated Families with Young Children. Paper presented at the Biannual Meeting of the Society for Research in Child Development, Baltimore, MD.

Yanagisako, Sylvia Junko. 1977. Women-Centered Kin Networks in Urban Bilateral Kinship. *American Ethnologist* 4:207–26.

Zaretsky, Eli. 1973. *Capitalism, the Family and Personal Life*. New York: Harper.

Index

Caring work (*continued*)
ideologies of family life, 12–13, 15–16, 18; dimensions of, 4–6, 9–10, 229, 231–33, 237–41, 238–39 n. 11; language and, 4–6, 228; in larger community, 238–39 n. 11, 240; maintaining but obscuring gender relations, 2, 3, 18, 161, 227–32, 240; men's (non)involvement in, 1–2, 234 n. 7; needs for, 241; as organized by race and ethnicity, 20–21; as paid work, 238 n. 10, 240; vs. paid work, 2, 4, 235; producing "women" and "families," 12–13, 230, 232; and relations of subordination and dominance, 161–63; seen as central to women's identity, 1–4, 8, 10–11, 228, 233, 237, 239–40 (*see also* Feminist scholarship); socially constructed, 11–13, 229; supporting traditional family patterns, 2, 65; in *To the Lighthouse*, 6–10, 231; why women responsible for, 10–13, 96–97; women's perceptions of, 2, 7–8, 9, 10–11, 161, 231, 240; as valuable, 3, 4, 18, 161, 238.

Charles, Nickie, 242 n; on determinants of quality of diet, 44–45, 70; on division of labor of cooking, 143; on food practices and class, 172, 201, 223, 233 n. 15; on the work of pleasing, 41–42, 152 n

Child care: division of labor of, 13–14, 26, 96, 99, 101–6, 138, 183; learning of, through experience, 117; and women's paid work, 102, 138

Children: affecting meal times, 36, 37, 78, 80; behavior at meals, 50; contribution of, to feeding work, 63–64, 100–101, 105, 140, 155, 192–93; in different classes, 187–88, 191–93, 195–96, 212–13; and discourse of family, 16, 136, 200, 231; food preferences of, 40, 42, 85, 86–88, 113, 149, 187; monitoring and learning feeding work by having, 113–15, 116, 119, 187; monitoring of, and provisioning for, 67, 71–72, 78–84; nutrition and, 40, 113, 114, 223–24; organization of feeding

work around, 80, 83, 122–25, 149, 151–52, 231–32 n; in this study, 19, 22–23, 23 n. 7.

Chodorow, Nancy, 234 n. 7, 235 n

Class: assigned to households, 23–24, 24 n. 9, 168–69; and conceptions of work, 238–39 n. 11; and conduct and meaning of caring and feeding work, 2–3, 18, 30, 185–87, 191–92, 243; differences in social connections between households, 186, 193, 206–10, 209 n; and domesticity, 95–96; elements of, 23–24, 168–69, 230; gendered division of labor in feeding work and, 95–96, 98, 99, 193–95; ideology of family life and, 15–16, 18, 23–24, 167–68, 180, 181, 183, 225–26, 230; and importance of kin, 186, 206–10, 225; makeup of informants, 19–21, 23–25; and meals as events, 49–50, 54; organizing and maintaining, 224–26, 230; as process, 23–24, 168; -related constraints and provisioning, 59; and a "ruling apparatus," 23 n. 8, 207, 226; social organization of, and family/feeding work, 24, 30, 167–203, 221–22, 230, 231; and use of nutrition and health discourse, 69, 215–22; and use of text vs. tradition for sociability and style, 203–26. *See also* Income; Material resources; Occupation

Collins, Patricia Hill, 195

Comer, Lee, 235

Conflict: of caring work with paid work, 2–3, 100; effect of flexibility and perceptions of "choice" on, 104–5, 152–59; effect of gendered expectations on, 142–51, 161–63; effect of invisibility of work on, 139–42, 151. *See also* Division of labor

Connell, R. W., 16 n

Consumption, 58–59, 70, 167, 169, 200, 216

Cookbooks: as texts for learning, 205–6, 211–12, 215, 216, 221

Cooking, 4, 133; as affected by technological and economic changes,

Individuality: attention to, as part of
feeding work, 85–91, 114; and production of family, 78, 85–86, 90–91,
240–41. *See also* Family; Group
life; Sociability; Meal Planning

Inequality, relations of, 11, 18, 161. *See
also* Class; Division of labor; Gender

Informants, 19–28, 245–46

Interactionist studies: of work, 19

Interviews, 19, 28–29, 229; difficulty
of, and class, 185–86; "listening,"
229

Invisibility: of caring and feeding work,
9, 18–19, 25, 30, 48, 55–57, 60, 75,
122, 140–41, 228; of constructing
family, 5, 91, 168; of housework and
effect on the division of labor, 140–
42, 151, 162–63, 228; of production
of class, 226; of relations of power
in feeding work, 161–63; of requirement to serve men and please
others, 147, 157. *See also* Language;
Meal planning; Monitoring; Provisioning

J

Joseph, Gloria, 192

K

Kahn, Alfred, 242 n

Kamerman, Sheila, 242 n

Kerr, Marion, 242 n; on determinants of
quality of diet, 44–45, 70; on division of labor of cooking, 143; on
food practices and class, 172, 201,
223, 233 n. 15; on the work of pleasing, 41–42, 152 n

Kin, 21, 22, 23, 38; connections with,
and class, 193, 206–10, 209 n, 231;
help from, in feeding work, 188,
195; learning feeding work from,
106–11, 203–4, 221. *See also* Learning; Mothers; Traditions/customs

Knowing: problems of, and experience,
4–10, 11, 19, 29–30, 186

Knowledge: from attention and experience, 116, 122–23, 221, 227–28,
243; of care, 239; and class, 171–72,

198, 217–18; of feeding work, 48,
90–91, 106–7, 216; gaps in, 5–6,
229; importance of, to bridge household and market, 76; of nutrition,
47, 69, 112, 198, 217–18; shared, 12,
44–46, 221, 241. *See also* Discourse; Learning; Women's
experience

L

Labor force, 2, 3, 181, 216. *See also*
Work, paid

Ladd-Taylor, Molly, 134

Language: of "choice," 156–63, 233;
obscuring women's experience, 3–5,
29, 227, 238–40; and recovering
women's experience, 29, 227–29,
239, 243; social organization of
feeding work in, 10, 28–30, 228–29,
231. *See also* Discourse; Gender;
Ideology

Learning: and adapting knowledge to
own circumstances, 91, 116–17,
122–23, 126–27; attention from
mothering, 111–17, 112 n; attitudes
toward food, 50–51, 204–6; caring
work, 8, 12; through cooking discourse, 215–24; deference to men,
143–48; feeding work, 48, 90–91,
109–10, 149, 152; food preferences
of household members, 40–42, 62,
87–88, 90, 113–15; ideology of family life, 91, 96, 111; mealtime
behavior, 50–51; through monitoring the market, 66–74; through
participation in gendered activities,
96–97, 106–19; and resistance to
housework, 104–5; responsibility
from mothers, 63, 106–19; sources
of, about feeding work, 91, 112–15,
116, 119; through talk, 47, 90–91,
113, 115. *See also* Advertising;
Cooking; Discourse; Doctors; Gender; Ideology; Knowledge; Media;
Public assistance; Texts

Leibowitz, Lila, 13

"Leisure": vs. "work," 5, 238 n. 11

Lesbian/gay couples/parents, 16–17,
235–36

Z